Praise for *I'm Right and* ‍

This is a deeply thoughtful book about what it really takes to communicate, especially with people who we don't understand. A must-read for anyone trying to break the climate impasse, or indeed, make progress in any domain of social conflict.

— Naomi Oreskes, Professor of the History of Science,
Affiliated Professor of Earth and Planetary Sciences, Harvard University

The public square has been polluted by industry-funded propaganda when it comes to matters like climate change and what to do about it. Read James Hoggan's *I'm Right and You're an Idiot* for some ideas on how to fix that.

— Michael E. Mann, Distinguished Professor of Atmosphere Science,
Penn State University, and author, *The Madhouse Effect*

Hoggan has done an admirable job in getting to the root of the why public discourse on some of the most pressing problems facing society today is so fractured and toxic. His interviews with many of the world's leading thinkers on this crucial issue are essential reading for anyone who wants to understand how we got into this mess and what we can do to get out of it.

— Mark Jaccard, Professor, School of Resource and
Environmental Management, Simon Fraser University

Jim Hoggan's monumental study explores a wide range of thought about the babel that passes for public discourse today. Anyone concerned about how civil society can be better informed so decisions can be made for the public's long term interests must read this deeply thoughtful book.

— David Suzuki, science broadcaster and environmental activist

James Hoggan's book could not be more timely.... A must-read for anyone who despairs at the pollution in the public square. It doesn't have to be this way, says Hoggan. There is a way out.

— Gillian Findlay, Host, CBC News: the fifth estate

Conversation is the essence of being human. To converse is to listen, to respect, to love and so to be open to fresh ideas and perspectives. James Hoggan has illuminated a series of amazing conversations with thinkers and doers.... This is a text which should be thought, not just read, by all who seek reconciliation.

— Professor Tim O'Riordan OBE DL FBA

Impressive list of contributors; important topic; inspired insights.

— Brenda Morrison, Ph.D, Director, Centre for Restorative Justice,
Simon Fraser University

James Hoggan has interviewed a diverse group of thinkers, from pundits to psychologists, seeking explanations of and alternatives to the all-too-familiar "stubborn adversarial advocacy" that pervades public discourse. This engaging and important book offers a blueprint toward empathy, flexibility, and creativity instead of narrow-minded demagoguery.

— Scott Slovic, coeditor, *Numbers and Nerves:*
Information, Emotion, and Meaning in a World of Data

I'm Right and You're an Idiot

THE TOXIC STATE OF PUBLIC DISCOURSE AND HOW TO CLEAN IT UP

Second Edition

James Hoggan

with Grania Litwin

new society
PUBLISHERS

First edition © 2016 by James Hoggan.

Cover design by Diane McIntosh.
Cover illustration: ©Shutterstock 246114139.
Interior: p. 1 © Rahul Sengupta; p. 129 © vchalup / Adobe Stock.

Printed in Canada. First printing May, 2019.

Inquiries regarding requests to reprint all or part of *I'm Right and You're an Idiot* should be addressed to New Society Publishers at the address below. To order directly from the publishers, please call toll-free (North America) 1-800-567-6772, or order online at www.newsociety.com

Any other inquiries can be directed by mail to:

New Society Publishers
P.O. Box 189, Gabriola Island, BC V0R 1X0, Canada
(250) 247-9737

LIBRARY AND ARCHIVES CANADA CATALOGUING IN PUBLICATION

Title: I'm right and you're an idiot : the toxic state of public discourse and how to clean it up / James Hoggan.

Other titles: I am right and you are an idiot

Names: Hoggan, James, 1946– author.

Description: Second edition. | Includes bibliographical references and index.

Identifiers: Canadiana (print) 20190084235 | Canadiana (ebook) 20190084340 | ISBN 9780865719149 (softcover) | ISBN 9781550927078 (PDF) | ISBN 9781771423038 (EPUB)

Subjects: LCSH: Interpersonal communication. | LCSH: Polarization (Social sciences) | LCSH: Debates and debating.

Classification: LCC HM1166 .H64 2019 | DDC 302.2—dc23

Funded by the Government of Canada

Financé par le gouvernement du Canada

Canadä

New Society Publishers' mission is to publish books that contribute in fundamental ways to building an ecologically sustainable and just society, and to do so with the least possible impact on the environment, in a manner that models this vision.

Certified
B Corporation

MIX
Paper from responsible sources
FSC
www.fsc.org
FSC® C016245

*With gratitude and admiration for those
who struggle to turn combative shoving matches
into healthy public discourse,
and as a tribute to the public intellectuals
who light their way.*

Contents

Acknowledgments

When I started the journey to write this book, I had no idea how long and difficult the road would be. The scope of the project became massive. The more I researched and the more people I spoke to, the more I realized that I had to draw a line somewhere and tell myself to stop. Having the opportunity to interview some of the world's leading thinkers on the issues I have explored in the book was an exhilarating privilege, but it was also painful at times. It opened my eyes to the very difficult task we face in moving toward a level of public discourse that will allow us to discuss and resolve the most critical issues of our time. Everyone I interviewed added to my own knowledge and understanding. I would not have succeeded without their insights and guidance. Many of them are featured in the book, and the views of others are on the website imrightandyoureanidiot.com. Those who I have not quoted in the book contributed nonetheless by helping guide me to the final product and I thank them all most sincerely.

This book began with an almost impossible question and endless curiosity about its answer. I would never have been able to come close to finding that answer without the support, encouragement, advice and friendship of many people.

Grania Litwin, who helped me transform the interviews and my jumbled thoughts into eloquent prose, is a very special person. What she thought would be a one-year project turned into a six-year commitment, but she never wavered. And just as important as her writing and editing skills was her real-world view that kept me focused as we worked through the massive volume of information

I had gathered in the interviews. Thank you Grania; I was blessed to have found you.

I had the great fortune early on in the project of attracting the interest of Ashley Arden, one of the smartest young people I have ever met. As my thought partner and fellow adventurer, Ashley contributed invaluable research, assisted with interviews and helped guide me in the right direction. She also told me when to stop, or I might still be travelling the world doing interviews.

I also owe a debt of considerable gratitude to my friend Alex Himelfarb whose thoughtful advice and generosity of spirit through many stages of the project added shape and meaning to the book.

To Nick Anderson for his forthright guidance and for nudging me to focus on rhetoric, and for introducing me to the work of Bruno Latour.

And to my long-suffering executive assistant, Kirsten Brynelsen, who successfully battled the chaos and knuckled down to learn new skills like editing, social media, website development, infographics, marketing, etc., etc., etc.

I also thank my long-time friends and supporters David Suzuki, Miles Richardson and Tara Cullis for their ongoing encouragement and guidance.

Thanks to Brendan DeMelle at DeSmogBlog and Carol Linnitt and Emma Gilchrist at *The Narwhal* for their inspiration and dedication to following the facts and telling it like it is.

I didn't interview Deborah Tannen, but I studied some of her vast body of work on linguistics to help me understand how the language of everyday conversation affects relationships. I found her book, *The Argument Culture, Stopping America's War of Words*, particularly helpful. I also borrowed her quote, *Smashing Heads Doesn't Open Minds*, as the title for Section A of the book. Thank you Deborah for inspiring me.

Thank you also to friends and colleagues who very generously gave up their time to read an early draft of the book that had no right to see the light of day. You helped identify the gems buried deep inside those 120,000 words and provided thoughtful advice on how I could make the book better: Ed Levy, Emma Gilchrist, Nancy McHarg, Peter Robinson, Chris Hatch, John Lefebvre, Chris Freimond and Freydis Welland. Thanks to Jesse Hirsh for helping me understand the problem that Facebook has become.

Apart from reading the early draft, John Lefebvre was a constant source of generous support. His wisdom and sage advice on the state of public discourse kept me on track. Thank you my friend.

Thanks to Emma Pullman for support in the early stages of the project, and to Simon Kelly for his research skills and to Gary Ross, who helped with the title as we moved to the conclusion.

Most of all, I am grateful to my wife, Enid Marion. Without her quiet patience, loyal support and endless enthusiasm for what I was trying to achieve, I would never have concluded what became such a time-consuming and costly distraction from our normal life. Thank you, Enid, from the bottom of my heart.

Prologue: A Beginner's Mind

In the beginner's mind there are many possibilities,
but in the expert's there are few.

Zen master Shunryu Suzuki

O NE HOT DAY in Sonoma Valley, my wife Enid and I were on a bike ride from Glen Ellen to Santa Rosa, which meant we had to climb a long, narrow, steep mountain road. I got to the top first and, while waiting, noticed a sign that read SONOMA MOUNTAIN ZEN CENTER.

Someone in well-worn farm overalls was raking gravel in the parking area, so I introduced myself and asked him when the small bookstore might open.

After chatting for a while, he suggested I come to the center for a retreat. I asked how long it was, and when he told me, I gasped: "SIX MONTHS? Who has six months for a retreat?" He responded by saying a healthy mind requires a break from the busy world from time to time, otherwise it's like using a calculator over and over, and never pushing the clear button.

When Enid made it to the top, we went into the bookstore and I asked the clerk who the gardener was. "Oh, that's the Roshi," he said, the group's leader and a prominent student of Shunryu Suzuki. I'm not really religious, but I became interested in Zen Buddhist meditation in my early 20s, and few months after this meeting, I returned for a four-day retreat, with family in tow, to learn Soto Zen meditation and push the clear button.

The idea of a beginner's mind is a caution given to students of Zen meditation. Students are encouraged not to "know" too much because it gets in the way of learning. When it comes to deep meditation, open-minded innocence is considered more helpful than the knowing expectations of an expert.

Suzuki Roshi, who popularized Zen Buddhism in the San Francisco Bay area in the 1960s, explained a beginner's mind this way: "All self-centered thoughts limit our vast mind. When we have no thought of achievement, no thought of self, we are true beginners. Then we can really learn something."[1]

From personal experience, this advice is the road to success in meditation. To transcend the flurry of thought and worry, you must release opinions and expectation. Then you can experience the deep silence and stillness that attracted you to meditation in the first place. An open beginner's mind is also valuable in understanding how to walk in today's hyperpolarized public square. The habitual stories we tell ourselves about the world create patterns of thought that interfere with a deeper, more creative understanding of human relations and public discourse. We need to free ourselves and rewrite these stories.

This is particularly true of the complex questions being considered here. Writing this book has taught me the wisdom of approaching such a vast subject with a beginner's mind, to be open to a wide range of ideas even if they appear to contradict each other—and especially if I strongly disagree with them.

☙

The environment is not the main subject of this book, but a seed was planted in 2003, shortly after I was appointed to the board of the David Suzuki Foundation, Canada's best-known science-based environmental organization. I was invited to join because of my experience as a public affairs consultant. After my first board meeting, we all adjourned to dinner at a French bistro in Old Montreal where I was seated across from David Suzuki. Board members at our end of the table were having a lively conversation about the lack of action on environmental crises when Suzuki looked at me and asked one of his famously blunt, straight-to-the-heart-of-the-matter questions: "Why aren't people paying more attention? There is enough evidence we are destroying the planet. Why aren't people out in the streets? How do we motivate the public to demand action?"

A silence followed and I didn't produce much of an answer, but the question struck a chord with me for two reasons. First, because I was talking to "Mr. Standing Ovation." David Suzuki is an inspiring speaker, one of the world's great environmental educators, and here he was asking my advice and expressing frustration at not being able to motivate people. That was humbling.

Second, since hanging out my public relations shingle in 1984, I have dealt with all kinds of prickly, front-page, public relations controversies and crisis situations—food poisonings, labor disputes, market crashes, animal cruelty charges, bodies disappearing from funeral homes, Taser deaths, multimillion dollar bank fraud, exploding sawmills, leaky condos, election and sex scandals—and I'm seen as one of the gurus in my field. But this was a communication dilemma of a different class, and the question baffled me. I remember muttering something about the sad state of politics as I fumbled for an answer, but the truth was I had no idea.

These questions have troubled me since that evening in Montreal, and I've come to realize that not knowing the answer to complex questions is not always a bad thing—sometimes it's better to keep an open, wondering mind than leap to a comfortable explanation that we mistakenly think is the answer.

In *The Undoing Project*,[2] Michael Lewis highlights this point when he recalls a speech Amos Tversky gave at the University of Minnesota in 1972 to a group of leading historians. At that time, Tversky and Daniel Kahneman were studying how the human mind works in the face of uncertainty, and especially the role of cognitive bias in decision-making and risk assessment. The soon-to-be-famous psychologists hoped that greater awareness of our own biases, and efforts to reduce them, might lead to improved decision-making. Their work eventually led to a Nobel Prize in Economics.

Tversky's speech, "Historical Interpretation: Judgment Under Uncertainty," described how a particular shortcoming of the human mind often leads us to believe we know things that we don't. He explained how when we come upon a puzzling event that we don't understand, in spite of our ignorance and without any new information to shed light on the surprising event, we begin to create an explanation to make the event understandable.

He pointed out that humans are very good at "detecting patterns and trends even in random data" and creating stories to make sense of events. Even worse, once we construct our explanation, we tend to stick to it. Tversky described this as a flaw in human reasoning: "All too often we find ourselves unable to predict what will happen; yet after the fact we explain what did happen with great confidence."

In other words, we prevent ourselves from learning by inventing stories to explain things we really don't understand, and then we defend them. We end up believing the stories and explanations we concocted, and this gets in the way of new learning, something we desperately need if we are to answer David Suzuki's important question.

The experts in this book challenge us to see things differently, to step beyond our blind spots. Otto Scharmer, an authority in social systems thinking at MIT, coaches his students to learn from the emerging future, not the past. He counsels them and us to move beyond "downloading" ingrained thoughts, default positions and deep-rooted habits.

This is done through openness, a conscious, deep listening that requires practice in the same way we exercise muscles to improve our fitness. "This is training the muscle of empathy, getting out of old patterns," Scharmer says.[3] It starts when we suspend old habits of judgment and begin to see problems through the eyes of others. By letting go, we allow other ideas to come in. He believes an open mind, open heart and open will are invaluable because "disconfirming data is the source of innovation."

I set out to write this book with a beginner's mind and to learn big lessons from the most thoughtful people I have ever met. I interviewed more than 70 political pundits, philosophers, moral psychologists, media gurus and social scientists and found the intellectual environment is ripe for this discussion.

They all agree that today's public discourse is an enormous obstacle to change—and many have been looking into some aspect of this problem for a long time, some for their entire careers. During early interviews, I came to understand that, as Yale Law School professor Dan Kahan said, "Just as we can pollute the natural environment, we can pollute public conversations."[4]

While the experts disagree about why this is happening, they concur when it comes to the damage it does: Toxic conversations stall our ability to think collectively and solve the many dangerous problems that are stalking everyone on Earth.

Kahan also noted the science of science communication is still in its infancy while the science of how to mislead people about science is more advanced, and there are plenty of people interested in fueling division.

Long before starting to write this book, I became interested in the role that propaganda and pseudoscience play in change resistance, and the ways in which manufactured doubt and controversy can be used to stall the growth of public concern and block public policy solutions. In 2006 I co-founded DeSmogBlog[5] to help dispel the public relations fog that swirls around climate science and global warming, to raise awareness and help people become savvy about the problem of spin. It gained millions of readers and was named as one of the best blogs of 2011 by *Time* magazine. In 2009 I wrote *Climate Cover-Up* with Richard Littlemore,[6] to take a deeper look at anti-science propaganda and the widespread echo chamber of media and think tanks that magnify it. The book won awards, became a Canadian bestseller, was translated into

Mandarin and was reprinted in Spanish, yet I was shocked that people were not more outraged by all the evidence of deception.

I wrote this new book to explore how we arrived at a time when facts don't matter and how can we begin the journey back to where they matter once again. I wanted to find out how we can recreate the space (needed for real conversations again) for higher-quality public debates where passionate opposition and science shape constructive conversations.

This is not a book that tries to change people's behavior as consumers or voters. It isn't about persuading people to become environmentalists or prodding them to take action. This book is about something much more fundamental: With all the swirling lies, tribalism and name-calling around us, with all the offensive rhetoric and misinformation, how do we begin to communicate and reconnect authentically again? People are turning off and tuning out because they can't believe a thing they hear, and as a result, we are closing down the public square.

Georgetown University linguistics professor Deborah Tannen[7] suggests that our habit of attacking the motives and character of those who disagree with us distracts the public from the real issues and undermines genuine opposition as it discredits the passion and outrage at the heart of real public debate: "Accusing opponents of venal motives makes it easy to dismiss valid criticism." She added this combative style of public debate leaves little room for the middle ground, and what's worse, "when extremes define the issues, problems seem insoluble and citizens become alienated from the political process."

Caustic dialogue is not limited to issues of the environment or climate change. The problem is evident whether people are talking about immigration, gun control or the economy, and it comes from all quarters, including advocates, elected officials and industry.

All of the interviews for the first edition of this book were done long before a reality TV star named Donald Trump was elected President of the United States. Fueling division, calling people names and demonizing the opposition seemed central to his communication strategy, and this brought me a lot of news media attention. Every interview started with comments such as "best title ever" and "great timing for the book," which was odd because Trump wasn't mentioned in the first edition. That has changed with this second edition.

Although polarizing, fact-free pollution of the public square was on the rise before Trump came on the scene, he took public discourse to new lows with his mean-spirited and destructive invective. Demonization of the other side went from sideshow to center stage, and it's now more flagrant, unashamed and menacing.

Donald Trump told CBS's *60 Minutes* that climate scientists have "a very big political agenda," and advised the Associated Press, "I agree the climate changes; it goes back-and-forth, back-and-forth."

The president, who says he has an "instinct for science" and an uncle who was a "great professor at MIT," halted Obama's regulations that reduced GHGs from coal-fired power plants. He rolled back improved fuel-efficiency standards in cars and trucks and pulled out of the Paris Accord.

But he also pulled back the curtain on a dark and dangerous side of society. He has exposed exactly how public spaces have been shut down through manipulation of facts, tribalism and ugly discourse. This kind of rhetoric has gone on for years, but it's now in our faces, out in the open, and it's on steroids. There is some good to come of this because Trump's actions are urging many right-minded people to speak up, to re-examine their values and to not be part of it. His emphasis on fake news is also sharpening the media.

It would be naïve to suggest that the only reasons we fail to take action on the serious problems we face is polarized debate, aggressive rhetoric or pollution in the public square. Nor is it merely a matter of information deficit. The inertia that Suzuki pointed to can be blamed, in part, on the scope and scale of problems such as ocean acidification, species extinction and climate change, which is the mother of all systems problems. As French philosopher Bruno Latour explains later, solving this critical situation will require seven billion people to completely transform almost every aspect of their lives. So it's small wonder there is change resistance.

However, as a PR specialist, I have spent 30 years dealing with tough issues, straddling the worlds of government and industry, business and the environment, and I see this dysfunctional dialogue and corruption in the public square as a pressing problem. If we don't find a way to work this out, to disagree more constructively, we may never arrive at timely solutions to critical collective problems. When faced with an onslaught of over-the-top advocacy, not to mention corrupt or inept conversations, people lose interest, lose hope or simply lose the thread of what they're being told. And this leads to escalating polarization and eventually to gridlock.

Spirited discussion and debate are necessary in a healthy democracy, and we have to defend that right while protecting our public square for generations to come. This imperative reminds me of the famous tragedy of Guernica, poignantly captured in Picasso's painting of the same name. In 1937 the German Luftwaffe bombed this small town in northern Spain, but by some miracle, an oak tree in the town square survived. Ever since Guernica was founded in 1366, that tree, or its descendent, has stood in the town square, and under its branches, citizens gathered to create laws, swear oaths of fealty and discuss community matters. Whenever the tree became sick, another sapling grown from its acorn was planted in its place, because residents valued and understood its symbolic role in the community. Although the aerial bombardment caused widespread death and destruction, the town's "freedom tree" survived along with the spirit of its people.[8] We need to strenuously defend the commons from the bombardment of propaganda and tribalism while we explore ways to open up space for higher-quality pluralistic, public conversations.

PART I

The Polluted Public Square

The public square is that literal and symbolic place where we meet to discuss and debate problems of the commons. It may be a church basement, a television studio or around a water cooler, but most importantly the public square is a place where citizens gather to discuss important community matters, governance and participate in democracy.

Our public squares should be forums for open and honest, higher-quality debate, but sadly, these meeting places have become polluted by a toxic mix of polarized rhetoric, propaganda and miscommunication. A dark haze of unyielding one-sidedness has poisoned public discourse and created an atmosphere of mistrust and disinterest. In this first part of *I'm Right*, we will examine how we all pollute the public square, and how we can make space for healthier dialogue.

Smashing Heads Doesn't Open Minds

1

Like Ships in the Night

with Daniel Yankelovich *and* Steve Rosell

We have an almost extreme situation
where the very intelligent elites are sort of
mumbling, and bumbling, and proceeding
as if they were communicating—when they're not.

DANIEL YANKELOVICH

W HEN I FIRST began thinking about writing this book,
I invited Steve Rosell to lunch at a little Italian restaurant across the bay from San Francisco in Sausalito, California. I
wanted his reaction to my early thoughts. I also wanted to convince
him that my ideas were worthy of an interview with his famous
colleague, social scientist Daniel Yankelovich, whom I had first
met more than a decade earlier. I had read his brilliant books and
valued his thinking tremendously. Born in 1924, Yankelovich is the
author of twelve books and has held professorships or other academic affiliations with New York University, the graduate faculty
of the New School for Social Research, the University of California and Harvard University.[1] Together, Rosell and Yankelovich
are pioneers in an evolving field that uses dialogue to deal with
highly polarized public conflict.

During my lunch with Rosell, I mentioned I was considering
calling my next book *Duped and How*, and he immediately expressed concern that such an inflammatory title would set the

book up, right at the outset, as a polarizing piece of work. Starting with a title that seems to say "I'm right and you're an idiot" is
not the best way to influence people or help them move toward
considered judgment, said Rosell, who has a doctoral degree from
Cornell, has been an advisor to numerous international agencies
and major corporations and worked with four Canadian prime
ministers.[2]

Rosell emphasized his point by recalling the 2011 debt ceiling
crisis in Washington DC, when everyone argued up until the last
minute. This kind of debate, or "debacle" as he called it, is totally
ineffective and seemed to him like a stalled airplane was hurtling
toward Earth, while everyone in the cockpit argued about what to
do. Rosell said conspiracy theorists assume there is a clever plan
behind such combative exchanges, but the scarier truth is that
when it comes to today's political posturing, there is no great and
clever plan: "Nobody is pulling the strings. It's just out of control,"
he said.

I was conflicted by this conversation. On one hand, I was reluctant to change the title I proposed because I was angry about
the pervasive propaganda and underhanded public relations trickery I was witnessing, deceit that conceals the gravity of so many
environmental issues. Few speak out about this dark art, and I
was keen to expose its perils, the spell it casts over unsuspecting
victims. At the same time, how could I dismiss his wisdom? Rosell
argued that assuming this stance would slam the door on many
thoughtful, open-minded readers.

Later, I realized that by starting out with a polarizing position
and aggressive posture emblazoned across the cover of my book,
I could ironically and precisely illustrate the conflict-heavy tone I
disapprove of. So, thank you, Steve, for the title.

I wanted to hear the reactions of these two social scientists to
David Suzuki's question, and also learn more about the power of
dialogue, how to mend broken conversations and achieve clear,
collaborative communication so we can triangulate issues in inno-

vative ways and find creative solutions. I was interested in their thoughts about the state of public discourse, propaganda, polarization, activism and the work I had described in my book *Climate Cover-Up*.[3]

Rosell set up the interview,[4] we three sat down together in San Diego, and Yankelovich got right to the point when he said polarization is dangerous because it interrupts lines of communication and leads to gridlock. It stops us from tackling urgent problems because without consensus we cannot take effective action. Rather than highlighting our differences, he said we should be working toward finding common ground, and moving into a place where we can reserve judgment until we have considered other ways to approach controversial issues.

Yankelovich once wrote: "Democracy requires space for compromise, and compromise is best won through acknowledging the legitimate concerns of the other. We need to bridge opposing positions, not accentuate differences."[5] He added that any unyielding one-sidedness creates a mood of corrosive bitterness. Worst of all, it is a formula for losing the battle, whether it's a war on terror or combating global warming. Taking a polarized attitude toward critical issues will inevitably yield answers that are dogmatic—and wrong—and keep us from arriving at truth.

"It's sad to say, but our culture favors debate, advocacy and conflict over dialogue and deliberation," Yankelovich said. These adversarial forms of discourse have their uses when attacking special interests in a courtroom or on television when we want our talking heads to be entertaining, but they're the wrong way to cope with the gridlock that threatens to paralyze our society. He said today's typical model of mass communication—"where people are not listening, being mistrustful, being polarized, not sharing the same basic understandings or mental frameworks"—distorts any possible discussion. We desperately need to find common ground.

Yankelovich believes the quality of public discourse today is "very poor" partly because people are generally inattentive to public affairs and because the media plays by its own rules. In addition, our public discourse is undermined by a lack of understanding about the rules of communication.

In particular, the scientific community is largely innocent of the rules of public discourse. So we have very gifted experts offering abstract, technical, difficult, highly qualified statements, and a media that presents what these people say in the form of controversy. "And since it involves an awful lot of inconvenience, people prefer to ignore it saying: 'If you people can't agree, what do you expect of us?'"

The scientific community assumes the same rules of communication are always applicable and rational, that people are attentive, open-minded, persuaded by facts and believe that those who are presenting information are people of goodwill, and not deliberately trying to manipulate them. But none of those things are true.

Communicating under conditions of mistrust requires a different approach, said Yankelovich, who spent the first 30 years of his career in market research. Under these circumstances, the first step is to acknowledge the skepticism or concern people feel, and then encourage them to reason why in this particular instance it isn't applicable. The approach should be: the burden of proof is on us; performance should exceed expectations; promises should be few and faithfully kept; core values must be made explicit and framed in ethical terms; anything but plain talk is suspect; bear in mind that noble goals with flawed execution will be seen as hypocrisy, not idealism.

When dealing with conditions of inattention, the objective is obvious: get people to listen. If they are mistrustful at the start, they won't listen, even to fair and balanced points of view by distinguished and credible scientists. So a key place to begin thinking about this is for policy makers and scientists to recognize that communication is not going on when they think it is. "We have an almost extreme situation where the very intelligent elites are sort of mumbling, and bumbling, and proceeding as if they were communicating—when they're not."

Yankelovich explained that university professors are used to communicating under conditions of trust and assume the public knows they act in good faith and will therefore accept their version of things. Well that's not true either, said the expert. Communicating under conditions of mistrust and political polarization is very different than communicating under conditions of trust. When we understand these elements—inattention, mistrust and polarization—it's clear why the truth about global warming has become so distorted.

Yankelovich added that the advertising profession has developed ways to communicate under conditions of mistrust and inattention, and others should too.

This is also where authentic conversation comes in. Yankelovich believes dialogue is not an arcane and esoteric intellectual exercise. It is a practical, everyday tool that is accessible to all, and when we use dialogue rather than debate, we gain completely different insights into the ways people see the world. Those who say they are "dialogued out" are actually tired of the lack of real dialogue, because most dialogue is just disguised monologue.

During our interviews, Yankelovich and Rosell explained the clear differences between dialogue and debate: in debate we assume we have the right answer, whereas dialogue assumes we all have pieces of the answer and can craft a solution together. Debate is combative and about winning, while dialogue is collaborative and focuses on exploring the common good. Debaters defend their assumptions and criticize the views of others, whereas in dialogue we reveal assumptions and reexamine all positions, including our own.

I especially appreciated their comment that debate is about seeing weaknesses in other people's positions, while dialogue is about searching for strength and value in our opponents' concerns.

This means approaching environmental issues with an attitude that we could be wrong and others could be right.

Yankelovich stressed the special form of communication called *dialogue* is only needed when people don't share the same framework, when ordinary conversation fails and people are passing each other "like ships in the night." Authentic dialogue takes some effort to achieve and would not be worth the trouble if we could accomplish it with something simpler. In other words, when everybody is singing off the same sheet, shares the same values, goals and framework, we can all communicate just fine. But when we have highly educated scientists communicating with poorly educated citizens, as well as policy makers and people from the oil industry, it's obvious that everybody brings a different frame to the issue.

Climate change is a perfect storm when it comes to communication, because it involves a broad array of stakeholders, people with differing values, frameworks and levels of education—all being whipped up by winds of passion and emotion. Rosell added that a growing gap between elites and the general public breeds mistrust between those different universes of discourse. "Government folks talk in jargon, and scientists talk about data. The public talks a different language, and you have to earn their trust. You can't assume trust anymore."

In our lawyer-ridden society, the dominant mode of communication is advocacy, Yankelovich observed. Advocates are trying to sell something, whereas dialogue needs people who will listen, pay attention and suspend judgment so there is enough shared framework that even if people disagree, they can find some common ground.

When I asked Yankelovich how he became absorbed in the world of dialogue, he described an interesting journey. After having trained in philosophy and psychology, he moved into market research and public opinion polling, but was disappointed in the level of public discourse and the fact people rarely gave thought-ful, considered responses. He noticed this kind of "raw" opinion has certain structural characteristics. For one thing, it is full of contradictions. Ask people the same question at different times and you get different answers. Change the wording slightly and answers change again. People's views are inconsistent, and most importantly, people don't tend to think through the consequences of their views.

Having isolated these characteristics, Yankelovich determined to find out under what conditions people could move from raw opinion to more thoughtful judgment, where their views would be consistent and where they would be aware of the consequences. In the course of trying to answer these questions, he came upon dialogue, and that led to his ongoing work on how to improve the quality of public discourse and public trust.

Yankelovich and Rosell have identified a process they call the *public learning curve* that describes maturing public opinions, where people's views evolve from poorly informed reactions to more thoughtful conclusions. The three-stage process begins with building awareness and consciousness (where advocates and the media typically do a good job). The second stage involves working through wishful thinking and denial, resistance to change and mistrust, grasping at straws, deliberate obfuscation and lack of urgency (which is where dialogue comes in). The third part of the learning curve is when people come to resolution (which is handled by decision makers and governance institutions). "Much of our work focuses on improving the 'working through' stage, which our society does not handle well and where critical issues like climate change can get stuck for years or decades," said Rosell.

The dialogue specialists have developed tools and techniques to accelerate this process, but it still takes time and Rosell explained that's to be expected. Experts in all fields have taken many years to master a sphere of knowledge and understand an issue. "There is an assumption that somehow the public will do that instantly, but they don't. They need time to work through the learning curve, and it can take decades in some cases."

In conclusion, Rosell emphasized: "Public discourse matters, public confidence matters, and trust matters if you want to achieve anything collectively. But what's going on now is not competent, not effective, not legitimate, and it's undermining public trust."

The ability to have an honest conversation is a tremendous national and public resource, but what Rosell sees happening now is a deliberate attempt to fracture society. We've all been exposed to this during election campaigns, when we hear outlandish attacks, out-of-control PR and distorted information, but Rosell said this conduct has a cost when it enters everyday life. "You keep doing that, and doing that, and you basically pollute the commons."

Protecting the public square and the public good is an objective worthy of support, he said, and by working to create a climate of trust, a community of discourse, we build up capital that we can use to deal with tricky issues in the future. On the other hand, when public conversations are corrupted, when we can't think things through because of a tangle of polarization, attack rhetoric and failure of experts to communicate, it is difficult if not impossible for people to move from raw to considered opinion. It is hard enough to go through these stages when we are exposed to clear arguments and healthy discourse, he said, and added that people can surprise themselves when they find common ground and manage to talk and disagree in a different way.

The Advocacy Trap

with Roger Conner

There are a few profoundly evil people in the world,

but if you think you're surrounded by them,

you probably need to change your own psyche.

Roger Conner

WHEN WE LOOK at the miserable state of public discourse today and how we are polluting the public square, it's plain to see that many people believe the problem derives from evil on "the other side." But this kind of pollution comes from all around the square—including our side—and as long as we think somebody else is the source of it, we're unlikely to ever see our way through it. The problem is structural and derives from human psychology, the way we look at the world and ill-intentioned and well-intentioned sources alike. It also arises from the nature of advocacy.

My ideas about this book were still developing when I came across the work of lobbyist, litigator and consensus builder Roger Conner. Conner has spent close to half a century studying public discourse and now teaches a course on non-litigation strategies for social and political change at Vanderbilt Law School in Nashville, Tennessee. Conner told me that my pollution analogy is particularly apt when applied to climate change because smog was long believed to come from factories. Eventually we acknowledged the possibility that it was individual car drivers who were causing the greatest harm—a controversial view when first advanced.[1]

Conner says that most of us aren't evil, and good people sometimes do bad things for good reasons. If we don't understand that, we fall into something he calls the *advocacy trap*, which happens when we come to believe that people who disagree with us are wrongdoers. This judgment causes us to become locked into such a foe stance that we lose sight of our purpose. People can't collaborate to solve global or systemic problems when we treat one another as enemies.

Roger Conner acknowledged he spent the first part of his career as a "name 'em, blame 'em, shame 'em advocate" and thought he had learned everything he needed to know about advocacy in Sunday school: "There was David and Goliath, and I was always David. There was Moses and Pharaoh, and I was always Moses." What these Biblical heroes did exceedingly well was identify the source of evil, name it and crush it.

Conner was caught up by that brilliant simplicity, and his first gig as an advocate was in the environmental movement, running the West Michigan Environmental Action Council. His motto there was We fight evil and do good. But then Conner went to Washington DC to work on immigration issues and was in for a shock. He discovered a whole other cadre of people who thought that they were David and he was Goliath; "they wanted to destroy me" Conner realized. Still, he decided the way to be a successful advocate was to redouble his efforts to overcome his enemies. The media loved him, and soon Conner was appearing on every major talk show in the US and was a regular on CNN's *Crossfire*.

One day he was invited to the US National Institute of Justice to work on crime and disorder issues "at a time when big cities in the US were falling apart"; while working at the local level, Conner had a eureka moment. For the first time in his life, he found his tried-and-true approach—identifying the correct solution, identifying the enemy and overcoming the enemy—didn't work.

"If you're trying to get rid of a group of drug dealers, maybe that works. But you can't deal with police that way, or neighborhood organizations or the public defender." He went back to the drawing board and began earnestly researching local communities all around the US that were successfully tackling crime. In every instance, Conner found people who were historically on the Left working effectively with people on the Right.

Solutions were evolving wherever members of the community and police worked collaboratively, where people were suspending areas of disagreement and seeking common goals. Perhaps most importantly, Conner realized it was impossible to understand the problems, let alone create solutions, without deeply hearing what people were saying. The result? At the end of his research, he found himself "essentially unemployable," as he no longer believed in the effectiveness of any of his former advocacy tools.

The solution must lie in more peacemakers, Conner surmised, and for a decade, he toiled as a professional peacemaker on public policy issues. But he realized the greater challenge was to create new, more sophisticated advocates. At Vanderbilt Law School, while consulting to a couple of foundations, Conner witnessed how many public policy issues devolved into shoving matches in which neither side fully understood the problem. He saw people blinded by their own resentments and hatred.

Conner set out to understand why this was happening and began reading works by people like Harvard public policy lecturer and author Marshall Ganz and Martin Luther King, "people who are less theoretical and more practical." He had previously thought that professional Washington lobbyists were bad people engaging in polarizing conduct, but then asked himself, "Could it be that we have good people doing bad things for good reasons?" On the whole, yes, he said, and he added this is at the root of polarized public discourse.

Concerning environmental campaigns against oil and gas pipelines in Canada, Conner admonished, "If you think that the whole movement of people advocating for the pipeline in Canada is made up of people who are either evil or idiots, I can almost assure you with great certainty that's not accurate."

I found his answer surprising and slightly irritating, but Connor sees effective advocacy as a way to change the flow of events in the public life of a community by altering the way key individuals and groups think, feel and act. "The flow of events is complex, like a river with many tributaries," and the effective advocate seeks to alter that stream by guiding individuals and institutions to change their behavior.

Conner said there are two obvious ways to change behavior—by pushing and pulling—and one less obvious way involving collaboration. The push approach makes a person do something whether they want to or not, and the pull strategy involves cajoling someone through education, incentives or warnings. The third option operates like a well-functioning community team and entails solving specific problems through deep forms of collaboration in which participants may agree to disagree on other matters. The collaboration strategy requires all participants to step off their narrow paths, surrender individual egos and agendas. No one ever does it perfectly, and at first Conner thought these three fundamentals were the whole answer.

But it soon occurred to him there is another dimension. Conner calls it *stance*. Stance is about attitudes we hold toward another person or group, and allows us to describe others as friend or foe, from bosom buddies down the spectrum to bitter enemies. (Conner uses the term *friend* not in the sense of liking a person but to signify that we respect them and accept they are decent, even though they hold other opinions.)

Conner explained that the most common strategy when trying to overpower someone believed to have evil interests is push-foe, whereas push-friend would be utilized when working with a government official or legislator who agrees with you. Pushing in this instance is done from a place of respect and care. You wouldn't want to cause this person to lose her or his job. You wouldn't call them names. A pull-friend or collaboration-friend strategy is usually stable and sustained over time, as is a foe-push strategy. Why in the latter case? Because unfortunately, most of us have attitudes toward other people or groups that are determined by their behavior toward us. "If you behave like my enemy, I understand you are my enemy." If you behave like a self-interested, profit-seeking, care-nothing-for-the-environment person and call me a liar, I see you as my enemy, Conner said. So we commonly allow our stance to be determined by other people's behavior.

This leads to what Conner calls the advocacy trap. People don't start out as enemies—it happens in stages. When people disagree with us, we first question their views, but eventually we question their motives and intentions. When they persist in their disagreement with us, we start to perceive them as aggressors. When they criticize our cause or condemn our reasoning, our defense mechanisms kick in. We are offended and start to get angry. When both sides in an argument draw their stance from the perceived behavior of the other, people eventually start treating each other as not just wrong but as wrongdoer, and then as enemies. Once that happens, it is almost impossible to do anything over a sustained period of time other than futilely push one another.

Conner observed that the advocacy trap is very much like other seductive but ultimately self-destructive pleasures. In the short run, it provides attention, "from the all-important media and applause, not to mention money, from their base, but in the long run this behavior prevents them [advocates] from fulfilling the calling that drew them into public advocacy in the first place."

Effective advocates need to shift from push, to collaborate, to pull as circumstances change. It's very difficult to engage in genuine collaboration or even compromise with someone you consider untrustworthy, evil or despicable. In a sustained dispute, if both parties draw their impressions from the perceived behavior of the other, each of them mirrors what they think the other is doing. It doesn't take long for them to look at each other with profound distrust. Once the advocacy trap is set, breaking the circle of blame is extraordinarily difficult. To escape this rancorous circle, an advocate needs to stand up and walk away. In three decades of experience, Conner has seen no other solution to such inflamed situations. To explicitly and consciously choose a stance of respect, or better yet empathy and compassion—and to do so without expectation of reciprocity, is exceedingly hard. But letting go of the foe stance can break a stalemate.

Conner does not suggest people stop fighting for what they believe in, but he counsels us all to police our attitudes so we can learn to push sometimes, pull sometimes, collaborate sometimes and remain limber enough to sway back and forth, like a light-footed boxer, as the situation demands. Too much aggression will automatically and absolutely increase the energy the other side is devoting to an issue, he explained. "Nothing's so common as powerful groups creating resistance by overplaying their hands and dealing in ungenerous or resentful ways."

Roger Conner, who is also a consultant on advocacy strategies, conflict resolution and polarization, said it takes conscious thought and discipline to generate our attitudes toward others from the inside, rather than having them develop from the outside. But people who monitor their attitudes toward others, and don't allow resentment to boil up, can actually hear what others are saying. A good police officer employs that skill so an angry drunk can't provoke them. A wise doctor does not become emotionally upset when a child with multiple gunshot wounds comes into the ER. Parents do this too, when raising children. Of course, some kids are smart enough to get under their parents' skins, but a smart parent can overcome that, just as a good CEO does. Few of us practice this skill of not letting our perceptions control our attitudes, and as a result, we hand over control of a vital part of our cognitive machinery to someone else.

In a 2005 paper titled "Strategy and Stance,"[2] Conner said a leader such as Martin Luther King refused to fall into the advocacy trap because he refused to allow his stance to be a reflection of the behavior of others. He did not give others the right or the power to determine his attitude. The same was true of Mahatma Gandhi, who refused to hate those who imprisoned him. To use the entire range of strategic options, a public advocate must avoid thinking of others as foes.

Conner observed that it is no surprise that good people do bad things for good reasons. And the advocacy trap is to be expected in a political arena where people disagree, just as it's normal for a swamp to stink at night. "But what has changed in the current environment, compared to when I first started 40 or 50 years ago, is the increasing number of people involved in advocacy." Sheer volume is creating more polarization as more people are treating one another as enemies.

The antidote is to develop a greater capacity for self-awareness and self-control because "resentment is like a drug. It feels good to go home and say: 'Those assholes! Those jerks! Those liberals. Those conservatives…I'm right, they're wrong.'" Self-righteousness becomes a fuel that can justify "damn near anything." Conner has seen how resentment escalates in groups that start out only mildly resentful of each other. Discussion grows about how the other side is misusing information or ways in which they're making unjust attacks. "The truth is we all have some degree of uncertainty, and we go to this self-righteous place to protect ourselves from that uncertainty." Righteous indignation is necessary to act in the face of injustice, but self-righteousness develops when you cannot admit there may be an error in your point of view—or the possibility the other side is motivated by something other than evil. "I believe it's possible to think somebody is completely wrong, but also to believe they are a decent person who has somehow got it wrong." If you can hold that thought, you will avoid falling into the advocacy trap.

In conclusion, Conner urges advocates to abandon the foe stance and hold every person in your vision with respect. If you need to do it for religious reasons by saying every person is a child of God, try that. If you need to do it for psychological reasons and say, "I don't know what childhood experiences this person had that led them to behave this way," try that. Start by assuming others' intentions are good, and believing the leader of an organization deserves respect.

In Conner's experience, it's better to be clearheaded and respectful when pushing a strategy. It leads to greater understanding. Push strategies are often essential to wake someone up, but you need to switch to pull and then move toward collaboration as soon as possible. Success comes from understanding another's needs so fully that you can reshape the future together.

3

Mistakes Were Made
(But Not By Me)

with Carol Tavris

The brain is designed with blind spots, optical and psychological, and
one of its cleverest tricks is to confer on us the comforting delusion
that we, personally, do not have any. In a sense, dissonance theory is
a theory of blind spots—of how and why people unintentionally blind
themselves so that they fail to notice vital events and information that
might make them question their behavior or their convictions.

Carol Tavris *and* Elliot Aronson

AFTER LISTENING TO Roger Conner explain how people base
their stance on the perceived behavior of others, I wanted to
learn more about what it is in our human nature that makes us
stumble again and again into these advocacy traps. What drives
good people to do bad things? What fuels human beings' obstinate
behavior, irrational justification and confrontational opinions in
the face of convincing evidence.

A few years ago, I was reading an interesting book called *The
Social Animal* by David Brooks,[1] and some members of my book

club said, "That's great but not nearly as good as the one by Carol Tavris and Elliot Aronson called *Mistakes Were Made (But Not by Me)*."[2] They were right. I picked up a copy and read it three times. Tavris and Aronson explain so simply, so elegantly, why a person can discard your point and adopt a counter position, almost regardless of what you say. I began to understand that some people are not listening because of a whole set of reasons I had not previously considered.

I contacted Carol Tavris to see if she would be willing to talk about climate change denial and the psychology behind our current environmental conflicts. She agreed. She is a very take-charge person, and I was amused when she started the interview herself by asking the first question.[3]

"I assume you want to know why many people aren't receptive to the message of global warming, right? It's the latest version of a question that has puzzled me my whole life: why is it when you say to somebody: 'Here's some really wonderful evidence that explains ever so clearly why you're wrong,' the person doesn't say, 'Oh thank you, Carol. I've been really waiting for this evidence. I'm just so appreciative.'"

Scientists are used to changing their thinking, are constantly putting their ideas to the test, risking being shown their hypothesis is wrong. But *cognitive dissonance* is uncomfortable for most people. Tavris defines this as "a state of tension that occurs whenever a person holds two cognitions (ideas, attitudes, beliefs, opinions) that are psychologically inconsistent," such as "smoking can kill me, but I smoke two packs a day." The smoker can reduce the dissonance in one of two ways: either quit smoking, or justify smoking by denying or minimizing the evidence that it's harmful. The mechanism of cognitive dissonance keeps us committed to our beliefs—especially beliefs that we have acknowledged publicly, that we have a commitment to or that we have invested time, effort and money into maintaining. This discord produces mental discomfort, which people seek to reduce in ingenious and self-deluding ways.

And so the answer to Carol Tavris's question is twofold. One relates to social psychology (the study of a person in his or her social context, what's happening in their world), and the other relates to what's going on inside that person. Fundamentally, people are resistant to climate change data because of the human resistance to changing our mind, the psychological response to fear messages—especially fear messages we can't do anything about—and the inherent biases in human perception. These are biases that make us seek and remember information that confirms what we believe—and reject, distort or forget information that dis-confirms what we believe.

But another set of factors has to do with the economy and ideology. Tavris recalled a time many years ago when she was a young editor at *Psychology Today*, reviewing a book on the Japanese town of Minamata, where people had been severely harmed by industrial pollution. She was struck by the fact these people decided to stay there because that's where their jobs, their homes and their livelihoods were. Even risking that their own children would be deformed, they would not leave. "On a global scale, this is what we see everywhere. In the aftermath of Hurricane Sandy, you would think the logical reasoning would be, 'Let's not rebuild here. We're losing our shoreline, let's build further inland.'" But no, people resist change and want to stay in their community.

She said enormous economic and ideological forces reinforce this tendency when it comes to climate change. "People don't want to acknowledge the danger to the world because of the economic consequences to their work, to their families, to their ways of life. That's a huge and realistic concern." Furthermore, those who have made enormous financial investments in doing things a certain way are unlikely to say: "Right. We'll just take a tremendous loss, close up shop and move into some other business." When you have a combination of economic, ideological and psychological biases all in play, it's very difficult for human beings to easily accept large-scale social and economic change.

I told her that when I did my book tour for *Climate Cover-Up*, not once did I have a climate change denier say, "Okay. You caught me. I was wrong. I admit it. I've changed my mind." The psychologist smiled and said that before we make a decision about anything—"Do I believe in climate change? Do I want to buy a Prius?"—we are at our most open-minded, and we will look for information supporting both choices. But the minute we make a decision, we begin to see all the reasons that were right about it. "We start to overlook and forget any information that suggests we were wrong." Self-justification protects us from the uncomfortable feeling of cognitive dissonance that comes from recognizing we made a mistake; the longer we hold fast to that original decision, the harder it is to change our minds.

In *Mistakes Were Made*, Tavris and Aronson use an image they call the *pyramid of choice*: "Two young men who are identical in terms of attitudes, abilities and psychological health, are standing at the top of a pyramid." They are pals and they are undecided about some issue—cheat or don't cheat in an exam, buy this car or that, take drug company money for their research or not. Now one of them makes a decision in one direction, and the other makes a decision in the opposite direction. The minute they do that, they both start looking for evidence to confirm the wisdom of their choices. As they justify their decisions and their beliefs, they each begin moving farther and farther away from each other until, over time, they are standing at the bottom of the same pyramid, miles apart, and they might have come to dislike or even despise each other.

This image can describe most important decisions involving moral choices or life options, Tavris explained. By the time these two former buddies have slid to the bottom, their ambivalence will have morphed into certainty. The two will think they have always felt this way because self-justification works to keep our beliefs consonant with our behavior and our commitments. What's worrying is that their original decision may have been spontaneous, impulsive, perhaps not very well thought out—but every step they take afterward sets them on a path that they must increasingly justify.

Over time, the more time, effort, money and public face we attach to any of our decisions, the harder it is to climb back up that pyramid and say, "You know what? Gee, halfway down I really should've changed my mind." This is called the *justification of effort phenomenon*. It is very powerful. "We make an early, apparently inconsequential decision, and by justifying it, we start a process of entrapment that increases the intensity of our commitment," Tavris told me. Justification of effort explains why people who invest in a project that tanks will generally find a way to defend that mistake rather than face the alternative, which is to say: "I'm a good, smart, decent person—and I just did something stupid, unethical or incompetent."

Tavris further explained that cognitive dissonance—that state of having two conflicting cognitions or beliefs that clash with each other—is as uncomfortable as being very hungry or thirsty. The mind is highly motivated to reduce that discomfort: "Dissonance is especially painful when the conflict arises between my view of myself and information that disputes that view."

"Most people think of themselves as being better than average," Tavris said with a smile. "We think we're smarter than average, more attractive than average, more competent, more ethical, and so on. (It's very funny: 88 percent of all Americans think they're better drivers than average.) That's good for self-esteem, but actually people with the highest self-esteem have the most trouble accepting the evidence that they made a wrong decision, did something harmful or are holding an outdated belief."

As I listened to her, I realized this is why advocates in any field of conflict have to be careful not to make their opponents more entrenched in their opposition. This is why it's so important to delve into this modern research, to understand these psychological underpinnings of inaction and denial cycles.

Tavris concluded: "The greatest danger we face on the planet is not only from bad people doing corrupt, evil and bad things, but also from good people who justify the bad, evil and corrupt things they do in order to preserve their belief that they're good, kind, ethical people." This is why it's so hard for physicians to hear they need to correct medical errors in hospitals, or prosecutors need to help release those who've been wrongly convicted—in other words, to correct wildly significant errors in their professions.

In *Mistakes Were Made*, Tavris and Aronson noted that self-justification is more dangerous and powerful than intentionally lying to others because it allows people to convince themselves that what they did was right. The thought process often goes something like this: "There was nothing else I could have done... Actually it was a brilliant solution...I was doing the best for the nation...I'm entitled."

This self-talk minimizes our mistakes and poor decisions and interferes with our ability to self-correct. Everyone knows when he or she is lying, making excuses, finessing their income tax, doing something illegal or immoral. They may consciously lie to avoid being punished, "to duck the fury of a lover," to avoid being sued or sent to prison. But self-justification is completely different and more pervasive because it allows us to lie to ourselves. It is a self-protective, unconscious mechanism that allows us to keep our self-image intact. Tavris said the feeling of dissonance is sharpest when we have to resolve a conflict between evidence and some important aspect of our self-concept. "You can criticize me for something that isn't part of my self-concept, but criticize something I try to do well and it will really sting. That's the sting we have to pay attention to because that sting is the sign of dissonance."

Cognitive dissonance and justification of effort play a role in politics too. If a member of your party does something stupid or corrupt, you tend to minimize it, but when someone from the opposing party does exactly the same, you'll say, "That's typical of those bastards." One example was Newt Gingrich criticizing Bill Clinton for having an affair in the Oval Office while he himself was having an affair with one of his own interns. Gingrich's ability to blame Clinton, while excusing himself, shows how far people will go to reduce their own cognitive dissonance.

There is no point hectoring people or telling them they are wrong, Tavris and Aronson explained in *Mistakes Were Made*. Anyone who understands dissonance knows that shouting "What were you thinking?" will backfire because it translates as "Boy, are you stupid." Accusations like this cause already embarrassed victims to clam up, withdraw and refuse to talk about what they are doing—"What was I thinking? I thought I was doing the right thing." People need to feel respected and supported, not criticized. This is the inherent risk of advocacy, because if you accuse someone of being stupid, or make them feel foolish or dim, it only serves to reinforce their default position—which is to activate their self-justification.

How does this insight help us in our environmental conflict discussion? What are the factors that cause somebody to jump off the pyramid at the very top and take a position on a problem? And perhaps more importantly, what do we do when we have two polarized camps at the bottom, both justifying the choices they made?

During my interview with her, Carol Tavris stressed again there are two things to be concerned about: factors that cause us to come to a belief in the first place and factors that cause us to maintain that position. "In all social movements, you are not only justifying the beliefs you've acquired, but you become part of a group of like-minded people, all echoing the reasons you're right."

To understand resistance to information about climate data, we can look at the history of seat belts, smoking or environmental protection laws that were once thought impossible to enact.

Revolutionizing people's smoking habits required more than changing people's belief that smoking could kill you. Everyone knew someone who lived to be 93 and smoked every day. To change people's habits, we had to apply peer pressure, change laws, change taxes, change social norms and force people onto the street if they wanted to light up.

From Tavris's perspective, you don't transform societies through a change of heart alone; you have to first change the laws, change public notions of what is acceptable or unacceptable behavior and change the economic consequences of the practices you want to alter. "When that happens at a national or systemic level, people's attitudes begin to change." Going back to her image of the pyramid, the goal is to help people form opinions at the top of the pyramid (for the first time), or, when people have dug in their heels, find out what it would take to get them to alter their minds.

I suggested that people likely don't spend a lot of time at the peak of the pyramid, and Tavris agreed. Most have strong beliefs and have already slid down the pyramid, one way or the other, on environmental issues. So the stronger power of persuasion may lie in getting people who believe in social justice and protecting the environment to become more actively involved in changing government regulations and citizen passivity.

Tavris said one of the most important findings in social psychology is that when you just give people a frightening message— "If you have sex, you'll get AIDS. If you smoke, you'll die"—people tune out. But if the scary message comes with something you can do to avert the disaster, such as "Condoms will keep you from getting AIDS," then people are more likely to listen. "One of the great problems with climate change arguments is that we have been made to feel helpless; the problem is overwhelming. 'I could get a gas-efficient car, but every time I fly to England, that's the equivalent of, what, how many thousands of miles that I've driven in my car?'" One of the best ways to help people change their behavior is to give them feedback, show them how much money or water they have saved, by practicing methods of conservation.

Tell them it's working and give them hope. Hope is the narrative of freedom and change. It is the great motivator. "Otherwise, let's just dance on the cliff until we fall off. Social reformers and activists are all acting with hope. What keeps us going is seeing how much change has occurred in the past as a model for the kind of change that can occur in the future."

I asked if activists often make things worse by stimulating people's self-justification response. Tavris believes we need two kinds of activists: both extremists and persuaders. "Shell Oil is not going to listen to reasoned persuasion and say, 'Oh, thank you so much for providing us with this information about how we're spoiling the environment. We hadn't realized that.' Nor are the big pharmaceutical companies going to say, 'Oh, thank you for the data showing our drug has actually been killing far too many people.'" These companies want to hide and suppress data, she said. So one tactic of more extreme opponents has been to go after the worst offenders and polluters. They're not going to do the right thing until they're forced to, until there are regulations and penalties, and enough consumer protests to warrant making changes.

But change also happens through persuasion, when the public becomes more aware of the kinds of harm these companies are doing. The danger for the accuser, however, arises when they put on the mantle of the do-gooder, the valiant David taking on Goliath. "All of us need to keep reassessing our beliefs, our goals and our methods because we too can be vulnerable to justifying our methods and our beliefs without stopping to ask ourselves if this is the most effective thing we can be doing."

It's not easy for any of us to ask those questions, and Tavris illustrated her point with a personal example of her own dissonance. She used to be opposed to hormone replacement therapy, which she felt was unnecessary, possibly dangerous and most likely another effort by the pharmaceutical industry to sell more drugs than necessary. But when she and a colleague, an oncologist who has studied the issue for many years, looked at the evidence that has accrued over decades, they found that for most women HRT is actually beneficial in prolonging life and quality of life. "That was a big dissonance-inducing discovery for me as I am a big critic of Big Pharma and opposed to taking just about anything. So I know how uncomfortable it feels when you are forced to say, 'Here's something I believed for many years and I'm wrong.'"

Self-righteousness is a barrier to self-change, and an impediment to persuading others. We don't relish listening to a moralizer or proselytizer trying to persuade us of something without recognizing where we are coming from and what our needs are. Tavris said it is important to have passionate beliefs because they help motivate us to improve the world, but the key is "to hold those beliefs lightly so that if evidence comes along suggesting we might be wrong, we can give them up without feeling like we are idiots."

She said an ideal way to live with dissonance is by understanding that we can both see ourselves as good people and admit to doing something wrong. We can admit a mistake and seek ways to rectify it in the future. Cognitive dissonance is a blind spot that enhances our pride and activates our prejudices, she and Aronson wrote in their book. When we spoke, Tavris urged us all to watch out for blind spots (just as good drivers do) and to watch ourselves for any signs of post-decision dissonance. We can all stay aware and open-minded by asking ourselves, at certain intervals: "I made this decision or I came to this belief three years ago, is it still the right one? What do people with different points of view have to tell me about this now?"

And be aware of *naïve realism*, the built-in bias that we are not biased. Naïve realism allows people on two sides of any issue, whether it's the Middle East or climate change, to each think their view is the only reasonable one. Social psychologist Lee Ross gave a sample group of Palestinians a peace proposal designed by the

Palestinians, but he labeled it as coming from Israelis. He also gave Israelis a peace proposal that had come from Israelis, but was labeled as a Palestinian proposal. Each side soundly rejected the proposals.[4] "They weren't rejecting the idea in the proposal; they were rejecting who they thought it came from."

One way out of this built-in trap, Carol Tavris explained, is to do our best to hear and repeat the opposite camp's point of view. For those of us trying to get more people concerned about climate change, we need to be able to hear deniers' arguments if we are to persuade them to hear ours. Listen openly, and see if you can understand the sources of people's fears and concerns. And then don't ask them to repeat their views—see if you can repeat theirs.

4

Morality Binds and Blinds

with Jonathan Haidt

If you want the truth to stand clear before you,

never be for or against.

The struggle between "for" and "against"

is the mind's worst disease.

Seng-ts'an

A S THE THEMES in this book began to crystalize, I arranged an interview with social psychologist Jonathan Haidt. A professor of ethical leadership at New York University's Stern School of Business, Haidt looks at how ingrained tribal behaviors can bind and blind us, and shut down open-minded thinking. Looking at the dynamic of polarization from the point of view of tribes and teams is enlightening and useful in this discussion.

Many of those who read my last book, *Climate Cover-Up*, have asked me why people try to discredit scientists, confuse the public and deny climate science. What motivates this kind of activity? How can these paid lobbyists and bogus experts sleep at night? I used to say it was because of money, but I no longer believe it's that simple. The strength and doggedness of these campaigns calls for a deeper look, and Haidt is an expert in the morality and anatomy of persistent beliefs that fly in the face of evidence.

During our interview in New York,[1] the professor explained that human beings are tribal, oriented from birth to band together into groups and teams. And while there is much good to be said for this age-old drive, it is also a potentially dangerous trait that binds and blinds us. Banding together can lead to unreasonable behavior, disagreements and violent conflict because we are not driven by rationality, facts or compelling arguments. Haidt's and his colleagues' studies have found banding together causes some groups of people to pull apart from other groups, to not only go to war but to become polarized along distinct lines, whether it's over gun control or oil sands.[2] Division can be dangerous because when people share values and morals, they become part of a team, "and once they engage in the psychology of a team, open-minded thinking shuts down."

Haidt calls this perilous trap the *moral matrix*. And just like in the movie *The Matrix*, we all have a choice: "You can either take the blue pill and stick to your comforting delusions, or the red pill, learn some moral psychology and step outside the moral matrix," Haidt explained.

Based on research into what Haidt calls the psychological foundations of morality, he explained an awareness of our moral roots can help us learn to become more civil and more open-minded, to glean a deeper appreciation of the world around us and to balance the yin-yang effect of opposing forces. We come to understand how we can get stuck in a moral matrix and, more importantly, how to escape it. "Our righteous minds have been designed by evolution to unite us into teams and divide us against other teams, to blind us to the truth," but if we can step outside our moral matrix, we can find balance and truer understanding of each other.

I first learned about Haidt's work while watching his 2008 TED talk, titled "The Moral Roots of Liberals and Conservatives,"[3] and later I read his book *The Righteous Mind*, which explains how and why good people become divided by politics and religion.[4]

Haidt began his TED talk by declaring that the worst idea in all of psychology is that the mind is a blank slate at birth. Far from

it, he stressed. Children come into the world neurally prepro-
grammed to easily learn certain things and have difficulty learning
others. Brain scientist Gary Marcus said the initial organization
of the brain does not rely heavily on experience. "Nature provides
a first draft, which experience then revises."[5]

So the question for Haidt is "What is written in that first draft
of the moral mind?" Haidt and his colleagues researched this concept across cultures and even species and came up with a theory
that identifies six moral foundations common to all.[6] They are
care/harm, fairness/cheating, liberty/oppression, loyalty/betrayal,
authority/subversion and sanctity/degradation. Loyalty/betrayal,
for instance, relates to patriotism and self-sacrifice, which is why
human groups so easily unite to fight other groups. This trait
likely evolved from a long history of intertribal struggle, and when
we don't have tribes to fight, we create sports instead so our teams
can compete in other arenas. "The aspect of purity/sanctity, on the
other hand, is an ideology that tells a person they can attain virtue
by controlling their body and what they put in it. This is seen in
our liberal moralized attitude about food. Purity's not just about
suppressing female sexuality."

Haidt said we come into the world pre-wired, organized in
advance by these six sources of intuition and emotion that enable
us to quickly bond with others, feel compassion, found religions or
defend ourselves. This "first draft" is revised and tuned by life experience and culture, just as audio equalizers in a complex sound
system regulate sound waves—but the basic human moral matrix
remains. Haidt's research has shown liberals celebrate diversity, are
more open to new experiences, crave novelty, question authority
and speak for the weak and oppressed, even at the risk of chaos.
Conservatives speak for order. They like things that are familiar,
safe and dependable, which is why they support institutions and
traditions.

Haidt believes it is important to acknowledge and cherish both
points of view because they bring balance. Once you accept that

liberals and conservatives each have something of value to contribute, the way is open to step outside the moral matrix. "Yin and Yang aren't enemies. Like night and day, both are essential. In the Hindu faith, both Vishnu and Shiva, the preserver and destroyer gods, share the same body." When diversity is understood and valued, we can step out of a battle between good and evil and "use every tool in the toolbox" to create cooperative groups. "Use that passionate commitment to the truth to create a better future for us all."

I asked Haidt about partisan polarization, and he explained that it has increased in the US since the 1980s, and especially in the last 10 years, partly because the two parties have become "purified." If you go back to the 1960s and 1970s, and even into the 1980s, there were liberal Republicans and conservative Democrats, but there is no longer any middle ground. The parties are perfectly distinct, not just in moral visions but in personality, Haidt observed. As the polarizing current becomes more and more powerful and increasing amounts of money are spent to influence policy, anything with even the "slightest valence" (meaning emotional charge) gets pulled to one side or the other.

Haidt said money for advertising campaigns is another factor that plays into growing polarization. Public relations machines are incredibly powerful, devious and manipulative; a confluence of factors around 2005 and 2006 made people congeal around the idea that climate change was a fraud. Haidt told me he once heard American radio host and commentator Glenn Beck say, "Climate change is not about the environment, it's about control." Americans don't like to be told what to do. They don't like the nanny state, and Haidt believes the Right very skillfully pushed certain moral buttons that sowed profound doubt.

I asked if there is any hope that conservatives can change their minds and start taking environmental problems seriously. He suggested those who want to make this happen should think less about direct methods and more about indirect methods.

A general principle of moral psychology is this: intuitions come first and strategic reasoning second. If people don't trust the Left, don't trust the environmental or scientific communities, the electromagnet again grows more powerful. If they see scientists and environmentalists as liberals, they won't trust them. Echoing Carol Tavris's image of the pyramid of choice, Haidt explained that *confirmation bias theory* tells us if you doubt, dislike and distrust something in your heart, you're going to look for evidence that confirms that. We human beings tend to say: "I think proposition X is true. Is there any evidence for it? Yes, I just saw some on Fox News. Okay. It's true." This theory explains why direct attacks are not effective. Results are achieved by draining the passion, changing feelings and opening up space for better reasoning.

Haidt cited the gay marriage movement as a prime example. For many years, the Left argued: "How does it hurt your marriage if other people marry? Don't they have a right?" But the rights of gay people to marry did not start to change until more people came to know gay people, and they became just people who happened to be gay. The passion to oppose their rights drained away. "Twenty years ago, to be homosexual was laughable, disgusting and strange—but now everybody knows gay people," so gay marriage is losing its emotional charge.

Similarly, Haidt suggested that as climate change advocates focus on issues such as fuel efficiency standards, better light bulbs and ways to make us all less energy dependent, the negative charge will weaken. "If you begin to associate combating climate change with the Apollo program and a gigantic national effort to find technologies that will wean us off the carbon-heavy fuel sources, then it won't seem threatening anymore." Suddenly people will trust the scientists. Change the feelings, and then evidence has a chance.

Polarization is extremely predictable, Haidt explained, and part of the blindness involves perceiving issues increasingly as threats. The more you make something central to your team's mission, the more blind you become, which causes the other side to become blind to your issue. For example, in the US now, more than 50 percent of kids will not live with their two biological parents throughout their childhood, either because of divorce or non-marital childbearing. It's a concern to many, "but people on the Left are unwilling to say marriage is good or necessary because they don't want to risk offending feminists, African-Americans and gay people. So the Left is effectively blind around the issue. If you hitch your environmentalism to a polarizing issue, you can pretty much guarantee that you're painting it with a cloak of invisibility, and the other side is simply not going to see your concern."

Haidt paraphrased a quote by Jesus: "Why do you complain about the speck in your neighbor's eye when you cannot see the plank in your own?"[7] In general, our social cognitive abilities are extremely accurate in our perception of others, but extremely inaccurate in our perception of ourselves.

He added that although it's very difficult to remove people's biases, when in conflict with a person or group, an incredibly valuable tool is to acknowledge where others are right because in almost any conflict each side is right about something. "If you're Shell Oil, you could start by saying: 'Environmentalist, we understand that you're concerned. The oil and gas industry has done some bad things. We've had some major screwups, we have killed seabirds.' The Left could say to Shell Oil: 'You're not crazy to worship markets. Markets really are amazing things.'"

This is true acknowledgment, the power of empathy, and it lies at the heart of Haidt's message. If our goal is to seek a deeper understanding of the world around us and clear the public square, we must move from self-righteousness to moral humility. It's all about shifting the tone and not being accusatory because, as Haidt explains, each of us has a thin-skinned moral matrix that is the source of our most sacred beliefs.

5

Why We Want to Be Misled

with Dan Kahan

People will find the person whose values they think
are more like theirs to be more credible.
And that's how they figure out what to believe,
because they trust people like them.

Dan Kahan

ONE OF THE FIRST interviews I did for this book was with
Dan Kahan at Yale Law School. Yale Law has an interdisciplinary faculty where professors and scholars specialize in everything from economics to psychiatry. Kahan's primary research
interests are risk perception, science communication and the
application of decision science to law and policymaking. I had
come to interview him after reading about his work on the Cultural Cognition Project, which features a team of interdisciplinary
scholars who study how cultural values shape people's beliefs and
perceptions of risk. I wanted to learn how group values impact
risk perceptions and how our interpretation of scientific evidence
is shaped by our cultural affiliations.

Cultural cognition describes the tendency of individuals to
conform their beliefs about disputed matters of fact—whether
relating to global warming as a serious threat or the death penalty
as a deterrent to committing murder—to values that define

their cultural identities. Kahan and his colleagues employ social psychology, anthropology, communications theory and political science to chart the impact of this phenomenon and identify its operating mechanisms. In a study published in 2010, Kahan and his colleagues looked at why some members of the public disagree—"sharply and persistently"—about facts on which expert scientists generally agree. The study confirmed that cultural cognition does indeed shape individual beliefs about the existence of scientific consensus, whether about climate change or the disposal of nuclear waste.[1]

My interview with Dan Kahan took place in his office over the course of two hours—time I now affectionately refer to as "My Class at Yale Law."[2] What began as an interview about the impact of corporate misinformation on public denial of climate change became a fascinating lesson in how the public forms opinions about risk and science. It reconfirmed in my mind how futile public arguments involving facts and evidence can be, and deepened my view about how industry misinformation creates confusion. I went into the interview well versed in how people are misled by misinformation and propaganda, but I wanted to learn more about how we mislead ourselves—and about the complicated process of how corrupted cultural networks affect our understanding and our judgments.

While misinformation campaigns certainly play a role in public confusion, Kahan argued that there are more powerful forces at work and that more accurate information on its own will not fix what he calls a *social pathology* that leads to underestimating or denying climate change risk. Nor is the pathology of climate change denial as simple as one group agreeing with real climate scientists and another aligning themselves with charlatans.

Kahan said there is a reason why people allow themselves to be misled and are predisposed to being misinformed. He described two primary influences that play into this vulnerability: confirmation bias and motivated reasoning. *Confirmation bias* is a type of selective thinking in which a person tends to notice and look for what confirms their beliefs, while prompting them to ignore or not favor information that contradicts those beliefs. He described *motivated reasoning* as, "the unconscious tendency of individuals to process information in a manner that suits some end or goal extrinsic to the formation of accurate beliefs." Motivated reasoning is a unifying theme or general class of mechanisms that makes people resist information that threatens their identity.

These influences propel people to confirm what they already believe and ignore any data to the contrary. These forces can also drive them to develop elaborate rationalizations to justify those beliefs, even if false, and even if logic and evidence point in another direction.

In a paper titled "Motivated Numeracy and Enlightened Self-Government," Kahan studied subjects who were presented with a difficult problem that called upon their ability to draw valid "causal inferences from empirical data."[3] Subjects with high scores in numeracy (the ability to use quantitative information) did much better than others in the group when asked to interpret data about a new skin rash treatment. But interestingly, the subjects' responses were more politically polarized and less accurate when they looked at results from a gun control ban study. In fact, the polarization increased in high numeracy subjects who used their greater reasoning capacity to make sure their interpretation conformed to their politics.

Kahan referred to another paper that showed when two experts argue about something, even if the issue is remote from the values of those involved, "people will find the person whose values they think are more like theirs to be more credible. And that's how they figure out what to believe, because they trust people like them[selves]."[4]

Kahan stressed human beings are "really good" at figuring out who to believe about what. This is a critical skill since not one human being could possibly reproduce all the world's knowledge alone. Every scientist builds on previous researchers' work; this is why Sir Isaac Newton said he was standing on the shoulders of giants. Kahan illustrated this point further by saying he hasn't been to the North Pole himself and even if he had, he wouldn't know how to measure whether the ice was melting. "If you gave me the measuring equipment and I got readings out of it, I wouldn't know what they meant." Kahan explained that we make the sensible decision to go with people who certify for us, in a reliable way, what's true.

We all rely on such trust networks or systems of certification and communication to make the right choices, but sadly these systems sometimes end up being distorted and corrupted. "We wouldn't have the problems we have today if there wasn't the kind of concentrated, orchestrated effort to try to cause division.... Just as we can pollute the natural environment, we can pollute public discourse."

Public controversy over climate change is often attributed to ordinary citizens' limited knowledge of science, their poor reasoning capacity or assumed inability to assess technical information. But a study conducted by the Cultural Cognition Project and published in the journal *Nature Climate Change* found no support for this at all. "On the whole, the most scientifically literate and numerate subjects were slightly less likely to see climate change as a serious threat," reported Kahan. Those with the greatest science literacy and capacity for technical reasoning were, in fact, among the most polarized.[5] Kahan theorized that this discrepancy arises from a conflict between belief systems—a conflict between *individuals* who form beliefs in line with those held by others with whom they share close ties and the *collective* in which everyone shares in making use of the best available science to promote common welfare.

I asked Kahan, "Isn't the whole idea behind critical thinking that you try not to let your beliefs get in the way of facts and evidence?"

Yes, he said, but belief is not a function of will. You don't choose what you believe; you believe what you believe because you are furnished with the kinds of evidence that impel a certain kind of cognition. People have what Kahan called a "commonwealth" of sensibilities, values and dilemmas that exert control over them and can cause them to misunderstand things. We all rely on people who confirm what we think and on systems of certification, but because our beliefs are connected to who we are and our personal history, they are sometimes distorted.

The Cultural Cognition of Scientific Consensus study showed that when people get new information, they can update prior beliefs. This only happens, however, if they recognize the new information as valid. He explained: If you put people in a room and give them a really hard math problem, 90 percent of them won't know the answer. What typically happens is that the people who are ignorant of math will converge on the 10 percent who have that knowledge, not because that group tells them how to do the math problem, but because the 90 percent know something—how to identify others who know what they're talking about.[6]

The process hinges on trust networks and the human skill of being able to find the right kinds of affiliations, so each person can plug into "different networks of certification." That's the normal science communication organism working: you don't have to be an expert in medicine to be adept at choosing a competent doctor.

But Kahan pointed out something is happening in current discourse to cause systems of certification to be less reliable than usual, to corrupt trust networks. Sometimes it is because people are manipulated, "and there are some fringe groups out there that say, 'Screw science!'" But Kahan believes there are two more significant, reciprocal elements at work: "one is the orchestrated and deliberate attempt to misinform, and the other is a kind of vulnerability and disposition to being misled." How far you can get with the former depends in large part on the latter.

Dan Kahan believes we need to improve the science of science communication so we can transmit knowledge accurately, especially now because people are not paying attention to debates about science. Also, there is a science of how to mislead people about science, and there are plenty of people who have a big interest in fueling division. They are not playing a constructive role because they may have vested interests or are mired in "the error of zealotry."

When I asked Kahan how we can move toward healthy dialogue and agreement, he said an effective way to strike communication gold is to start mining more pluralistic narrative resources.

"We know from cognitive psychology that people process information in narratives." When there is a good guy and a bad guy; some kind of recognizable drama; a beginning, middle and end; as well as a moral and a conclusion, people resonate with the story and make sense of what you are saying. Culturally diverse people are motivated by different kinds of narratives, characters and dramas, so we need an inventory of narratives to convey information across different groups.

He stressed that there is also a narrator in every story, a speaker somewhere, and an audience will be very attentive to that; this is another influence that should affirm identity and not threaten it. Pluralistic advocacy needs to think about the message and the messenger, about the right narrative and the right spokesperson to deliver it, across myriad groups. When all these align, each person is able to converge on truth in their own way. A pluralistic advocacy environment is one where "people can see people like them on both sides of the issues, and also people who are not like them on both sides." The goal is to find a narrative that people relate to and embed a message that will lead to open-minded consideration.

Kahan explained that we must converge on the truth and respond to problems by respecting each other and letting go of intolerance. "It's not healthy to be imperialistic about one's own story and meanings." We need to acknowledge that other people have different sets of values, and we need to give up our compulsion to be right. That is zealotry. "We are thinking human beings and we're opinionated, and there is going to be a plurality of different kinds of ways people think.... We should agree that that's something we're going to promote."

A Failure to Communicate

6

Facts Are Not Enough

with George Lakoff

Get clear on your values
and start using the language of values.
Drop the language of policy.

George Lakoff

I FIRST BEGAN READING the works of linguist and cognitive scientist George Lakoff about 15 years ago and was struck by the Berkeley professor's now famous ideas about what he calls *frames*. In public relations, our stock-in-trade is messaging because our role is to create understanding with maximum clarity and brevity. We work in the world of sound bites and elevator pitches that are designed to be short and pithy, and we rarely have the time or budget to delve into frames or deeply moving narratives.

I wanted to better understand the difference between messages and frames, to know how frames work, how to manage them and how frames impact facts and scientific evidence in public discourse, or when shaping opinion.

When we met, Lakoff described *frames* as metaphors and conceptual frameworks that we use to interpret and understand the world.[1] They give meaning to the words we hear more than the other way around, because words don't have objective meanings independent of these metaphors. Frames are structures of thought that we all use every day to determine meaning in our lives; frames govern how we act. They are ultimately a blend of feelings, values and data related to how we see the world.

We can't think without frames, Lakoff explained. "Every thought you have, every word is defined in terms of a frame. You can't say any word that's meaningful without it activating a frame." Frames permeate everything we think and say, so the people who control language and set its frames have an inordinate amount of power.

Lakoff explained that if you do a bad job of framing your story, someone else will likely do it for you, and his comments reminded me of something my mentor in the PR business, Mike Sullivan, once said: "If you don't tell them, someone else will—and it will be bad." What Mike meant was if you are an unwilling or ineffective communicator, you leave yourself wide open to someone else doing serious damage.

A frame is a way of looking at the world that is value laden, and like a metaphor, it conjures up all kinds of thoughts and emotions. Jackie Kennedy used a frame when she referred to her life as Camelot. "Ethical oil" and "tax relief" are also frames. Such words evoke subconscious images and meanings, as opposed to factual statements such as "10 million scallops are dead," a headline that appeared in February 2014 in a Vancouver Island newspaper.[2]

What came to be called Climategate was an international campaign to discredit scientists on both sides of the Atlantic just before the 2009 Copenhagen summit on climate change. It took the momentum to set targets out of the conference. I was astonished to see how a group of legitimate climate scientists, with stacks of peer-reviewed evidence on their side, could lose debates to a group of people who had none—all because of a lens created by mischief-makers. Climategate was a battle of frames versus facts, and the frames won.[3]

The truth is, facts alone don't change minds, said Lakoff, who wrote a book called *Don't Think of an Elephant*, which explains how to frame political debates in terms of values, not facts.

Lakoff believes that the progressive community contributes to confusion in the public square because of an outdated understanding of reason and consequent lack of persuasive communication. During our interview, he told me that progressives need a mental model that goes beyond cold, logical messaging that's directly correlated to reality—a model which should embrace metaphors, a marriage of emotion and logic.

Liberals have an unemotional view of reason that dates back to French philosopher Descartes. Lakoff explained that when conservatives want to go into politics, they study business, marketing and what makes people tick, whereas progressives study political science, law and public policy. Progressives don't study cognitive science, neurology or how the brain works. "They learn a false view of reason that goes back to the 1600s…that says reason is conscious, logical and unemotional."

It wasn't long ago that risk communications experts, who study the power of facts, also assumed that giving people more information and evidence would ensure they made better decisions. But research shows facts don't change minds, at least not in the way we think they do.

Lakoff explained that cognitive and brain science research has shown that reason is not rational without emotion, without an overlay of values to make sense of facts. Simply put: frames trump facts. "We have thousands of metaphors structuring our brains," Lakoff told me. "We think in terms of them all the time, and they're not random, they're not mythical, they're things that allow us to get around in the world. We have to use them. Words aren't neutral"; they are the structure we use to think.

We should all have a commitment to the truth, he continued, but not let an understanding of facts overwhelm our job, which is to change the brains of people out there. "Every time you argue, you change your brain. Every time you tell somebody something else, you're changing brains, because everything you think is physical; it's all in the circuitry of your brain." But just speaking the truth isn't enough to convince people of new ideas. If facts are to make sense and be perceived as urgent, they must be framed in terms of deep, deep values.

George Lakoff's advice is short and sweet: To be an effective communicator, get clear on your values and start using the language of values. Drop the language of policy. "People do not necessarily vote their self-interest. They vote their identity. They vote their values."[4] Lakoff believes so-called inaction and apathy should warn progressives that the conservatives are winning the communications battle between moral imperatives: "It's time to decide, either we are all in this together or it's every man for himself."

Progressive morality says citizens act responsibly to provide infrastructure, education, health care, transportation and basic research for one another. Progressives constrain stock markets and protect bank accounts. They believe that private profit depends upon public provision. Conservatism is all about personal responsibility. The importance of public services is minimal when compared with the benefits of private enterprise. Conservatives promote stock markets and regulate banks. They believe that human effort creates wealth.

Of course some people are conservative about some things and progressive about others. Lakoff calls this *bi-conceptualism*; it means you can have both moral systems operating in your brain at the same time, each inhibiting the other from time to time. The more active one is, the stronger it gets, and that's where language and communication come in. It's also why media influences matter so much, as do the ways we communicate.

In politics and social issues, frames are hierarchically structured, and at the top of that hierarchy are the moral frames. So the question often is: Is this a frame where citizens care about each other, act responsibly and where there is a robust sense of what's good for all? Or is the frame telling us that someone believes they have the freedom to access their own self-interest but need not care about the interests of others?

When it comes to environmental issues, Lakoff explained that these conflicting moralities are tied to two very different ideas of our relationship with nature. For progressives: we are a part of nature and dependent on the environment. Nature has inherent value. For conservatives: we are separate from and dominant over nature. Nature's value is determined by its direct utility to people. Lakoff was quick to note that this is a simplification because most people aren't ideologues, and bi-conceptuals are generally open to persuasion in either direction. The moderate has no ideology.

Every word is defined by an individual frame. A frame is a neural circuit. A neural circuit is made up of connections of neurons joined together by synapses. When a circuit is activated, the synapses get stronger. If that circuit inhibits another circuit, then that other circuit's synapses get weaker. When the synapses are stronger, it is easier to activate an idea in someone's mind and therefore easier for it to spread to other issues. "So, repetition is what strengthens synapses. And it doesn't matter if it is accurate."

Suppose you're a conservative, he said, and you want to create a frame that fits your moral system, but let's suppose it has nothing to do with truth. You may be saying, for example, that cutting corporate taxes will create jobs. We know that's false. Corporations are making more profits than ever before and are not hiring people because they're outsourcing work, reaping the benefits of cheap labor in other countries or using more technology. They're not "creating jobs." So this is a false statement. But if conservatives call themselves job creators and repeat it over and over, people will think that cutting corporate taxes will create more jobs. The words are like a recurring jingle, stimulating a synapse and creating a thought pattern. That frame is activated over and over, and every time it is reactivated, it grows stronger.

I asked Lakoff if it's possible to set the record straight. Every time we say "Those are not job creators," do we step into the job creator frame and imprint it again? By outlining facts, even in a logical statement of contradiction, do we always help reinforce the other side's point of view?

Yes, he said. You lose the persuasion battle when you consistently step into your opponent's frame; it reinforces their morality and their argument in the minds of your audience. The way to respond is to not mention the other frame. Only mention yours. Always start with your frame and stay in it. Always be on the offensive; never act defensively.

Framing is a system that has evolved because it works for everyday life, said Lakoff. "Free will is not totally free. It is radically constrained by the frames and metaphors shaping your brain and limiting how you see the world. Those frames and metaphors get there, to a remarkable extent, through repetition in the media."[5]

Everything you have learned is stored physically in your brain, Lakoff stressed. Every frame is in a brain circuit, every metaphor is in a brain circuit, every image is in a brain circuit. Your whole moral system is in your brain. If you hear something that doesn't fit with what's in your brain, it will go in one ear and out the other unless you are the type of person who remembers things that don't quite fit and worries about them. But most people don't.

Progressives must realize that their old-fashioned view of reason is false—that Descartes and the information injection theory of communication have not panned out.

Matters Of Concern

with Bruno Latour

It's not a question of getting the facts straight
and sorting out truth from the rhetoric once and for all....
It's a question of changing the conditions of existence,
not just of a few people, but of seven billion people.

Bruno Latour

FRENCH PHILOSOPHER Bruno Latour agrees that facts don't change minds. They don't clear up controversies, and they don't solve problems, especially regarding environmental science communications, where arguments cyclone around facts, confusing the public and getting in the way of action. We need a different approach, said Latour,[1] who is a professor at Sciences Po Paris where he founded and directs a groundbreaking social sciences facility called médialab. It is a high-tech hub for leading-edge research that applies digital tools and technologies to enhance research in the social sciences.

When we met in Paris, Latour told me we should put aside matters-of-fact and focus instead upon matters-of-concern, a conclusion he arrived at after having studied everything from environmental crises to atmospheres of democracy. His advice seemed simple enough, but why is this necessary and what does it mean, exactly?

Latour has authored dozens of books, including *Laboratory Life*, *Pandora's Hope*, *We Have Never Been Modern*, *Science in Action*, and *The Politics of Nature: How to Bring the Sciences into Democracy*, all of which explore the intersections of science and politics.[2] In 2013 he also won the Holberg Prize for his ambitious analysis and reinterpretation of modernity, which led the committee to state his work reaches far beyond the "studies of the history of science, art history, history, philosophy, anthropology, geography, theology, literature and law."[3]

In a 2005 essay called "From Realpolitik to Dingpolitik: An Introduction to Making Things Public,"[4] Latour referred to an infamous address given by former US secretary of state, Colin Powell, to the United Nations. In this 2003 speech, Powell attested to the "unambiguous and undisputable fact of the presence of weapons of mass destruction in Iraq." Of course, it wasn't long before the world realized that this "fact" was groundless, but at the time, Powell prefaced his remarks by saying: "My colleagues, every statement I make today is backed up by sources, solid sources. These are not assertions. What we are giving you are facts and conclusions based on solid intelligence."

Never was the difference between facts and assertions more abused than on that day, wrote Latour. "Mr. Powell tried to distinguish the rhetoric of assertions from the undisputable power of facts. He failed miserably. Having no truth, he had no eloquence either. Can we trace again the frail conduits through which truths and proofs are allowed to enter the sphere of politics?"[5]

Latour explained that this question is actually moot because the solution lies not simply in getting facts straight and sorting out truth from the rhetoric once and for all. "Transparent, unmediated, undisputable facts" have become so rare today that to offer a public proof—big enough and certain enough to convince the whole world of the presence of a phenomenon or of a looming danger—seems now almost beyond reach.

And so Latour said it is important now to put facts aside, to abandon the worn-out cliché of incontrovertible so-called truths and to compare assertions instead. With these inferior types of proof, we may come to a conclusion at last. He suggested that turning to matters-of-concern suits the modern era because we are in a time of huge sea change, of transformations that will encompass our conceptions of science and understanding of objectivity. The enormous complexities of both scientific research and political activity at every level are leading us to a growing appreciation that objects and issues "are much more interesting, variegated, uncertain, complicated, far reaching, heterogeneous, risky" than we have ever believed.

Even today, people like Powell are accustomed to sweeping away opposition by claiming the superiority of their facts, but Latour explained that, after studying real scientists in action during his 40-year career, he understands that in the realm of science facts are always the source of careful scrutiny, inquiry and discussion. Whereas in the realm of politics, matters-of-fact are too often held to be self-evident weapons to be used to end a debate rather than foster discussion or dialogue.

We talked about the complexity of climate change, and Latour explained that the field involves a vast body of research that encompasses the knowledge and practical work of thousands of scientists, the multifaceted accomplishments of an immense number of individuals. The problem, he asserted, is not a lack of information or facts. Quite the opposite. Climate science has produced masses of information, but Latour points out "knowing is made up of so many different loops and different layers that it takes a lot of time to measure out what we know." He sees a disconnect between what is known—what facts are, what knowledge means and why those facts are significant—precisely because of the time it takes to evaluate data, to discuss and project its implications and to consider how to act on that knowledge. We will never have such good data on climate change as we have today, he stressed, "because now we have put the thing out of whack" (referring to Earth's climate balance).

Latour believes that action on climate change has been stalled because our knowledge has been muddled by political wrangling and because of the daunting demands that climate change action requires: "the complete transformation of all the details of existence of seven billion people." It's no easy task to ask the entire world's human population to change their lives completely, and small wonder people respond with an unwillingness to believe we must change. We have all become what Australian public ethics professor Clive Hamilton refers to as climate skeptics because adopting this stance allows us to avoid doing what we should.[6] It's not a question of knowing and not acting—what we are witnessing is global resistance to change.

The transformation we need is on a scale that even the most radical revolutionaries—whether Marx, Lenin or even Stalin— could never have imagined. Their ideas of revolution were superficial compared to the colossal shift now necessary, said Latour, who is actually pleased that climate change has become so controversial because it drives home the reality of what we are facing, even if people are still unwilling to act.

He noted some positive advances were made during the last 30 years, when Republicans and Democrats in the US managed to agree on many laws about climate and the environment, but now people have marched farther apart and are more opposed than ever. Such polarization is propelling issues of climate change into the political arena.

This is a realm where we clearly witness the chasm between matters-of-fact and matters-of-concern. Latour explained we used to have an idea that action followed facts, and that those who didn't follow were ignorant or irrational. "Actually, this has never been the case in the whole history of science, but this was our idea, that you settle the facts first and then get into the question of politics and values." Even if this were true, it would not work in the case of climate change because the event is ongoing, having lasted and developed for centuries. "Nothing of that could be put in the normal framework of an action following knowledge."

Because so many people disagree about it, and because climate change is becoming an enormous matter-of-concern, Latour urges scientists not to stay sequestered in their labs, simply doing their studies and clinging to the idea that they should be disinterested and impartial. Scientists put themselves in a precarious position if they hold fast to a position that they are "just stating the facts" and should not politicize science. At the end of the day, scientists are human beings who have to make a living: they are drawing salaries and competing for grants from government, industry and other institutions. Latour wants them to stand up and fight, with full disclosure, full respect, scrupulous honesty, honoring of the democratic process.

We have long passed the point where we can talk about a fight between good, clean science and science that has been sullied and distorted by personal and public interests. It is time to fight, to get political and "fly under one's own colors"; as the US intellectual Walter Lippmann once said, "It is a fight for the world." Otherwise, Latour said flatly, if world temperatures continue to rise, we will be living in a very different place, and that will end the argument. Latour is currently writing a play, and at the end of the debate between his central characters (a scientist and a climate skeptic), the audience is told the scientists are now on the warpath. "I think that's a powerful way of putting it."

We need scientists to become more political because pure evidence—facts, figures and flowcharts—cannot form an adequate basis for public debate. Why? Primarily because the public is not equipped to get to the bottom of such a discussion, or analyze all these facts. "And having to work within a notion of consensus closes off argument and authority. We become completely mired in all the epistemology of getting the facts straight." We must talk about concerns and interests instead.

So what exactly is the public's role?

One answer lies in what Latour considers to be one of the best books on democratic politics of the 20th century, Walter Lippmann's *The Phantom Public*.[7] In this famous tome, Lippmann described the public as being like someone who arrives late, in the second act of a play, glances around the stage, leaves before the performance is over and makes a snap judgment as to who are the bad guys and who are good. And yet despite this "incompetency," as Lippmann called it, members of the public are asked to align themselves with one side or the other whenever they go to the polls. They do this by relying on experts to help them choose their alliances.

I asked Latour how a collective can operate if the experts can't be trusted, if the trust networks are corrupted and people are up to mischief? He said the problem becomes especially acute when the issues at stake are unprecedented—as in the case of climate change—and when there is a dispute in which experts fail to agree. Then it is up to the public "in all its incompetency" to try and align itself with one side or the other. Lippmann, who died in 1974, said we can never expect more from the public, and Latour agreed, saying it has become much worse since Lippmann's day.

If this is the case, what can we do? The only solution is to help the public detect partisanship, said Latour: "Lippmann had this marvelous definition of the role of the intellectual as the one who produced quick detection of partisanship." I was happy to hear that this is why Latour uses our DeSmogBlog in his research. "It is a bias detector," he said, adding that he created his cartography of controversy project because he, too, wants more bias detectors to be available.

At the Sciences Po médialab, Latour created a tool he calls *controversy mapping*, which is now used around the world. It focuses on controversies that swirl around scientific knowledge, rather than honing in on scientific facts or outcomes themselves. Because knowledge of the truth is always complicated, something like controversy mapping can offer insights into the process of producing knowledge, of how something comes to be considered true. Mapping reveals how a view of pure science often ignores important facets and perspectives.

The best thing the public can do is to try and detect partisanship, said Latour, adding this is what he endeavors to do with controversy mapping. Lippmann does not suggest a person can ever achieve a state of complete nonpartisanship, but at least we can learn to detect biases faster and more effectively, "by crude and oral signs. That's all you can do."

A key part of the process is learning to decipher who the experts are. Debate is the weapon of the epistemologist. Climate skeptics say they want a fair debate—"and for every climatologist there seems to be a climate skeptic"—but Latour advises against participating in any debate about science and facts because there can be no resolution. This doesn't mean we should back off, be disinterested or neutral, which he likens to taking part in a boxing match with your hands tied behind your back. Instead all parties in a decision-making process need to declare their interest.

The French scholar said if he were mapping climate change, he would totally ignore the critics and individuals who sow mischief. "They would not even appear because they are not publishing scientific papers." These disputes are politically motivated and arise because we are faced with a revolutionary transformation that no one has ever lived through. We need to adjust our philosophy of science to the new situation so "let's talk about interests instead of disinterest." We may not agree on the interpretation of measurements and there may be disputes about instruments of calibration, but if we have scientific papers that are peer-reviewed, this eliminates the so-called other side.

When uninformed people talk about ineffective climate change models, Latour labels such public misinformation and confusion "science of deliberate ignorance." Deliberately misleading comments were put forth years ago about smoking and have been used to deny the Holocaust during World War II in Europe; Stanford

University's Robert Proctor calls this phenomenon *culturally induced ignorance* or doubt.[8] According to Latour, struggles between rhetoric and science have been waged for 20 centuries, from Socrates to Powell, and everybody uses rhetoric, even scientists. But it need not make any difference—because the real gap is between well-constructed and badly constructed science, not between rhetoric and reason.

However, Latour does worry about the way scientific facts are wielded by environmentalists who deliver dire warnings. These may be well-intentioned, but Latour suggested that many ecologists are frightening people with their apocalyptic predictions. "We are talking about seven billion people having to convert to other energy resources, but after seeing films showing a series of catastrophic exponential curves paired with very strong music, the only reasonable consequence is that we do nothing." There is little point in creating a message that leads to paralysis. This is a Fox News attitude and should be fought by all possible means; Latour said.

Another source of pollution in the public sphere comes from an argument about inevitability, says Latour, adding this was Al Gore's position in his film *An Inconvenient Truth*. It is not a wise strategy to define a situation as inevitable or out of our control. "This is a negation of politics—because you don't do politics with inevitability," explained Latour. If you send a message to people that there's no other possibility, that it's too late—the result is inaction. To get people politically interested, Latour suggested that the message must give them the will to find a way out of the dilemma. If you produce a message that removes the will, even if it's a completely informed message, a factual message supported by 200 Nobel Prize winners, the result will be inaction. This is not the situation we want; "science is not about inevitability and ineluctability."

To remedy this situation, Latour suggested that we "abandon the notion of truth," at least the cumbersome perception of truth which either plays the role of an arbiter or gives us solid ground on which to stand together. People only assemble, he said, when there is no arbiter and when they don't yet stand on common ground. People assemble politically because "they share the dispute," because they are concerned about the same issue and need to reach a settlement. He noted there is debate about every single infrastructure topic these days—whether it's oil, windmills or solar panels—not to mention arguments about everything from tuna to whales, from vitamins to meat. This is another source of pollution. We used to believe that experts would deliver a disinterested set of facts that were then discussed by politicians who made sound decisions based on good information. We, the public, do not believe this anymore.

While he encourages and welcomes the move away from matters-of-fact toward matters-of-concern, Bruno Latour stressed it is a dangerous time because we have not learned to navigate these waters yet. He used two examples: In the past, if you were troubled about whether or not to vaccinate your children, you discussed it with your doctor and an epidemiologist. Now there is much more information in the public sphere, and controversy overflows around this and almost every topic. If you want to know whether to support the development of windmills in your area, you will find myriad opinions on the topic. Few experts agree, and they don't just talk about windmills, but about law and the price of electricity.

In the past, revolutionaries sought to change the way people lived, but not in every aspect. Now every detail of the way we live comes under scrutiny. People attack you because you bought cherries in winter, because of your carbon footprint. Every single detail is disputed, and we are made to feel guilty. When we seek advice today, we find disputes by experts who hold different sets of values. In France, for example, there is a fierce controversy being waged in the newspapers, "not in the scientific papers," about genetically modified organisms. "And now we have people privately auditing science—which would not happen in a world where people believed the scientific community. It's completely impossible, completely implausible."

And while he shakes his head at this turn of events, he believes it is healthy to have disputes because they lead to the next step which is to ask the question: What kind of world do we want to build, and how can we organize a discussion about that without a political institution or forum which has been designed for the purpose?

Latour did not develop his theory of abandoning facts, and setting truth aside, because he believes there is no truth. What he believes is that absolute truth only exists in a laboratory, and truth has many faces in the public sphere. When everybody declares they speak in the name of truth, what do we achieve in public discourse? Nothing. Instead we have *modus vivendi*: we agree to disagree. "Truth distorts the situation, because it is not really a scientific term, and it asks too much from the conversation."

"So let's abandon the notion of truth, not because we don't want objectivity, but because it plays the role of a referee which would be arbiter of our dispute." When there is no arbiter, we need to assemble; where we don't share the common ground, we can share the dispute. If someone comes to the assembly and says "I have my values, and this value can't be trampled on" or "I have matters of fact and they are indisputable," then no assembly is possible. This is why he believes we are witnessing a civilization shift where we can't use old epistemology on climate change.

Latour explained it is impossible to make a successful argument for climate change "in the straitjacket of normal politics. This is what happened in Copenhagen." They tried to find solutions, but the problem of course is that to have an assembly of this shape and magnitude we need to employ the God of Politics as our arbiter.

People could introduce themselves very politely to each other and say: "I am presenting the CO_2 curve with these instruments, and it cost this to produce. I have my own interest as a scientist. I hope to get the Nobel Prize for this beautiful thing here. And now, what is your card? Yes. Ah, you work for the oil industry, and it's perfectly respectable. We need the oil industry. What world do you want to build? And are you representing the penguin? Ah, very good." In other words, full disclosure, full respect between everyone participating in the conversation.

We are in a fight for the Earth, said Latour. This is the big political point that is missing from disputes about the environment: Who is the enemy? Are we the enemy of the Earth, or is she our enemy?

Duped and How

The Self-regulating Psychopath

with Joel Bakan *and* Noam Chomsky

The corporation's unbridled self-interest
victimizes individuals and society.

Joel Bakan

AN OVERRELIANCE on facts and dependence on a false view of reason contribute to today's toxic conversations and acrimonious dialogue, but another area of great concern is propaganda, a polluting and polarizing behavior that is arguably as vast and destructive as any of the cultural or social forces already discussed. What's more, in the case of modern corporations, deregulation has allowed the legitimate use of unbridled propaganda and created a regulatory, legal and financial system that virtually demands it.

In his book *The Corporation: The Pathological Pursuit of Profit and Power*,[1] author, filmmaker and law professor Joel Bakan traced the corporation's rise to dominance, right back to its origins centuries ago. He illuminated how these juggernauts are required by law to elevate their own interests above those of others and pursue their goals with rampant self-interest, sometimes without regard for moral limits.

After seeing the film Balkan made from his book,[2] I was keen to speak with him. I was interested in his views on the role some corporations play in corrupting public discourse, something

I had occasionally seen up close during much of my career in PR. I asked Bakan what inspired him to write *The Corporation*, and he explained the project was driven by a passion to inform people about an institution that increasingly governs their lives and poisons public discourse. The law professor sees the contemporary corporation as a "very strange, potentially dangerous and destructive institution."[3] Back in the late 1990s, he started to observe the power of corporations as they exploded into public awareness, spearheading the development of globalization, deregulation and privatization. Governments began to abdicate much of their regulatory oversight and free corporations from legal constraints. As a result, corporations emerged as self-governing institutions with the single goal of serving their own interests and those of their shareholders.

Bakan's work does not seek to vilify or analyze the people who run corporations or work for them. He critiques the institutional nature of the corporation as legally created, saying it is an invention which has been imbued with characteristics that, if observed in a human being, would swiftly be diagnosed as psychopathic.

This view initially seemed a little extreme to me, as I built my business around representing successful corporations and never saw anything remotely like this in the companies I worked with. But then Bakan outlined the characteristics of a psychopath, including: callous unconcern for the feelings of others; incapacity to maintain enduring relationships; reckless disregard for the safety of others; deceitfulness, repeated lying and cheating people for profit; incapacity to experience guilt; failure to conform to social norms with respect to lawful behavior. Looking at this list in relation to the excesses on Wall Street, the guiles and machinations of big banks, the environmental record of oil and gas companies, the misinformation campaigns we wrote about in *Climate Cover-Up* and the lies and lack of guilt in the tobacco industry, I began to see Bakan's point.

"Not only have we created an institution in the image of a psychopathic human being, but we've actually conferred personhood on it…and as a society we've given it immense power to govern every aspect of our lives," Bakan said. Increasingly, corporations have limited legal obligation to be concerned about the environment but are compelled to do what's best for their shareholders, whether that means investing to ensure a favorable scientific environment, favorable public opinion environment or favorable political environment so that they can lower production costs and increase profits.

That's not a conspiracy, Bakan stressed. "That's just the logical dynamic of a particular institution."

Corporations do an excellent job of churning out masses of marketing materials that suggest they are doing the right things, but when you look at the actual record, they are not being responsible to social interest, nor can they be expected to be. "How can you expect a psychopath to be self-regulating? The concept doesn't make any sense," said Bakan, who calls corporate social responsibility an oxymoron.

I found Bakan's analysis more believable than the evil CEO explanation or any conspiracy theory. The current system makes it incredibly difficult for a corporation to behave any differently. These companies run on shares, return of stock options, and their whole structure demands they do nothing to jeopardize profits. It's an oversimplification to turn this fact into a good guy/bad guy narrative because corporations are required by law to act this way.

Bakan noted that some of his best friends work in corporations, and many excellent employees are genuinely committed to social values such as the environment. They want to see their companies doing good things in the world, not causing harm. But when they walk into their offices, they are "metaphorically and practically" bound by the institutional demands of their corporations, and that means "social responsibility to stakeholders can only be strategic." Their critical path must be to serve shareholder profits—that's been the unique nature of the institution and its legal obligations since corporations were first formed.

Corporations were first conceived in the late 19th century as immensely powerful tools to attract large sums of capital; they created massive projects such as railroads and more recently airlines and the Internet. They were mighty, effective investment capital vehicles, and they were constrained so they would not cause more harm than good. Beginning in the 1930s, "there began to develop a robust regulatory system and regulatory state," Bakan observed, but in the 1980s, we began to see a dismantling of regulation, which continues today. "Now the notion is let's let the powerful vehicle do its own thing and hope it constrains itself…somehow everything will trickle down and play out, and the market will take care of it so everything will be fine. Well, everything isn't fine," said Bakan.

Today's corporation, as an institution, lacks any intrinsic or internal ability to constrain itself morally or ethically, and Bakan sees this as very dangerous: "If you put blinders on a donkey, that donkey is going to do a much better job of going straight down the street and pulling the cart. But it will not see what's happening at the sides, and it won't have any responsibility for that."

Over the last 30 years or so, "there has basically been a deal, and the deal is that government would become less involved in demanding that corporations be socially responsible, providing corporations would take on the task of regulating themselves and becoming more socially responsible." It used to be that public laws demanded that corporations toe the line, but now we rely on the private choices of individual companies. Many corporations talk the talk of social and environmental responsibility, but Bakan sees a huge gap between words and action and said the deal has not been a good one for the people, for the environment or for stakeholders.

Chief Justice Leo E. Strine Jr. of the US State of Delaware has written that corporate sustainability misunderstands Delaware law and that it "is not only hollow but also injurious to social welfare to declare that directors can and should do the right thing by promoting interests other than stockholder interests."[4]

Corporations are invested in creating a scientific domain that is favorable to them and hostile to those who criticize them. For instance, a pharmaceutical company is legally bound to act in ways that serve its shareholders, and it will naturally seek to shape public perception about science, "to control science for its own ends."

Bakan observed that public relations machines have worked hard to repress the true nature of corporations and convey the notion they "are just like you and me...warm and fuzzy, like a good neighbor. They are the Michelin Man and Ronald McDonald." Massive amounts of money have poured into efforts to paint a caring human public face on corporations, to present them as benevolent servants of humanity. "The extent to which this has been successful has been a disaster for democracy and for various values like the environment," Bakan said flatly. A good example of how companies edit information to promote their point of view was an Enbridge Northern Gateway Pipeline's campaign which showed a map that erased about 1,000 square kilometers of islands from the Douglas Channel, in an attempt to make the company's proposed oil tanker route look less treacherous. This campaign also included the slogan "It's a path to world class safety standards and low environmental impact." In another Enbridge ad, accompanying an emerald-green underwater scene, was a poem that included the lines: "A limitless pool of life / A playground for the tiny and giant things that live within it / And a gateway to the other side."[5] Bakan commented, while corporate social responsibility in some instances does some good, it is most often merely a token gesture that serves to mask the corporation's true purpose.

Bakan stressed that because the corporation as an institution lacks any moral or ethical constraints, it is necessary to impose constraints externally through regulation "and find a balance between what it can do well and the harm it will inevitably cause if not constrained."

I asked Bakan why the public has failed to demand more regulation. "That's the $64,000 question," he said, and it has to do with the manufacture of ideology, with the manufacture of public opinion, with the role that for-profit, advertising-driven media plays in forming public opinion, the lack of critical-thinking training in our education system—and all the various ways in which knowledge is constructed in our society. "We citizens have been asleep at the switch."

Public awareness is seen as a danger by governments and ruling elites, said linguist and cognitive scientist Noam Chomsky, one of this continent's leading political commentators and a Professor Emeritus at MIT. That's because it can interfere with the primary concern of business, which is the enrichment of the very rich in the short term. Chomsky explained that an oil company executive, for instance, may be personally concerned about greenhouse gases or habitat loss, but in their institutional world, they cannot express that worry or step out of their corporate role. "These are very deep problems; they are institutional, not individual."

Chomsky wasted no time telling me exactly what he believes is at the root of the problem: "The government is not our government. It is not a government of the people. It's a government of the overwhelmingly rich, of the corporations and the wealthy... and so it does what they want." He explained that big business is interested in short-term gain and cares little about what are called, in the economics literature, *externalities* (consequences that are not part of market transactions). In other words, large corporations are self-interested and unconcerned with making a deal that's good for everyone. For example, a company that manufactures or sells cars is not worried about pollution, traffic congestion, accidents and injuries, said Chomsky.

He noted the financial crisis of 2008 as a prime example of people ignoring externalities. "This [economic collapse] is what happened when Goldman Sachs, JP Morgan Chase, Barclay's Bank and the rest of them made fraudulent or semi-fraudulent [transactions] in the housing market to try to maximize short term gain."

Big enough mistakes create what's called *systemic risk*, meaning the danger that one company getting into trouble can spread and destroy the whole system. In the financial world, systemic risk is not lethal because the public can bail a company out. "So AIG didn't go bust as it should have, and Goldman Sachs didn't collapse as it should have," Chomsky observed. In the case of Earth's natural environment, however, the risk of destruction is high, but an executive with Exxon Mobil or an official at the Chamber of Commerce is focused on short-term gains, so externalities are ignored. "And there's nobody to bail you out."

"Market systems are designed to create lethal catastrophes," Chomsky warned. These market systems and structures can be overcome with regulation, government control and popular pressure, in theory, but all of these require a political democracy, and one of the effects of a high concentration of capital inequality is that democracy is weakened.

Chomsky pointed out the American public favors higher expenditures and efforts to deal with climate change, but that doesn't matter. "What matters is what the rich and powerful think." And they are quite transparent in their opposition to such expenditures. "The American Chamber of Commerce, the business lobby, the petroleum lobbies have openly proclaimed they are carrying out efforts to undermine popular beliefs in anthropogenic climate change." He referred to the organization called ALEC—American Legislative Exchange Council—that creates legislative programs for states in the US and recently rolled out a school program they call *balanced teaching*.[6] The name may sound nice, but it means in practice that if a Grade 6 class is given "information" about climate change, that information has to be balanced by "information" about climate denial, which comes out of Exxon Mobil. "It's like a totalitarian state," said Chomsky. "It's a way of ensuring that the public is as stupid and ignorant as possible, and it makes perfect sense from the business lobby point of view."

I described the Canadian oil industry's appeal to Americans to buy Canadian oil because it's more ethical. I explained how this campaign surprised me because it is the message we are used to hearing from the American Petroleum Institute or the US Chamber of Commerce, not something we normally hear in Canada. Chomsky responded that in recent years Canada has abandoned many of its more decent characteristics. "Canada used to be a relatively tolerant, open society and less violent than the US. There's plenty of crime, but it was much more moderate and humane than in the South...but that's changed in recent years."

He believes this change happened, in part, because of the North America Free Trade Agreement, which has brought Canadian and American societies closer at an economic level and increased the power of the corporate sector in both countries at the expense of the general population. "It's also due to policies which are quite openly driving Canada to the right. Canada has changed in international affairs and many other things."

When it comes to rancorous debate, Chomsky sees the same pollution of the public square on both sides of the border. "If you can't answer an argument, shriek. That's true in corporate relations, true in international relations. Just rant. Call people names. Slander them. Anything to undermine an argument you can't respond to." He said there are no magic keys, no simple ways out of such issues, whether it's slavery, women's rights or the environment. "It's going to be a long, hard struggle."

Despite the structural failings of corporations, Joel Bakan believes change is possible but the solution ultimately has to come from us: "We need to feel we have the right and the obligation as citizens in the public domain of democracy to do something about this." This is critically important, and why I am writing this book. People need to become savvier about the systems we're creating, more aware of how propaganda works and how public discourse gets polluted.

It occurred to me how wrong-headed the demonization of corporate leaders is. We invented corporations for good reasons—to raise immense amounts of capital to build infrastructure such as bridges, railways and air transportation systems. But we also made them furiously focused on creating shareholder value, and in the wake of the anti-regulation movement that started with Thatcher and Reagan, we removed many balancing mechanisms and constraining regulation. Corporate CEOs are required to make money for their shareholders, and if they fail to do so, they can be in serious trouble, even legally.

No doubt there are some greedy psychopaths at the helm of a few large companies, but there is a much deeper, systemic problem here. Increasing deregulation and unchecked corporate independence, combined with legal constructions which encourage the pathological nature of these institutions, means they can and must act in the interest of shareholders, sometimes to the detriment of communities and the environment. When things go wrong with products—when it's found that tobacco causes cancer, or oil and gas are changing the climate, when their license to operate is threatened—they are of course motivated to become skilled at propaganda.

The result is a more corrupted debate and more misleading PR and advertising being pumped into the public square. It can be relentless, not because corporate leaders are bad guys but because it's systemic and large companies have deep pockets. By allowing corporations to self-regulate, we place them in a position where they may actually have a corporate responsibility to their shareholders to pollute the public sphere, both physically and conceptually. Corporations are motivated to manipulate public opinion and perception because if they don't, and things go wrong, shareholders may be outraged by poor stock prices or companies might lose their licenses to operate.

Vast amounts of advertising dollars are being spent by big business to influence public opinion and boost sales. In the next chapter, we will see what happens when this fearsome expertise is applied in the realm of politics, and how the power of algorithms combined with devious social media surveillance techniques are used to manipulate voters in populations around the world.

9

Steve Bannon's
Full-service Propaganda Machine

with research by Carole Cadwalladr

And here's the tragedy.
We are building this infrastructure of
surveillance authoritarianism
merely to get people to click on ads.

Zeynep Tufekci

O N A WINTRY Sunday evening back in December of 2016, top British investigative journalist and feature writer Carole Cadwalladr started typing "Did the Hol" into a search bar on Google.[1] She was astonished when the auto-complete suggestion suddenly prompted "Did the Holocaust happen?"

What followed was even more disturbing. Topping the list of choices provided was a link to a neo-Nazi and white supremacist website called Stormfront and an article headlined "Top 10 Reasons Why the Holocaust Didn't Happen." In another search, the auto-complete suggestion came up with the offering "Are Jews evil?" after she had typed "Are Jews." Shocked but curious, she clicked, and another page of Google search results popped up with 9 out of 10 results confirming Jews are evil. She continued playing with the search engine and learned women are evil, Muslims are bad, and Hitler was a good guy.

On Monday morning, she contacted Google to relate what had happened. Google refused to edit the results and said, while the company was "saddened" to know that hate organizations do exist in this world, the fact that such sites appear in the platform's search results "does not mean that Google endorses these views."

Appalled, Cadwalladr wrote a story about what she saw as "grossly irresponsible" and noted Google had declined to remove the offending articles. This pleased Ku Klux Klan former leader David Duke, who tweeted his support for Google's decision. The columnist was so annoyed, she personally paid £24.01 to place a Google ad at the top of this search result and wrote a headline that read: "The Holocaust Really Happened." After her articles ran in numerous esteemed publications, a Google spokesman finally apologized and said, "Clearly, we don't always get it right, but we continually work to improve our algorithms."

The journalist went on to write articles in the *Guardian* and *Observer* about how Google is not just a platform but also a medium that "frames, shapes and distorts how we see the world." She explained how extremist sites are able to "game" this search engine, using it for their own propagandist agendas.

As part of her follow-up articles, she interviewed Jonathan Albright, an assistant professor of communications at Elton University in North Carolina, who confirmed Google's algorithm had been gamed by alt-right extremist sites. He was also the first person to mention Cambridge Analytica to her, calling the company a center point in the Right's propaganda machine. Soon after this interview, she went on to break the Cambridge Analytica (CA) scandal, which involved the mining of millions of Facebook users' private information. It released a torrent of outrage about personal data theft.

This massive invasion of privacy gave us just a glimmer of a much bigger problem: The deeper concern is how that data, once stolen, was manipulated and deployed to help skew elections and public thinking, to help elect Donald Trump and to help the Leave.

EU campaign win the UK Brexit referendum. We can't begin to understand the growing problem of toxic public discourse without recognizing the looming threat posed by political consultancies like CA and the damaging role that Facebook and Google can play when they help spread divisiveness and extremist propaganda.

The general public began to grasp the full extent of CA's covert operation when whistleblower Chris Wylie contacted Cadwalladr and went public early in 2018. The young Canadian is former director of research at the British political consulting firm that is principally owned by billionaire American hedge fund manager Robert Mercer. President Trump's chief strategist Steve Bannon is former vice president of the company and has been linked with Mercer in various projects over the years. Wherever Bannon is found, Mercer and his money are not far away. For instance, when Mercer started funding Donald Trump's presidential campaign, Bannon became campaign manager.

Mercer is also part owner of the alt-right Breitbart News Network, an ideological site that its critics call racist, xenophobic and misogynistic. Bannon was a founding member and former executive chair of the site, widely known to publish conspiracy theories and fabricated news. Bannon encouraged Mercer to also buy SCL Elections, which became the parent company of CA, which he created.

Wylie first met Bannon in 2013 when the older man was editor-in-chief of Breitbart. They chatted about using Facebook profiles to garner insights into people's psychological makeup. By 2014 Wylie was working for CA.

Four years later, the disillusioned Wylie gave Cadwalladr secret documents that revealed the inner workings of CA and explained how it harvested information from Facebook and then melded that data from a carefully designed questionnaire, to determine personality traits and emotional triggers of swing voters. Wylie said CA built hundreds of algorithms that allowed the company to create a model to predict people's personalities, political preferences, affiliations and orientation. This psychographics study enabled the company to draft narratives, craft messages and refine ads to specifically appeal to people's different personalities, values and emotional buttons.

CA's controversial role in recent American political races as well as the Leave.EU campaign in England is now the subject of criminal investigations on both sides of the Atlantic, led by attorney and former FBI director Robert Mueller in the States, and in Britain by Information Commissioner Elizabeth Denham. There is ongoing coordination between the two.

In May 2017, Denham launched a formal investigation into the use of data analytics for political purposes, specifically looking at the misuse of personal data to manipulate political ads in the EU Brexit referendum. Her investigation became the largest of its kind ever undertaken by any data protection authority and focused on online social media platforms, data brokers, analytics firms, academic institutions, political parties, and campaign groups. It involved 71 witnesses, a review of 30 organizations' practices, and examination of 700 terabytes—which equals 52 billion pages— of data.

Facebook and CA became the focus of her investigation when evidence emerged about the harvesting of data from 87 million Facebook users and friends across the world. In her interim report, Denham announced an upcoming criminal prosecution against SCL Elections, the parent company of CA and a firm with decades of experience in military disinformation campaigns and "election management."[2]

Denham's deputy James Dipple-Johnstone also noted, at that time, that there was potential evidence of a direct link "between the company at the heart of the Trump campaign...and the Russian government's disinformation campaign."[3]

Facebook was heavily criticized by her office and fined the maximum penalty of £500,000 for its failure to protect user data.

Denham made it clear she considers such data abuse a serious crime:

> Facebook has not been sufficiently transparent to enable users to understand how and why they might be targeted by a political party or campaign.... We are at a crossroads. Trust and confidence in the integrity of our democratic processes risk being disrupted.
>
> New technologies that use data analytics to micro target people give campaign groups the ability to connect with individual voters. This cannot be at the expense of transparency, fairness and compliance with the law.... Fines and prosecution punish the bad actors, but my real goal is to change and restore trust and confidence in our democratic system.[4]

In her November 6, 2018 report to the British Parliament, the Information Commissioner stated "multiple jurisdictions are struggling to retain fundamental democratic principles in the face of opaque digital technologies," and she warned there is a need for new laws and measures to protect against the risk of interference if we are to "preserve the integrity of our election process."[5]

"Parliamentarians, journalists, civil society and citizens have woken up to the fact that transparency is the cornerstone of democracy," she wrote in the report. "We may never know whether individuals were unknowingly influenced to vote a certain way in either the UK EU referendum or in the US election campaigns. But we do know that personal privacy rights have been compromised by a number of players and that the digital electoral ecosystem needs reform."[6]

"Without a high level of transparency and trust amongst citizens that their data is being used appropriately, we are at risk of developing a system of voter surveillance by default."[7] Her investigation uncovered a "disturbing disregard" for voters' personal privacy, as well as invisible "increasingly sophisticated marketing techniques" and behind-the-scenes use of personal data to target political messages.

The report noted the ICO office has issued monetary penalties and enforcement notices ordering companies to comply with the law, instigated criminal proceedings, and referred issues to other regulators and law enforcement agencies. The Commissioner concluded: "Data protection agencies around the world must work with other relevant regulators and with counterparts in other jurisdictions to take full advantage of the law to monitor big data politics and make citizens aware of their rights."[8]

"This is a global issue, which requires global solutions," Denham said.[9]

The CA scandal is not simply about normal political dishonesty. It's darker than that. This data breech exposed a frightening campaign of surveillance and manipulation of political beliefs on both sides of the Atlantic.

Cadwalladr has continued to write extensively in the *Guardian* and *Observer* about these digital stealth operations and how they were set in motion. Wylie, the young British Columbian who had begun to question the ethics of his role in launching these events, has since described himself as Bannon's "psychological warfare mindfuck tool," a weapon Bannon designed to fight his culture war.

Cadwalladr describes the CA story as "the weirdest" she has ever researched, one of the most profoundly unsettling and one of the most important political scandals of our time. Unlike many journalists, she understands the complex world of digital propaganda and its cozy relationship with social scientists and technology giants like Facebook. She is part of a team of reporters at the *Observer*, *Guardian* and *NYTimes* that has linked Brexit to Donald Trump to Russia and Facebook.

Wylie was the data scientist who originally came up with the concept of how all this could work and then built the "machine" using Facebook data, psychology and micro-targeting techniques.

He told the UK media that his former employer, CA, inappropriately used Facebook profiles harvested by a psychology lecturer and data scientist named Aleksandr Kogan at Cambridge University. The academic is also affiliated with the University of St. Petersburg in Russia and has consulted for Russian interests.

Kogan developed a Facebook app featuring an online personality quiz, and CA paid people to take it. About 270,000 downloaded the app, and this gave CA access to not only the participants' Facebook accounts but also their friends—ultimately allowing the mining of 87 million users' data, some say more. Facebook confirmed the access, saying Kogan's sharing with CA was a breach of his academic agreement.

Many people have missed a critical element in the CA scandal, which is the enormous value of such a sample. Much concern has focused on the people who took the quiz, and those whose information was harvested, but what's important to understand is the enormous sample they represent. Researchers used that sample to model the population as a whole.

Wylie has since come to deeply regret the sinister way his ideas were used. In his interview with Cadwalladr, he explained how CA's "full service propaganda machine" began to take shape. After harvesting millions of profiles, "we built models to exploit what we knew about them and target their inner demons. That was the basis the entire company was built on," he told her.[10] The company then organized massive amounts of information using new insights from psychology to determine people's personalities through their values, opinions, attitudes, interests, aspiration and lifestyles. This psychographic research was then melded with micro-targeting technology.

Wiley now describes this as "a grossly unethical experiment" that played with the psychology of an entire country, "without their consent or awareness in the context of the democratic process." He said there is no doubt that CA was tampering with democracy. That company's chief executive, Alexander Nix, confirmed the meddling with people's minds and their reality when he admitted to undercover reporters for Britain's *Channel 4 News*: "It sounds a dreadful thing to say, but these are things that don't necessarily need to be true as long as they are believed."[11]

Andy Wigmore, the Leave.EU director of communications, admitted that whipping up concerns among voters about immigration was the main thrust of the campaign during the Brexit referendum. He acknowledged this during an interview with Emma Briant, a senior lecturer in journalism at the University of Essex who specializes in media and propaganda.[12]

Wylie told Cadwalladr that CA could anticipate what kind of messaging people would be partial to, as well as the kinds of topics and content they would like and how they would want to receive it.[13] The company learned how to push emotional buttons to prompt changes in people's thinking. All this required a sophisticated team of data experts, psychologists, creative thinkers and artists to craft content and then feed it into the Internet in whatever form that person was most likely to respond to.

This was acknowledged by CA's Alexander Nix when he was secretly recorded by Britain's *Channel 4*: "We just put information into the bloodstream of the Internet and then watch it grow, give it a little push every now and again over time to watch it take shape."[14] The company's CEO went on to say these messages can infiltrate the online community but do so with no "branding," so they cannot be attributed or tracked. The company often used "proxies" such as charities and activist groups to feed the "infection," without leaving a trace.

Instead of communicating in the public square, listening to and airing ideas in full view, the company sent underground messages so there was no shared narrative. In effect, Wylie said it was like murmuring quietly in a voter's ear, with a different message drafted to specifically appeal to them alone.

After following this story for months, Cadwalladr concluded we risk fragmenting society when we have no shared experiences or shared understanding. Without a common narrative, how can society function?

This is not a unique or isolated incident but a widespread corrupt form of rhetoric designed to manipulate rather than persuade the public. Computer scientist and philosophy writer Jaron Lanier does not believe the CA scandal is the worst of it.[15] He believes Facebook's algorithms and business model are designed to enable precisely the mass manipulation that CA unleashed. The algorithms of Facebook and Google are constantly watching people so they can manipulate them, and as long as these "machines" drive social media, bad actors will find ways to do the same.

Initially these platforms used such technology to boost sales and keep advertisers happy. But unfortunately, companies like CA, that want to flog bad political ideas, can use the same technology to manipulate political beliefs just as effectively as purchasing power. Google and Facebook are free, but the sites are loaded with ads, and as algorithms got better and better, what started as normal advertising turned into behavior modification. Even if Facebook puts reforms in place to protect public data, bad actors will still find a way to use its manipulative powers for dark purposes, said Lanier, who knows what he is talking about when it comes to algorithms. He has been around Silicon Valley from the beginning and is considered the father of virtual reality.

One of the original scientists who scaled up the Internet and developed early chat rooms, Lanier believes Facebook and Google have darkened society with their relentless advertising and content scheme of surveillance and behavior modification. Their algorithms have so warped our political processes, we no longer know if our elections are real.

One of the key concerns is that Facebook ads are different from television ads. TV ads don't watch back, which is something algorithms managing Facebook ads are capable of. This is how they learn about our interests and are able to use that data to manipulate us and determine the next bit of content to show us.

Whereas everyone can see television ads and there is a collective experience, Facebook and other online marketers can now target just a handful of voters or even a single person.

Martin Moore of Kings College told Cadwalladr that CA could use up to 50,000 variations of an ad in a single day, measuring responses, then tailoring them to individuals. These campaigns were opaque and focused on particular locations, a strategy the company described as micro-targeting.[16]

That's a problem because we have no idea what advertising or news content voters are seeing. As long as everyone gets the same information, even if misleading, we have a fighting chance to deal with the propaganda. But the micro-targeting that Facebook does takes social discourse and community norms out of the conversation. In fact, there is no conversation, and this undermines human dignity and agency.

When we are on Facebook or Google, we are under surveillance by algorithms that make assumptions about us and are constantly deciding what to show us next. They persist until they find something to change a viewer, without them realizing it happened.

According to Lanier, these algorithms "are looking for quick responses. Negative responses, like getting startled, scared, irritated or angry.... The positive responses like building trust or feeling good rise more slowly. So algorithms naturally catch the negativity and amplify it, and then they introduce negative people to each other."[17] For example, algorithms were able to determine there is more public engagement and response when using the word ISIS than when Arab Spring is mentioned.

"If you are doing rapid measurement of human impulses instead of accumulated human behavior, it's the negativity that gets amplified," said Lanier. "You will find engagement more often by irritating people than by educating them."

This is precisely the same point being made by techno-sociologist Zeynep Tufekci who warns this is a danger with YouTube because it amps up negativity to hold its audiences.[18] She was watching YouTube videos of Trump rallies during the 2016 presidential election as part of her research and was surprised when YouTube started to recommend and autoplay white suprem-acist rants and Holocaust denial videos. She is not in the habit of watching this type of video, so she was curious.

The academic, who is an associate professor at the School of Information and Library Science at the University of North Carolina and was an Andrew Carnegie Fellow in 2015, decided to experiment. She started watching Bernie Sanders and Hilary Clinton videos to see what YouTube algorithms would recom-mend for her. Sure enough, she began receiving left wing con-spiracy videos. The videos YouTube offered her were increasingly extreme, unrequested and a long way from the mainstream search she began with.

Tufekci then tried non-political videos and found the same thing. Searches about vegetarianism lead to videos about veganism, while those about jogging gave her videos about ultramarathons. "You are never hard core enough for YouTube's recommendation algorithm," she said in a TED talk. It promotes, recommends and disseminates videos in a manner that appears to constantly up the stakes. "Given its billion or so users, YouTube may be one of the most powerful radicalizing instruments of the 21st century."

Tufekci, who specializes in the social implications of emerging technologies as they relate to politics and corporate responsibil-ity, does not believe Google and Facebook are maliciously intent on making the world more polarized or encouraging extremism. But this is what's happening due to artificial intelligence and the Google business model.

This is the fox guarding the hens problem. Growing, unre-stricted and unregulated access to data is similar to the problem I wrote of regarding large corporations, which Joel Bakan calls dangerously "self-regulating psychopaths." It reminds us of the concern we should all have about modern corporations, which have been unregulated to the point that governments unwittingly encourage their use of unbridled propaganda and rampant self-interest, sometimes without regard for moral limits.

Google sells the "attention" of its users to advertisers. The longer people stay on YouTube, the more attention the advertisers get and the more money Google makes. And algorithms have decided people crave more and more incendiary content. A *Wall Street Journal* investigation of YouTube content found that YouTube often "fed far-right or far-left videos to users who watched relatively mainstream news sources," and such extremist tendencies were evident with a wide variety of material.[19]

Tufekci says YouTube algorithms are biased toward inflammatory content and "leads viewers down a rabbit hole of extremism, while Google racks up the ad sales."

She worries that YouTube may radicalize billions of people as our natural curiosity keeps us on websites that lead us into hoaxes, lies and misinformation to make a buck. She warns, "People in power will use artificial intelligence from machine learning to control us, to manipulate us, in novel, sometimes hidden, subtle and unexpected ways."

What algorithms choose to deploy in this "persuasion architecture" can affect people's emotions and political behavior. "And here's the tragedy. We are building this infrastructure of surveillance authoritarianism merely to get people to click on ads." She echoes Lanier's concerns regarding micro-targeted messages that ensure we no longer know what others are seeing online. "Without a common basis of information, little by little public debate is becoming impossible...we're just at the beginning stages of this."

Tufekci believes this type of authoritarianism is different because it quietly watches and nudges us without our knowing. It can manipulate individuals one by one using their personal weaknesses and vulnerabilities, and it can do that at scale.

The CA scandal is not an isolated episode of corrupt business practices. It is a systemic problem enabled by the algorithms of Facebook, Google and others that have turned advertising and news feeds into behavior modification machines. This is propaganda on a titanic scale. As of the second quarter of 2018, Facebook had 2.23 billion active monthly users; Twitter, 336 million; and Google had more than 2 billion monthly active devices.

It's clear from the CA scandal that Facebook has had a negative effect on politics and the quality of public discourse. Facebook was involved in manipulating people in the 2016 presidential election and the Brexit referendum, and for the first time in human history, we have a global ability to spy on, target and manipulate hundreds of millions of people and modify their behavior without them knowing and in ways we never imagined.

Lanier says we should get rid of this manipulation machine: "I don't believe our species can survive unless we fix this. We cannot have a society in which, if two people wish to communicate, the only way that can happen is if it's financed by a third person who wishes to manipulate them." If we are going to face existential threats like climate change, our society has to be sane. We can't drive ourselves insane with a universal scheme of manipulation and trickery, he believes.

It wasn't sinister decisions or evil business people that caused this digital economy problem. It came about because of the well-intentioned idea that information should be free on the Internet, but Lanier argues it can't be free. If access to the Internet and social media is free (because advertisers pay), we get this surveillance and manipulation model to ensure Internet advertising is effective. And then this manipulative technology can be used by any bad actors for digital propaganda. He believes we need to disallow the commercial incentive and adopt a new business model, like a public library model or a user-pay model like Netflix.

Through this data breech scandal, we have come to see the inner workings of a social pathology that is more about divisiveness than misinformation. We have seen how CA's strategy was to sow division, how the Trump and Brexit strategies sowed division. The Russian strategy did the same, and the unintended consequence of the algorithms of Facebook and Google is also sowing division.

Psychometric targeting is an insidious and pernicious form of propaganda that spreads over the Internet under the cover of anonymity. It is a covert operation that allows carefully honed messages to worm their way into the public consciousness, whether it's to slam same-sex marriage, attack immigration policies or stir jihadist tendencies.

If anyone doubts the power of this new weapon, they can read a recent study by researchers at the University of Warwick that looked at 3,334 anti-refugee attacks during a two-year period in Germany.[20] It found one common denominator: Facebook use. Researchers discovered a phenomenon that was long suspected by those who study Facebook: that it stokes racial violence. They also found where Facebook use was higher than average, attacks on refugees increased by about 50 percent, a link held true in all kinds of communities, whether large cities or small villages, affluent or poor areas, Far Right or Far Left neighborhoods.

The jump in violence related to Facebook only, and did not correlate with Internet or web use per se, but a growing body of research shows social media of all kinds can influence users' perceptions of outsiders, not only through hate speech or blatant vitriol but through subtle and pervasive ways in which the platform indirectly infects and then distorts reality or social norms.

Human rights advocates say Facebook also played a role in the Myanmar government's campaign of ethnic cleansing, when it failed to monitor and moderate abusive content that inflamed violence against the Rohingya, Myanmar's Muslim minority.

Social media analyst Raymond Serrato,[21] who works at the UN Commission for Human Rights, studies the impact hate speech and misinformation on social media platforms have on vulnerable communities and human rights. He found that hate speech spiked dramatically among Myanmar's 14 million Facebook users before Buddhist mobs and the military massacred thousands of Rohingya

Muslims and burned villages to the ground. More than 700,000 have fled to Bangladesh to avoid arson, rape and violence. Civil society groups have since criticized Facebook for fueling violence and failing to provide the protection and platform oversight that it offers in Western countries.

We all need to know a lot more about where and how this is happening because it is messing with people's reality and undermining normal trust networks that operate through social mechanisms.

The Internet's early promise of a vast and vigorous public commons where people could participate in a robust democracy has never been realized. Instead its dark opposite emerged spreading false beliefs and driving the politics of division in communities around the world. It has become a place of bogus news, conspiracy theories, propaganda and phony debates. The hate speech and bigotry broadcast and promulgated by Facebook and YouTube have no place in a healthy public square.

As the largest distributers of news on the planet, Facebook, Google and Twitter have a moral obligation to be gatekeepers, and like other respected and trustworthy news media, they should seek to sort fact from fiction and prevent the spread of false, polarizing propaganda.

In the next chapter we take a look at another example of the widespread problem of polluted public discourse.

Note: Much of this chapter has been based on the extensive and outstanding reporting of Carole Cadwalladr in the Guardian *and* Observer. *I encourage readers to check out her stories and support these news organizations in their efforts to reveal the truth.*

Foreign-funded Radicals

Where would they (environmentalists)
draw the line on where they receive money from?
Will they take money from Al-Qaeda,
the Hamas or the Taliban?
Who is really making the decisions in Canada
if we allow foreign money to lobby against
what should be Canadian made decisions?

Senator Don Plett

THE WORLD'S LARGEST reservoir of crude bitumen—a thick, sticky hydrocarbon with the viscosity of cold molasses that smells and looks like tar—is located in northern Alberta, Canada, in a vast area larger than England. Formed over millions of years, small amounts of this gummy substance were used centuries ago by Cree Aboriginals to waterproof their canoes, but in 1967, a massive commercial operation began to release the energy that was locked into these deposits. Separating the heavy petroleum product from sand has been a challenge, but more difficult still, has been the contentious dispute surrounding this valuable resource and how it will be transported to markets.

This controversy is alarming because it stalls action and the threat of global warming is no longer just seen in ice core samples or minute laboratory measurements. It is larger than life, right before our eyes. In 2015, the world's seven billion inhabitants went through the hottest year ever recorded;[1] drought gripped California where the snowpack vital for water supplies fell to its lowest level in five centuries;[2] more than 3,000 people died in heat waves in India[3] and Pakistan[4] as temperatures hit 120°F (49°C); Cyclone Chapala battered Yemen—a country that has never before seen a cyclone hit its shores—drenching some areas with seven years' worth of rain in 48 hours.[5] That same year, the far eastern Pacific spawned Hurricane Patricia,[6] thought to be the strongest storm ever recorded; and rising ocean temperatures caused the third mass coral bleaching event in recorded history (following ones in 1998 and 2010), killing an estimated 4,600 square miles of coral around the globe.[7] Never has there been a greater disparity between what scientists say we should be concerned about and what members of government and the oil and gas industry are doing.

The wildfire season of 2018 was the worst ever recorded in California and British Columbia, with millions of hectares going up in smoke. It was also one of the most damaging in decades in Greece, Spain and even Sweden. Bush fires in Western Australia burned more than two million acres that same year in what has been termed a "gigafire."[8] According to data from the National Oceanic and Atmospheric Administration, 2018 was one of the hottest on record; only three other years had been hotter: 2015, 2016 and 2017. The World Meteorological Organization, in its State of the Global Climate report released November 29, 2018, stated the 20 warmest years on record have all occurred in the past 22 years.

In this case study, I highlight several extreme examples of polarizing spin and misleading propaganda that epitomize the extent to which the vested interests that Joel Bakan and Noam Chomsky described—and governments that support them—will go to confuse issues and discredit critics, on both sides of the Canada–US border.

A few years ago, Canadians attuned to such things noticed a peculiar shift in the international debate about the environmental impact and economic importance of this country's best-known natural resource. Phrases such as "ethical oil" bubbled to the surface as oil industry proponents sought to defend not only the resource but also the proposed Keystone and Enbridge Northern Gateway pipelines that would carry crude to the Gulf of Mexico or British Columbia's northern coast for export to Asia. At the same time, environmental groups that dared speak out against either the oil sands or the pipelines proposed to carry its crude were labeled by the Harper government and the oil and gas industry as "foreign-funded radicals," bent on undermining Canada's sovereignty and economic growth.

And then the peculiar term "ethical oil" started being used on national television. One day while watching a CBC interview, I remember EthicalOil.org spokesperson Kathryn Marshall repeating it like a mantra. She had a slightly unhinged tone, like a comedian on *Saturday Night Live*, as she refused again and again to answer the interviewer's questions about who was funding EthicalOil.org. Marshall tried to deflect the question with pat statements about puppet groups trying to hijack a Canadian pipeline process. Her desperate and comical efforts became a YouTube sensation, and her urgent plea to stop the so-called foreign-funded radicals ran on media outlets from coast to coast for weeks.[9]

In one interview, Marshall said Northern Gateway is good for Canada and will allow the export of "more of our ethically produced oil to different countries that can reduce their dependency on conflict oil from nations like Nigeria and Saudi Arabia and Iran that have atrocious human rights records and really don't care about the environment at all." She said Ethical Oil supporters should "make sure that foreign interests and their foreign-funded front groups and lobby groups" didn't interfere with the pipeline approval and didn't "hijack a Canadian process."[10]

As the ethical oil, foreign-funded radicals propaganda campaign rolled out, I listened closely to the rhetoric and shook my head as I watched the media's lapdog response. In spite of a lack of evidence of any wrongdoing on the part of environmental or community groups, the media seemed to play along with everything that was said. It was an astonishing—and apparently very successful—overreach.

Conservative Canadian Senator Nicole Eaton charged so-called foreign-funded radicals with political manipulation: "There is influence peddling. There are millions of dollars crossing the borders masquerading as charitable donations." She then launched a Senate inquiry into the funding of environmental charities by foreign foundations, alleging they were "audaciously treading on our domestic affairs and on Canadian sovereignty."[11] The Canadian Press started digging and revealed that most Canadian charities receive foreign funds, including many well outside the environmental realm. The CP analysis found only one of the top ten foreign-funded charities could be considered a conservation group—Ducks Unlimited Canada—while CARE Canada, which fights poverty in developing countries, reported the most foreign funding at about $99 million.[12] Amid these attacks by Conservative critics, it was revealed that the Canada Revenue Agency was auditing environmental groups that the Harper government had marked as enemies.[13]

There was even a suggestion of money laundering from Environment Minister Peter Kent, while Senator Don Plett asked about environmentalists: "Where would they draw the line on where they receive money from? Will they take money from Al-Qaeda, the Hamas or the Taliban? Who is really making the decisions in Canada if we allow foreign money to lobby against what should be Canadian made decisions?"[14]

Adversarial debate is an important democratic tool, but combative discourse is a problem when it is used to demonize, to obscure truth and steamroll dissent. As Steve Rosell, Roger Conner, Bruno Latour and Noam Chomsky have all pointed out, when campaigns do this, the result is public confusion, polarization and gridlock. And let's be clear, similar campaigns take place globally around all kinds of big issues—everything from gun control, tobacco and hydraulic fracturing to weapons of mass destruction—led by political parties and corporations.

Over the following months, I watched as the PR pollution grew more toxic and the echo chamber resonated. Attacks against scientists escalated, and a 2013 survey found 90 percent of federal government scientists in Canada felt they could not speak freely to the media, while 86 percent believed they would face censure or retaliation if they did. The survey of more than 4,000 scientists, commissioned by the Professional Institute of the Public Service of Canada, published in a report called *The Big Chill*, found almost one in four said they had been asked to exclude or alter technical information.[15]

I have taken on my share of PR battles over the years as head of my own public relations company, Hoggan & Associates. In fact, my Vancouver-based firm has a reputation for working on tough issues and sometimes taking opponents to the mat. When it comes to reputation management, we are known for hard-nosed tactics, and we have faced off with governments, unions and environmental groups. But even to me, these strategies used to defend tar sands oil and oil pipelines seemed excessive.

What Harper's government and the oil industry were promoting showed a serious disconnect with Canadian values, since almost 80 percent of Canadians I surveyed wanted stricter laws to protect the environment.[16] This PR campaign seemed to have been borrowed straight from the Harper government's allies at the Ethical Oil Institute, founded by controversial former tobacco lobbyist Ezra Levant, who himself borrowed from the US Republican Tea Party playbook. Levant devised a plan to brand Alberta's oil sands as "fair trade," versus the "conflict oil" of regimes supporting terrorism. He claimed: "Ethical oil is like fair trade coffee or conflict-free diamonds. Ethical oil burns the same as conflict oil in your gas tank and it costs the same, but it's morally superior and some people value that."[17]

In a book on the topic, Levant wrote: "If our goal as moral citizens is to make the world a better place, then there is only one choice: to pump as much oil as we possibly can out of Fort McMurray. Pump and steam and dig and drill and get that oil out of the sand in any and every way we can." He further noted: "Every drop of oil from Alberta is one less drop from some fascist theocracy, or some brutal warlord; one less cent into the treasuries of Russia's secret police and Al-Qaeda's murderers."[18]

Environmentalists poured plenty of gasoline on this controversy too. The Sierra Club compared the tar sands to heroin, and protesters at various events carried placards that read, "Tar Sands Kill" and "Tar Sands Oil is Blood Oil."[19] A 2012 campaign attacked fossil fuel companies with the slogan "Exxon hates your children."[20] None of this rhetoric was helpful.

Levant wrote about protestors in his blog: "If we were to take their advice (environmentalists) and shut down the oil sands, we'd simply be handing billions of dollars of business to misogynistic, terrorist-financing, nuclear bomb-building, union-busting, gay-bashing dictatorships like Saudi Arabia, Iran, etc."[21]

Meanwhile, the world was continuing to warm, and the Conference Board of Canada ranked Canada 15th overall in environmental stewardship among the 17 richest nations in the world.[22] Our failure to reduce greenhouse gas emissions placed us dead last among G-8 countries;[23] Canada's Arctic exceeded worst-case scenarios, with the most extreme sea ice melt in recorded history.[24]

In 2012 the Harper government passed Omnibus Budget Bill C-38, which was called the Jobs, Growth and Long-Term Prosperity Act. This sweeping bill was widely seen as an attack on environmental protection and science. The bill changed 70 federal laws and, concealing major amendments in a budget, made discussion of any single provisions difficult. Protection of fish habitat and species at risk were reduced in Canada's Fisheries Act.

Thousands of bodies of water, lakes and streams across the country were removed from oversight as Canada's Navigable Waters Protection Act became a Navigation Protection Act. The former Canadian Environmental Assessment Act was repealed, and a new act proclaimed which enabled fast-track approval of pipelines and oil sands expansion. In the same massive piece of legislation, the country's only high-Arctic data collection facility, the Polar Environmental Atmospheric Research Laboratory, was closed and the government removed Canada from the international Kyoto Protocol agreement.[25]

Canada now protects less than 1 percent of its oceans compared with Australia, for instance, which has a comprehensive network of marine protected areas covering 40 percent of its oceans.[26]

Few PR campaigns in Canada have been as extreme or well-funded as the one I have outlined here, and I've certainly never seen one as cocky. But it would be a mistake to dismiss it as a crazy sideshow or to think this only happens in Canada. In fact, this kind of oil and gas industry propaganda seems to have been born in the United States.

US Exemplars

The US firm Edelman, one of the largest PR firms in the world, was hired by TransCanada Corporation in 2014 after that company was stalled in its attempt to build the Keystone XL pipeline from Alberta to the US Gulf Coast. The PR giant was tasked with promoting an alternative route to carry crude oil from the Alberta tar sands to east coast refineries—entirely within Canada. The proposed pipeline would carry 1.1 million barrels per day of western Canadian crude to eastern refineries and export facilities, through some existing converted pipelines in Ontario, as well as new pipe through Quebec and New Brunswick.

Details of this PR aggressive campaign were revealed when Greenpeace Canada managed to obtain copies of draft documents that showed Edelman's strategy to garner public support for the $12 billion Energy East project. It included creating so-called grassroots advocacy groups to discredit and distract environmental groups that might jeopardize the proposed 2,858-mile project.[27]

Greenpeace's Keith Stewart characterized the firm's tactics as "dirty tricks" and said the documents exposed how worried the company was about the Energy East pipeline facing as much flak as the Keystone or Northern Gateway projects.[28] Edelman's strategy would counter opponents by "distracting them from their mission and causing them to redirect their resources" and by working with "supportive third parties who can in turn put the pressure on, particularly when TransCanada can't." The strategy would target groups such as the Council of Canadians, Ecology Ottawa and the David Suzuki Foundation (as well as their funders) and investigate any litigation issues or audits they might be facing. Edelman suggested this could be accomplished through *opposition research*, a term used to describe digging up dirt on your opponents.[29] It's a common tactic in US politics, but I wondered why it was being used as a weapon against ordinary citizens.

Edelman is used to controversy. The firm was at the center of a firestorm of trouble in 2006 after its founder Richard Edelman apologized for his firm using fake grassroots bloggers in a union fight with Walmart.[30] The company also ran a $52-million campaign for the American Petroleum Institute that allegedly involved pro-industry citizens' groups. The "Energy Citizens" campaign was designed to appear as if generated by ordinary people, but it was actually masterminded and run by oil company lobbyists.[31]

In the document entitled *Strategic Plan: Quebec*, the PR giant drafted plans to recruit "third-party" voices to help build an echo chamber of "aligned voices," and while the company's founder denied working with astroturf groups, Kert Davies, executive director of the Climate Investigations Center, was quoted in a *Huffington Post* article in late 2014 as saying this is precisely what's happening. "If astroturf is using artificial grassroots to support a corporate agenda, this is clearly it." He added it's not often you see "the full battle plan" of a major industry PR effort, but said this is a small window into the workings of big oil company campaigns.[32]

Astroturfing involves creating fake grassroots groups and makes it almost impossible to distinguish between a legitimate ground-swell and manufactured opinion. Some PR companies use such groups to garner synthetic support, to alter public perception or simply stir up doubt. On the Internet, astroturfing sometimes takes the form of bogus endorsements for products, hotels or restaurants, but in the larger sphere, blogs and comments that appear as seemingly spontaneous expressions of support are, in fact, masterminded and funded by big business, oil companies, chemical companies and more. In his book *Grassroots for Hire*, author Edward Walker defines this kind of false public participation as an elite campaign masquerading as a mass movement.[33]

"Win nasty or lose pretty...screw your enemy...Push fear and anger," and above all always work to give corporate cash "total anonymity": these are playbook mantras of another of big business's hired PR guns in the United States. Richard Berman is a Washington-based lawyer and political consultant whose stock-in-trade is exploiting fear and anger in what he has called "an endless war" against environmentalists. His PR game plan was exposed in 2014 when a speech to oil and gas industry officials was secretly recorded. The *New York Times* broke the story after Berman spoke to the Western Energy Alliance in Colorado Springs.[34]

Among other zingers in the leaked audio, Berman said, "If the oil and gas industry wants to prevent its opponents from slowing its efforts to drill in more places, it must be prepared to employ tactics like digging up embarrassing tidbits about environmentalists and liberal celebrities." His public affairs firm, Berman & Company, prides itself on exploiting fear, greed and anger, and in the secretly taped speech, he urged executives not to worry about offending people: "You can win ugly or lose pretty." The master of astroturfing explained he receives "anonymous" donations from businesses and has used the funds to create dozens of nonprofit groups that appear arm's length from industry, independent and community based. These front groups launch spin campaigns to influence public opinion against environmental advocates or industry critics.

"We run this stuff through nonprofit organizations that are insulated from having to disclose donors," he told the Colorado Springs meeting. "There is total anonymity. People don't know who supports us." During the meeting, he also advised the group that for $3 million he could battle their environmental foes with his Big Green Radicals campaign. This is just one in his network of front groups and so-called think tanks that he launched to block food safety legislation, to undermine environmental advocacy groups such as the Sierra Club, or groups opposed to fracking. Other pointers he offered the audience included using humor to marginalize opponents and tearing down celebrities by playing up their hypocrisy.

Misleading, deceptive PR campaigns have been used for decades in the US. The Americans had clean coal long before Canadians had ethical oil.

The term *clean coal* was coined in the late 1980s to deflect public concern from a dirty form of energy. The words were echoed by front groups with names such as Citizens for a Sound Economy, the Clean and Safe Energy Coalition and the Advancement of Sound Science Coalition. The Western Fuels Association teamed with the National Coal Association in 1991 to form the Information Council on the Environment, aiming to "reposition global warming as a theory (not a fact)" and "supply alternative facts to support that global warming would be good."[35]

Let's be clear, there is no such thing as clean coal. The greenwashing term sells the idea that coal is somehow environmentally friendly. The burning of coal combined with mist from the Thames Valley is what gave London, England, its infamous pea-soupers, the black fogs that were a lethal combination of soot particles and sulfur dioxide. London's Great Smog of 1952 killed an estimated 12,000 people in five days and left another 100,000 in respiratory distress. It also led to reductions in coal burning in England.[36] Coal pollution continues to take a deadly toll, and according to the American Lung Association, 13,000 people die prematurely every year because of it. Coal-fired power plants in the US burn more than a billion tons annually, emitting more CO_2 per unit of energy than any other fuel.[37] The industry contaminates drinking water, is a leading cause of acid rain and is the largest source of mercury pollution in the US.[38]

Clean coal is a myth perpetrated by industry PR and bank-rolled by mining companies such as Peabody Energy, Duke Energy and the Union Pacific Railroad. An advertising agency called R&R Partners is credited with coming up with the clean coal oxymoron—and is also responsible for the slogan "What happens in Las Vegas, stays in Las Vegas."[39]

Another PR company, the Virginia-based Hawthorn Group, worked on behalf of the American Coalition for Clean Coal Electricity to spread the gospel of clean coal, and subcontracted the Washington firm of Bonner & Associates to help fight the Waxman-Markey Bill which proposed limits on total greenhouse gases. It was approved by the House of Representatives in 2009 but defeated, in part, because of the astroturfing efforts of Bonner. The PR company was later accused of defrauding the federal government, and in 2009 Bonner acknowledged that his firm had forged more than a dozen anti-climate bill letters which were sent to members of the US Congress. The fraudulent letters, on fake letterhead, were intended to look as if they had come from minority groups opposed to the Waxman-Markey Bill.[40]

Trying to brand oil as ethical or coal as clean seems blatantly absurd, yet millions are spent on these campaigns because they sometimes work, not to persuade but to obscure and polarize (but more on that in following chapters). This is not just PR, it is propaganda, and I offer these examples here because they illustrate how far some corporations and institutions will go to block legislation, push pipelines and muzzle scientists.

By attacking the credibility of scientists and creating doubt about their findings—without actually doing any science themselves—critics poison the well of democracy and flood the public square with misinformation. These kinds of campaigns use abusive ad hominem attacks on the character of opponents in order to invalidate the concerns of scientists and environmental groups. If the media or public is duped into talking about foreign-funded radicals, then the discussion is no longer about climate change, tanker traffic or pipelines. Through repetition these assaults feed biases, stereotypes and prejudices, stirring up powerful feelings and distorted thinking. They are part of a public communication problem we should all be aware of and expect our leaders to shrink from.

As the interviews and conversations for this book continued, it became more and more clear this was a serious problem, and while these examples revolve around climate change—as that's an area I'm familiar with—such toxic forces are at work in many areas. Frankly, these tactics leave me speechless because I know the vast resources and amount of work that goes into organizing them, and getting away with it. They should leave us all speechless, but we need to move beyond being speechless and take a closer look at what's happening. We can't be truly effective in the public square without understanding these destructive and pathological barriers to honest communication and debate. In the following chapters, we will learn more about the process of propaganda, about silencing techniques, about gaslighting and other assaults on democracy to gain a better understanding of this serious form of pollution and ways to deal with it.

11

Assault on Democracy

with Alex Himelfarb

Minimize public spaces where dialogue might occur
and where it does occur, confuse it, obscure it.
The idea is to kill the debate, not foster it.

Alex Himelfarb

To better understand the significance of extraordinary
campaigns like those described in the case study, we must
now look at the role politics plays in today's over-heated climate
of acrimonious debate. When public discourse is invaded by this
kind of warlike political PR and the kind of personal attacks generally reserved for elections, the opportunity for authentic debate
evaporates. And if we blame the situation on a lack of facts, a failure to communicate or partisan polarization, we're not looking at
the whole picture.

I had invited Alex Himelfarb, a renowned social scientist and
one of Canada's leading political pundits, to speak at a David
Suzuki Foundation board dinner, and while strolling back to our
hotel, we discussed the foreign-funded radicals' campaign as well
as the over-the-top PR generated by the oil and gas industry and
Canada's Conservative government. I remarked upon how odd
it was that Prime Minister Harper, who was said to be highly
intelligent, could be ignoring climate change, dragging his feet on
regulating greenhouse gas emissions from the oil sands and tak-

ing such a combative approach to community groups opposed to pipelines and tankers. I suggested that Harper was either not as smart as people say he is or just evil.

Himelfarb responded, "Why the urge to demonize or diminish? Why would we want to buy in, however tempting, to the prevalent and corrosive junk politics that sees a world of heroes, villains and fools?"[1]

That stopped me, and got me thinking about how risky it is to view people behind such campaigns as dense or immoral. I understood Himelfarb was saying the situation required an entirely different attitude—and again I stress such an insight isn't just helpful on the Canadian side of the border. The problem of pollution in the public square is not a simple linear equation that can be quickly solved. It involves a complex set of variables and elements—and governance, or the lack of it, is a key factor.

The potential for positive dialogue hinges on our ability to bring collective issues to the table, said Himelfarb, who had a long career as a federal public servant, was Secretary to the Cabinet and Clerk of the Privy Council serving three Prime Ministers.

Himelfarb believes that the Right prefers to shut down public discourse, and that modern life makes it easy for this to happen. We live increasingly privatized lives, with scant time to devote to public policy. Issues of the common good often don't make it to the table. "Time is short. Mostly we're just trying to get by, deal with the kids who have a cold, pay our mortgage." It is increasingly difficult to engage people on issues like inequality, poverty or climate change. "From our private milieu, they seem pretty abstract; they don't seem immediate." Another reason collective issues don't make it to the table is that we spend less and less of our lives in public spaces interacting with people who have different views and experiences so that we can develop a sense of the common good. Divisive politics and growing inequality conspire to undermine social trust. These elements play perfectly into the right wing's hand.

Himelfarb explained that there is no evidence that Canadians have in fact moved to the Right. There are perhaps 20 percent who would self-identify as being on the Right and a similar number who would identify as being on the Left. But most have no wings, either right or left, and instead have internally competing Right and Left values.

In Canada, the federal Conservatives don't need to convince the public of anything or win any debate; they just need to avoid the debate. He called this do-nothing stance the default position, or *gravity*. In an age of heightened individualism and consumerism, it's pretty easy to undermine trust in public institutions. In an age of uncertainty, it's pretty easy to undermine trust in those who are different or to feed fear. To have a serious, moral debate and do something about fear and distrust requires an *anti-gravity* position, which is so-called because it takes energy, hard work and a real sense of the common good. Himelfarb explained that going along with gravity is easy. A number of thinkers have made the case that, without a crisis, we prefer to go with the flow, and that is the major reason we don't get action on the environment. We have a bias toward what is, the status quo. Making change is hard work.

The easiest thing for the Right to do is to spoil the public space and inhibit debate, to limit the public's capacity and will, Himelfarb explained. They don't have to convince the public that climate change isn't real. They just have to make it seem that all the proponents are pursuing their special interests—just as we all do—sowing doubt that anybody is telling the whole truth and then exaggerating the hazards of solutions to make them seem unbelievably risky. "The Right doesn't need to win hearts and minds, it just needs to make sure the Left doesn't. The key is to sow doubt and limit our sense of what's possible."

Like many others I interviewed, Alex Himelfarb noted the increasing and effective use of a classic rhetorical ploy called *ad hominem*—where attacks are aimed at a person's character, not their line of reasoning. This tactic can muzzle the voices of scientists and close down neutral bodies and scientific initiatives that might result in believable data or even parliamentary debate. All proponents have to do is close down public debate.

What we are seeing is an attack on democracy, and Himelfarb stressed that playing the same game isn't the answer. Progressives won't score any goals unless they have a better counterapproach. Himelfarb suggested several strategic moves.

First, paint a picture of a better future. The Right has been very effective at undermining everything that looks like a positive vision of the future, or at least the possibility that we could ever hope to achieve anything close to positive. Most citizens want a greener and more just Canada.[2] The questions then become: Do we think that such a Canada is likely or even possible? Do we trust one another and our institutions to believe we will all play our part? Environmentalists who hope to inspire people by prophecies of doom are actually feeding into a sense of fear. Himelfarb suggests that we create a compelling narrative and express why the public ought to care. Environmentalists must explain why every previous generation did what was necessary to secure the infrastructure and climate for people to succeed, and emphasize this generation's obligation to do the same. Learn to get better at the art of persuasion and don't be put into the conservative position that protecting what we have is the best that we can do, he explained. Also avoid polarization and present more voices across the spectrum, for example by bringing environmentalists, social and labor advocates together.

The Right has been very effective in promoting a vision of the world as nothing more than an arena for competitive individualism in which ordinary people are consumers and taxpayers rather than citizens with mutual and shared responsibility. Himelfarb pointed to British Prime Minister Margaret Thatcher's infamous "There is no such thing as society" comment, which framed all problems in terms of individual blame and merit, in which the rich deserve their wealth and the poor their poverty, in which there are no systemic problems or collective solutions.[3] Himelfarb argued that at the very time when our collective problems are most challenging, our collective toolkit is inadequate.

Himelfarb reminded me that, a few decades ago, the sociologist C. Wright Mills described sociological imagination as the ability to link private troubles and public issues.[4] That pretty well captures the progressive challenge: reconnecting people to collective solutions. Alex Himelfarb urged progressives to become hugely better at telling a positive narrative that expands what people see as possible, that engages people and gives them a plausible, feasible alternative to the status quo. And, he argued, we have to rebuild the public space where it's possible to hear a moral discourse and moral narratives that link to people's everyday lives, for example to their roles as parents.

Further, progressives must call the Right out on PR spin and its assault on democratic institutions. Democracy depends on engaged and informed citizenship. Any attack on reason, on information and on debate is an attack on democracy. And the notion that there is no society or "This is not a time to commit sociology" (as former Canadian Prime Minister Stephen Harper said in 2013)[5] undermines engagement on public issues. "We believe that if people had the information, knowledge and the ability to participate in these debates, they would not accept what's going on, and that's what the Right is worried about. For progressives, the key is restoring confidence that progress built on the best available evidence is not just desirable but possible. Of course we need to reengage on the moral debates."

But, said Himelfarb, most importantly we have to reject the line that there is no alternative to the current market triumphalism and austerity. Indeed, whenever politicians tell us there is no alternative, we can be assured there is, and it's likely one we would prefer, were it on offer. To turn things around is to expand our sense of what's possible. "And, notwithstanding the growing evidence that facts don't change people's minds, that emotion is the key to change, our best bet to turn things around is still an informed and engaged democracy—and that means opposing, at every turn, the attack on reason, on experts and expertise, on evidence and science."

And finally, he proposed, we need to realize that we are in a long game, not a short game. One speech or one clever strategy cannot turn the world around. We need to keep acting over and over again—not just focusing on the next election. Incessant repetition is something the Right has been doing very well, Alex Himelfarb concluded.

12

Silencing the Voices of Others

with Jason Stanley

Democracy only works

if you have normal, reasoned debate…

so you need to set the conditions

where that's possible.

Jason Stanley

J ASON STANLEY is a professor of philosophy and epistemology
with a PhD from MIT. He teaches courses on democracy and
propaganda at Yale. He is also an academic who explores new ideas
and techniques about mass deception that are directly related to
pollution in the public square.

Stanley explained there are a number of rhetorical and linguistic tactics that are being used now to silence people, and one of
the most blatant is the misappropriation of words such as *ethical*
or *clean* in relation to oil or coal. In an article he wrote in the *New
York Times* Stone series, Stanley said that using what he called
code words to win support has always been part of the arsenal of
politics, but it is now widely used in the popular media.[1]

When we met to talk, Stanley explained that making outlandish allegations, twisting meanings and making improbable
statements has the same effect. This is not really about making
substantive claims; it's what he calls a linguistic strategy for steal-
ing the voices of others, silencing people. Making bizarre claims

that President Obama is a secret Islamist agent, or was born in Kenya, painted the US President as grossly insincere. His voice was stolen, not by a legitimate objection to his platform or an argument but by undermining the public's trust in him so that nothing he said could be taken at face value. Simply put, when Fox News carried a story charging Obama is really a secret Muslim,[2] it damaged everyone's sincerity, and any opportunity for reasoned debate evaporated.

It's a simple tactic: When the public doesn't trust you and you can't rely on your own credibility to argue your views, when the public doesn't share your values or interests, when facts aren't on your side, why not attack and undermine your opponents' integrity while making them appear to have a vested interest?

When no audience or viewer expects truth in the media, only bias, political candidates cannot be held responsible for lying. Stanley made the case that then it becomes possible for everyone to lie with impunity; there is no downside to deceit. Every person has an "everyone's doing it" defense. People start to believe that no one is speaking authentically—that even scientists are massaging data to suit their ideological agendas.

Jason Stanley calls such strategy an attack on objective speech. When scientists' facts aren't clear, when everyone is trying to either complicate issues unnecessarily or promote a political agenda, public dialogue becomes confused. The people can easily believe that "climate scientists are just trying to get us to wear healthy clothing, or eat vegetarian food.... They are trying to change American cultural norms. They are just trying to sway you, not inform you about what is going on."[3]

In the PR business, there's a pressure to oversimplify issues, and the clarity of philosophy is the antidote—which is why I appreciated the precision of Jason Stanley's fresh way of thinking.

Stanley dives deeply into issues that Alex Himelfarb raised and believes the right wing media, such as Fox News, is not trying to communicate accurate, well-researched stories but is scrambling information intentionally, broadcasting noise so that it becomes difficult to hear the truth. This insight came to him a few years ago, when he was watching Fox News and began thinking about its claim of being "fair and balanced," something he and his friends thought nobody believed, including Fox News. He decided that the right wing news media is not trying to deliver fair and balanced coverage of events or reportage of issues. Instead, the message of Rupert Murdoch's media corporations goes something like this: In a world where everyone is trying to manipulate everyone else for their own interests and where no one can believe anything they hear, there is no point in being fair, no possibility of balance. Nobody is trustworthy.

Stanley argued further that Fox engages in a kind of silencing tactic when describing itself as "fair and balanced," especially to an audience that is perfectly aware that it is neither. The effect is to suggest there is no possibility of balanced news, only propaganda; this results in a silencing of all news sources by suggesting everyone is grossly insincere.

Stanley warned that democracy is in danger when we no longer expect truth or demand accountability from public figures, when there is no longer even a pretense of integrity. One early warning sign is an institution "having a problem" with facts; facts don't align with its interests, and a rival may have more credibility. The climate change debate is rife with examples of this, Stanley told me.

Public discourse has deteriorated to such an extent that the traditional debating model—based on accuracy, evidence and proof—isn't happening, so the typical fallback position is to tarnish another person's reputation. When it comes to climate change, for instance, the new technique is to first criticize the research and scholarship, then undermine and discredit scientists. How is this done? Rather than challenging facts, Stanley believes the general strategy is to co-opt vocabulary.

"It is difficult to have a reasoned debate about the costs and benefits of a policy when one side has seized control of the linguistic means to express all positive claims." This kind of dexterous management of language was brilliantly highlighted in the writings of George Orwell, whose Newspeak was designed by a one-party state to prevent freethinking.[4] Stanley said the diaries of Polish-born journalist and comparative literature professor Victor Klemperer are another rich resource when detailing this kind of propaganda.[5] Drawing on his experience in Germany from 1933 to 1945, the linguist recorded how propaganda changed the value of words. For instance, "special treatment" became a euphemism for murder; "intensified interrogation," another name for torture, and words such as "fanatical" were elevated to the rank of high praise.

It is difficult to have a sensible debate about a policy's benefits versus costs when the policy is labeled "Operation Iraqi Freedom" or "tax relief." Co-opted language takes many forms, even as oxymorons such as "clean coal" or "ethical oil." Stanley explained that seizing control of positive vocabulary makes naysayers appear to oppose something that is clearly beneficial. "It's possible to silence people by denying them access to the vocabulary to express their claims."

Democracy only works if reasoned debate in the public square is possible. If everything is mislabeled, then conditions for deliberative democracy do not exist. If people are deluded into thinking there is such a thing as clean coal, or ethical oil, if their ability to apply correct facts is circumvented, and the credibility of experts is undercut, where is the basis for reasoned debate? It's like trying to design a building without a level.

Stanley became concerned about the role of silencing in the public sphere through analyzing right wing media and its reliance on *truthiness*—a word coined by satirist Stephen Colbert to describe the "feeling" of truth based on a gut reaction, rather than evidence or logic.[6] Stanley explained when citizens have no access to reliable news, they become suspicious and untrusting: "The effects of a belief in general gross insincerity are apparent in societies in which the state media delivers only propaganda. Citizens who grow up in a state where authorities deliver propaganda have no experience with trust." In such an authoritarian society, "the public's trust in public speech, whether by politicians or in the media, disintegrates to such a degree that it undermines the possibility of straightforward communication in the public sphere."

Stanley used the example of North Korea: "Clearly something is really wrong with discussion in the public sphere in North Korea." No one trusts anyone, and no one believes what anyone says because they assume it is propaganda. We would hope that free speech guarantees the conditions for deliberative democracy. But if that is true, "how did we end up with public spaces in North America where nobody trusts what anyone says, and that look in certain aspects like North Korea—even though we've got free speech? That's a real mystery."

The answer is, when everyone has the right to make up his or her own facts, it weakens everyone's ability to speak with integrity, and he concludes: Free speech alone is not sufficient for delivering the conditions for reasoned debate. It is impossible without trust and sincerity, and Stanley suggests this is the first critical piece in the puzzle he calls *The Ways of Silencing*.

The whole "ethical oil" campaign in Canada sprang up after many, many years during which climate change was largely ignored by the oil and gas industry and Canada's Conservative government. Then suddenly, legislation started to pop up in Europe and California, and influential companies like Walmart started looking at low-carbon produce. The European Union threatened to stigmatize Canadian oil by proposing a Fuel Quality Directive designed to curb greenhouse gas emissions, and at one point sought to label all oil from the tar sands as particularly dirty, which would have made European refiners less likely to import it. When California passed a Low Carbon Fuel Standard, the Alberta oil industry and related US groups began pushing for bills to limit other states from passing similar standards.

Suddenly the Canadian government and oil producers couldn't ignore the trending legislation any longer. They needed an offensive position, and so they came up with the allegation that foreign-funded radicals were attacking Canada's "ethical oil." Suddenly, at home, criticism of Canadian oil producers could be interpreted as a threat to Canadian prosperity and sovereignty, and the new frame had the added advantage of putting the environmental community on the defensive.

This kind of frame can effectively silence opposition because it prevents people from communicating their message. Debates were no longer about tankers or climate change. Opponents had to refute claims that they were money laundering; NGOs had to spend enormous amounts of time explaining themselves. This messaging was not aimed at revealing the truth. It was aimed at silencing critics and diverting the public discourse. Suddenly the Northern Gateway Pipeline wasn't about Enbridge's safety track record or potential spills affecting shellfish—it's about foreign funding and sovereignty.

13

Gaslighting Blurs Our Reality

with Bryant Welch

When people hear the same message,

in the same language, over and over again,

it functions like an implant.

Bryant Welch

S OLUTIONS TO THE current environmental communication problems outlined in my earlier case study include figuring out forms of communication that are eloquent and persuasive and help people understand more—not less. We don't need people playing mind games, Harvard-trained lawyer, psychologist, lobbyist and author Bryant Welch explained to me. He wrote about a technique he calls *gaslighting* in his book *State of Confusion*.[1]

The term comes from a classic 1944 thriller, *Gaslight,* in which a manipulative husband tries to drive his wife crazy by adjusting the gaslights in their London townhouse. The husband's strategy is simple: he continually denies his wife's observations that the lights in their house are changing. The assault on her mind pushes her to the brink of insanity by undermining her sense of reality and belief in her own senses.[2] Welch said that today's gaslighters work in the public square to create confusion and prey on public vulnerability, using sophisticated forms of manipulation, mind games and PR spin.

Welch, who is past chair of clinical psychology at the California Institute of Integral Studies, believes the Western mind is increasingly gullible because it is overwhelmed by too much information and rattled by fear about what's happening in our world and to our climate. In recent years, our minds have been faced with a steep learning curve. Demands on our brains have increased exponentially because of the rapid pace of change and all that information we must assimilate, respond to and grapple with. Welch said more and more people are less and less able to make sense of, and rationally adapt to, this alarming onslaught. When the mind is overloaded, "we engage in increasingly archaic, increasingly primitive forms of mental solutions" which include wishful thinking, denial and turning away from unpleasant stimuli.[3]

When the mind is in a "state of collapse," we also turn to others to lead us, people who are attractive and hold strong opinions. Simple answers are less taxing for us to absorb, especially when we're faced with a complex issue such as climate change, Welch said. An authoritative person who takes command—"think of Fox News or Rush Limbaugh"— and spews strong feelings with absolute certainty is appealing to a beleaguered mind.

The darker side of public relations thrives on this legitimate longing for clarity. Welch said people today have become vulnerable to an "absolutist situation…a rationalization for doing away with the sacrifices needed to confront a problem" such as climate change. The choice is not easy when one person warns, "We're going to lose our planet" and another argues, "Not true; you don't have to confront that horrible possibility." When the first expert is painted as an elitist, "fuzzy intellectual," it's even easier to tune them out and turn toward "maladaptive kinds of mechanisms."

Today's assault on experts is combined with a new attitude that encourages people to believe whatever feels better, Welch suggested. Comedian Stephen Colbert had joked about this trend in 2006: "Who's *Britannica* to tell me that the Panama Canal was built in 1914? If I want to say that it was built in 1941, that's my right as an American."[4] Welch explained this mindset drives many primitive political processes. "It's what you see with the Tea Party group." Once you begin to eliminate supports for rational thinking and actively encourage people to indulge in beliefs that make them feel good, it's a downward slope. "People are drinking Kool-Aid," Welch commented.

Bryant Welch called this process of manipulation gaslighting because people begin to doubt their own perceptions and observations. When that happens, their autonomy is eroded and they become dependent upon those who foist their own versions of reality on others. People become less rational, less capable of thinking for themselves, "more and more beholden to Fox News." Welch noted that many people are now reliant upon a strong, forceful person telling them what to think.

He sees "gaslighting" examples everywhere: in mass communications, in the Iraq War, in the reaction to 9/11 and in climate change. He sees legitimate scientists describing how climate is changing, while ideologically oriented groups—such as the Competitive Enterprise Institute, the CATO Institute and the Heartland Institute—confuse people and reconstruct a different "scientific reality."

It's conscious, it's deliberate, and it is becoming an art form in government, said Welch who spent the first part of his career in private psychotherapy practice and later worked for the American Psychological Association in Washington. He was struck by the contrast: In individual practice the dialogue involves people struggling to be totally honest and see reality as clearly as possible. In the public Washington, Welch found the opposite: people trying to weave a whole new reality. Welch called this a Rovian approach[5] of fraudulent spin: "Let's see if we can convince people that John Kerry is unfit to lead. What's the guy's strongest point? His military service. So we simply start telling people that Kerry was a coward unfit to lead—and then you create that reality." The technique starts from a false point of view and manipulates other people to revise their reality.

Welch says it's propaganda, pure and simple—but why are we susceptible to lies or misinformation? Like a microchip implanted in a person's brain, the effectiveness of propaganda grows with constant repetition. American political satirist Jon Stewart occasionally runs a series of news excerpts showing a dozen or more talking heads from an administration—all of them spouting the identical language about an issue. As people hear the same language over and over, it functions like an implant. When you give a little chip to a mind that is struggling to come up with answers, the mind is grateful because it doesn't like to look stupid. People don't want to appear overwhelmed or confused, so they welcome the implant. It's easier than having to collect information, listen to differing points of view, talk to experts, read and make a decision.

People today cannot tolerate a state of uncertainty and anxiety. "The country's terrified. People are terrified," said the therapist. The less people can think for themselves, the more frightened they become; this is exacerbated by the pace of change. Yet as US President Franklin Roosevelt said, "The only thing to fear is fear itself."[6]

Bryant Welch believes that antidotes to fear lie in the wisdom of the ancients: "A lot of the contemplative practices from the East—meditation, yoga—are tremendously effective in treating trauma." If people were more centered in their own experience in the present, with less grasping and agitation, we would see a calmer and less gullible population.

Welch believes that nonviolent speech is effective because a lack of response from the victim undercuts "the projective devices that adversaries use to justify their aggression." If the victim remains silent, rather than responding with hostility, it is much harder to sustain any aggression.

Welch also said that the best response to gaslighting is awareness. Expose the manipulation, just like in the movie—when the

Scotland Yard detective reveals what has been happening to the wife. Her autonomy is restored the moment she recognizes how her husband has manipulated her.

I asked Welch what happens on a national scale when political leaders manipulate reality; he said it creates a dynamic very similar to that which existed between the husband and wife in *Gaslight*. At first, people are confused by the false reality. Then they doubt their own senses, become more and more dependent, more invested in bigger and more outrageous lies: "We're going into Iraq because he has weapons of mass destruction." Or, "It's because he was part of Al-Qaeda." Or, "Maybe he's just developing weapons of mass destruction." It changes by the month, and people end up not being able to think for themselves.

14

Summary:
The Polluted Public Square

A Personal Story

When I was seven years old, my friend Donnie Fisherman and I used to go to a park and play in an old dirt cave that stretched deep into the side of a hill. It had a small entrance, a little chimney exit in the roof at the back, and it was dark, spooky and exciting.

One day we were playing there, and a gang of bigger boys came along with boards and plywood and closed off the entrances. Donnie and I panicked in the damp, earthy blackness, and the more scared we became, the more we yelled and screamed, the more this gang of toughs laughed and taunted us.

It was my first experience with bullying, but it wasn't the last, because I grew up in a rough part of Calgary, Alberta. I ran into violence not only going to and from school but also at home because my dad was an unpredictable, violent man who used to thrash the hell out of me and my mother. One time, when my mother was in hospital having trouble with a pregnancy, my father decided to give me a haircut, and told me that if my mother died, it would be my fault. He went into a crazy rage and hit me with the razor. I still have a scar in the side of my face. I was a good athlete at school, and my high jumping ability came in handy that night when my father chased me into the backyard. Energized by terror, I vaulted over the high back fence and flew down the lane.

These experiences didn't crush me. I fought back. I didn't want to be a wimp, and as time went by, I too meted out some rough justice. I turned into a scrapper, got into fights, became friends with some very tough guys and sometimes slipped into bullying.

But as I grew older, I began to learn a pivotal life lesson—about the fine line between standing up against bullies and becoming a bully yourself.

My teenage years were confusing. I grew up with stories of the Lone Ranger and John Wayne dancing around in my head, and those romantic narratives told me that the good guys were right and justice prevailed. My own decisions to fight back didn't always unfold in such a heroic way, however, and in real life things were not so clear cut: good guys could be bad, and bad guys could be good. Sometimes the good guy got a black eye, a bloody nose and a fat lip. Sure, sometimes when I was fighting back, I was the good guy standing up for myself, but other times I was just a bully pushing around someone who couldn't really fight back. Now and then I was the coward who didn't want to fight. Fighting back wasn't always a story about courage and right triumphing over wrong.

A lot of people spiral downward because of abuse or bullying, but I was incredibly fortunate to become interested in meditation, Eastern philosophy and Buddhism. In the 1960s I fell in with a group of people interested in Eastern thought—from Zen philosophy and mysticism to Gandhi—and I turned in a new direction. I began reading Alan Watts and Aldous Huxley, and started going out with a young woman who was into Buddhism, a flower child. It was the 60s after all, a time of peace and love, and I realized that being a minor gangster was not cool.

Years later, after graduating from law school, I built a successful PR firm specializing in crisis and issues management, where I helped clients navigate through public controversy, difficult reputational problems and acrimonious court cases. From time to time, I ran across PR aggressors and intimidators, people who didn't know where to draw the line, who played fast and loose with the truth. These raw attempts to threaten and browbeat riled me, but it was on a small scale compared with what was to come.

At one time I naïvely believed that transparency was the answer. I thought that if you turned on the lights, the cockroaches would scuttle back into the corners. Then I got involved in David Suzuki Foundation and found out that sometimes when you turn on the lights, the cockroaches just get bigger, meaner and more aggressive. When I stepped into the environmental arena, a new world opened up to me, rife with muscular propaganda and PR pressure that was shockingly worse than anything I'd ever imagined. Discussions about climate change, energy consumption and the destruction of ecosystems seemed to trigger an ideological craziness that resulted in wild escalations of rhetoric and extreme polarization.

I found the attacks on scientists and volume of propaganda used to cloud environmental issues puzzling. I found myself becoming angrier about the deception and lack of fair play than I was about environmental damage itself. I wondered why, then one day it hit me: Bullies aren't just a problem in the schoolyard. They also try to take your lunch money and intimidate you in public.

Moving into the Square

When it comes to the environment, the public square is thick with bullies who want to protect their interests or assert their ideology with indifference. Just like the boys outside that dirt cave, they try to dominate others; I was angered about the attitude of people who feel it's okay to behave like this.

The foreign-funded radicals campaign in Canada was about bullying and demonizing. Climategate was the same, an attempt to malign scientists and disparage their work. When American marine biologist and conservationist Rachel Carson raised concerns about the health dangers of pesticides in her 1962 book *Silent Spring*, she was called a hysterical woman, a communist and a radical.[1] Such attacks are never intended to be part of a legitimate debate. These are all attempts to shut people up—bullying has always been at the heart of propaganda.

A core question—considering the insights and warnings from Kahan, Tavris, Conner and Haidt about being careful not to make matters worse—is how to communicate in a way that is more accessible to more people, regardless of their values or politics. How can we stand up for what is right and against what is wrong without becoming bullies ourselves?

As American linguist Deborah Tannen said, our argumentative culture is endangering our civic life because "when there's a ruckus in the street outside your home, you fling open the window to see what's happening. But if there's a row outside every night, you shut the window and try to block it out."[2]

There has long been a difference of opinion about how to advocate. Some suggest aggressive outspoken advocacy is needed while others prefer working with opponents and finding common ground. It's no surprise these issues have sparked many a debate at Suzuki Foundation board meetings. Even civil rights leaders such as Martin Luther King and Mahatma Gandhi had to defend themselves when followers questioned the effectiveness of nonviolent resistance.

My own experience fighting bullies in the rough and tumble world of PR has taught me these key strategies:

1. Be slow to pick public fights because fighting fire with fire seldom settles a dispute or issue in your favor. I have often told clients, who wanted to weigh in on a front-page controversy, to heed the warning of George Bernard Shaw who said, "I learned long ago, never to wrestle with a pig. You get dirty, and besides, the pig likes it." I usually add my own clarification, which is, after a while people can't tell the difference between you and the pig.

2. If you don't tell your own story, someone else will—and it will be bad. Not telling your own story is like not showing up for the game: You lose by default.

These can be contradictory pieces of advice: one tells you to step into the media spotlight and stand up for what you think; the other says don't react. But either strategy may be valid, depending on the situation.

The more I ponder David Suzuki's question about why we are failing to act, despite the warnings of scientists about looming environmental catastrophes, the more I realize we need to become much more savvy about the environment of public debate, so we don't slip into perpetual antagonism, anger and confusion. How do we communicate in a more persuasive and less polarizing, alienating and enflamed manner? And how do we navigate between strong, honest debate and the kind of narrative that drives us further into entrenched, defensive positions?

At its heart, *I'm Right* is about miscommunication resulting from narrative failure on the part of advocates. This has opened the floodgates to industry propaganda and polarization from all sides—whether from government, vested interests or environmental advocates—and miscommunication has created pollution in the public square, whether intentional or not. The results have been gridlock and shuttered windows.

It's a difficult balancing act, but we want to walk a fine line between speaking out against what is wrong while avoiding the advocacy trap.

New Directions for Advocates

If we truly believe that "the sky is falling"—and the vast majority of climate scientists say it is—we ought to be willing to question how we engage around this issue and learn to communicate better.

I hope that *I'm Right* will guide other communicators in government, industry and civil society who feel they are up against a rock wall. So this book is written for right-thinking people, on any side of these difficult issues, who care about what happens in their community and have an opportunity to influence the course of events. It may help people reconsider what they are doing, or for those not yet involved, who may be wringing their hands and wanting to do something, it may help them be successful.

We've learned about powerful psychological and social forces— part of the human condition—that cause us to line up in self-righteous teams and be blind to other points of view, and we've learned how unbelievably powerful it feels to believe we are on the side of Right, and to brand opposition as wrongdoers. But I can't help thinking it would be wiser to keep in mind, as Carol Tavris and others reminded me, that we could be wrong.

We have learned how the advocacy trap stirs up anger, and how we stop thinking clearly when we treat those who disagree with us as enemies. This drives people away from solutions and understanding. DeSmogBlog started there, and it took me a while to realize that attacking people's motives and intentions, even if they seem suspect, fuels their resistance as well as the resistance of people who believe them. And worse, it leads to gridlock and despair—which is the opposite of what those seeking climate solutions want. Even lawyers, duking it out in court, struggle to refer to each other as "my good colleague" or "my learned friend," and the older we get, the more we realize our parents taught us about civility for a reason.

Bryant Welch believes that nonviolence is effective because a lack of response from someone who is attacked undercuts "the projective devices that adversaries use to justify their aggression." If the victim remains silent, it is much harder for an aggressor to sustain an attack because "the perpetrator is left to stew in his or her own ugly juices. They are slowed in their attempts at self-justification," Welch explained.[3]

During this research, I developed a new perspective on polarization while watching a 2013 PBS special in which Bill Moyers and Harvard University social justice advocate Marshall Ganz discussed the power of social movements and how to achieve meaningful change. Ganz told viewers to never be afraid of controversy. He has no time for people who criticize polarization and say "Let's all just get along better." Ganz said we need more polarization, not less.[4] What? I yelled out loud. I was so shocked that I phoned him right away, but after a short conversation, I started to understand the difference between polarization and what I would call bullying.

Never shy away from an important argument or fear taking a combative stance, Ganz stressed when I spoke with him.[5] "This idea that contentiousness is somehow alien to democracy, that consensus is somehow what democracy is about, and that polarization is bad—is all wrong. We are really screwed up on that.... Paralysis is what's bad," explained the veteran activist. Polarization is a necessary precursor to negotiation, and our systems of decision-making should encourage more debate and controversy, not less. "Organizers have to be willing to be schizoids, because they have to polarize to mobilize, and then depolarize to settle." Without polarization and opposition, people never mobilize.

He said Obama made a huge tactical error in 2012 with his "shocking passivity" in the first presidential debate against Mitt Romney. Although seemingly rooted in the President's view that good leadership should avoid "having a good fight," such a conciliatory stance is not only an instrumental problem but a moral problem, "severely compromising the adversarial mechanisms that the citizenry must rely on to bring out the truth." Ganz said Obama had a responsibility to argue in the pursuit of truth, just as the prosecution or defense lawyer in a criminal case should never avoid argument, as that would undermine the entire function of adversarial litigation. His strategy of trying to sound like a statesman and elevate himself above the argument backfired.

Ganz added many of his students slip into conflict avoidance too often and too easily. They have a mistaken idea that if everyone talks things out, everyone will eventually agree and we can all move forward with consensus. Ganz argues that consensus is what you get in an authoritarian regime, not a healthy democracy where citizens are free to challenge injustice. But he was quick to note that debate, when used for reasons of power rather than truth, leads to gridlock in the halls of government. So while he believes contention lies at the heart of democracy, it must be constructive contention.

Ganz explained we should make sure that our argument is an "argument for the sake of heaven," described by Hillel and Panim in an early commentary on the Jewish Torah.[6] An argument for the sake of heaven aims to counteract injustice and bring out truth, not to defeat an opponent. Its goal is not focused on winning, crushing someone or grasping at power. In an argument for the sake of heaven, each side listens willingly and seriously to others' views and analyzes points using reason and respect. We will never solve problems such as climate change if we don't join discussions, and if we sit on the sidelines, our children's futures will be lost— but we need to be respectful of other human beings and not attack them or their opinions.

Communication is an art not a science, and we all learn in the doing. At its most basic level, *I'm Right* is about how we tell stories and how we treat each other. The best stories are iterative and interactive; they grow in the telling, and when they are powerful and compelling, they can withstand a maelstrom of negative PR spin. By telling inclusive stories that are well-crafted and relate to who we are, that help us and others understand the world around us, we can counter pollution in the public square. We also have a responsibility to our own narratives, to keep our own minds open and to seek to expand the minds of others.

This doesn't mean giving up on our principles or becoming wimps, but it does mean avoiding the unintended quicksand of anger-charged messages that drag us all down. The most effective stories enlighten and integrate; they're not selfish, greedy or abusive. We don't want to turn a right-versus-wrong narrative into an us-versus-them story that increases the amplitude of the opposition. Can we think of more culturally accessible ways to take on destructive propaganda, beliefs and values? Yes. And the rest of this book explores how we might argue for the sake of heaven.

PART II

Speak the Truth,
But Not to Punish

In this part of *I'm Right*, we consider how to clean up our polluted public square. Through the eyes of some of the world's great public intellectuals, we learn how to move beyond the one-sided rhetoric, warlike opposition and the ad hominem attacks that create toxic discourse.

We investigate the attitudes, knowledge and skills that can take public conversations to a deeper level, so that we can actually change people's minds about what's desirable and what's possible.

We look at how to communicate more effectively and disagree more constructively, using the language of emotions and deep values. Some people will be forever locked into their opinions, but for most others, it is possible to have an authentic, mind-changing conversation.

Leaning into the Future

15

Power and Love

with Adam Kahane

The tension between power and love
is at the very center of all social change work.

Adam Kahane

CANADIAN FACILITATOR Adam Kahane is an authority on social change and has spent much of his career outside Canada, working to find creative, durable solutions for some of the world's toughest problems. After starting his career in the 1980s at Royal Dutch Shell (a world leader in scenario planning), he co-founded Reos Partners and has since travelled the globe, helping resolve everything from thorny environmental, political and economic problems to issues of nutrition, energy and security—much of it through an advanced and specialized form of dialogue called scenario planning. Kahane is the author of several books about his methods.[1]

One of Adam Kahane's first high-profile successes was in 1991–92, just as apartheid was ending in South Africa and Nelson Mandela had been released from prison. At this crucial time, Kahane facilitated the Mont Fleur Scenario Exercises in which a diverse group of 22 leaders from across the ideological spectrum of South African society worked together to construct possible narratives about the future of their country. In the midst of great conflict and mistrust, this innovative and important project enabled him to work with South African politicians, business people, trade unionists, academics and activists—black and white—to establish a common vocabulary and mutual understanding for moving into the future.

Kahane enabled people to set aside their personal, political and business biases so they could discuss possibilities, and these exercises were part of many dialogues and negotiations that helped a new political landscape evolve.

Trevor Manuel, who chaired South Africa's National Planning Commission, said, "Every leader, policymaker and citizen can learn and take strength from Kahane's central message: by working together, setting aside prejudices and developing trust, we can change the future." Similar accolades came from Colombian president Juan Manuel Santos: "Sixteen years ago, Adam Kahane came to Colombia and worked with us on the future of our country. The four scenarios we built back then have come to life, one after another, and today we are living the best."[2]

With his immense knowledge and experience, I knew Kahane was someone I should talk to about the current state of public discourse. Yet Kahane's experience in more than 50 countries around the globe did not prepare him for what is happening now in his native country. "I'm surprised at the polarization," he said. "I could say, worse than that, the demonization of public discourse generally, but especially around environment issues. We see this in many countries on many issues, but I was expecting something better in Canada."[3] I interviewed him during the Harper period, and as people protested around pipelines, Kahane noted that he is witnessing levels of fragmentation, polarization and demonization almost as dramatic as those he's seen in other countries.

"In particular, this controversy over the so-called foreign funding of NGOs is extraordinary. I mean there are lots of countries that don't like foreign funding of NGOs—Russia, Uganda—but it's not normally an issue in the West." Kahane was also shocked by the delegitimization of opponents on both sides. "I've been surprised at the extent to which the people who work on climate change consider the elected majority government to be beyond the pale and impossible to engage with.... It's mutual demonization."

Kahane went on to explain that many issues can only be successfully addressed through collaborative, co-created work by actors from government, business and civil society.

Adam Kahane's work has shown him it is increasingly vital for people to work together, not just with friends and colleagues but also with strangers and opponents, even enemies, in order to address knotty challenges of which climate change is an extreme example. How do we get people to the table, and what should we do when we're there? First, he doesn't spend any energy trying to convince people to do something they don't want to. He looks instead for an attitude—whether from NGOs, corporations or governments—a shift that shows people finally recognize they cannot get where they want to alone. They are ready to come together because "usually they have bumped their head hard."

Kahane stressed that people need not agree on a vision in order to start working together. "The common theme in all our work is helping teams of actors from across different organizations and sectors who all think that something needs to be done in their system. They don't need to agree on the solution or on the problem. They don't need to understand each other, trust each other or even like each other." But they do have to recognize that the only way to move forward is together.

If actors are not initially willing to participate, he tries to find a way in, a crack. Even simply agreeing that the situation is dire can sometimes be enough of a toehold that will allow the actors to begin to engage with one another. He described this kind of work as a perpetual cycle that alternates between advocating and collaborating, "between pushing with all your strength for what you believe is true and right, and sitting and talking, trying to work with people who you don't understand, or trust, or like." The stress of going from the ramparts to the negotiating table is exacerbated by power imbalances—the power of money, or politics or ideas, Kahane said.

Adam Kahane calls the two basic pillars of his work power and love. Most people associate the word *power* with oppression and *love* with romance, but he quotes theologian Paul Tillich who said power is the drive of everything living to realize itself with increasing intensity and extensity, and love is the drive to unify the separated.[4] "The tension between power and love is at the very center of all social change work," said Kahane.

Both love and power have a generative and a degenerative side when taken to extremes. For instance, nothing happens without power, without an engine to drive us forward. But when taken too far, power becomes a destructive and confrontational steamroller. Similarly, love can engender a sense of oneness and collaboration, but can also be suffocating and emasculating. Kahane quoted Martin Luther King: "Power without love is reckless and abusive, and love without power is sentimental and anemic."[5]

Coming unstuck requires knowing when to exercise both power and love, and Kahane noted the elegance of this model applies at any scale of social system, from a family to a global issue.

He described a meeting he once had with a deputy minister who said, "We need a method for working on stuck files." This intrigued Kahane because whether you are working in Ottawa, Calgary or Washington, there are certain things you can't make progress on. You keep pushing, but can't move forward. Why? Because no single institution, even one as large as a federal government, can successfully address many of today's difficult problems. He recalled the beginnings of this in Ottawa 20 years ago when another deputy minister pointed out, "We've been trained to think that we can fix or deal with societal issues by pulling these levers, and we've discovered that these levers are not attached to anything."

Kahane noted that humanity is increasingly stuck in complex and polarized situations for three reasons:

1. We cannot solve the really tough problems by only working on our little piece.
2. We cannot transform large systems by only working with people we like, with our friends and colleagues.
3. We must learn to work with strangers and opponents, people we don't know or trust or agree with. Without this simple awareness, we will have gridlock.

One of the most effective ways to get unstuck is to tell stories that enable us to create new futures, hence Kahane's focus on transformational scenarios. These scenarios are not forecasts about what could or should happen. They are not attempts to make predictions or blueprints, or to come up with solutions. They are designed to generate new thinking about the future. "They are not about what people want, but about what's possible."

In the Mont Fleur process, each scenario was named for a bird. The Ostrich stuck its head in the sand so problems festered; the Lame Duck represented a new government, but with so many restrictions it never got off the ground; Icarus embodied the idea of elation and freedom, but ignored fiscal constraints and crashed the economy, but the Flamingo symbolized gradual rebuilding and flight as a group.

Kahane explained that transformative scenario planning contains a crucial paradox: those involved become very creative when they have to be absolutely objective and think deeply about fashioning a new situation. The actors do not have to understand, agree or trust each other in order to work constructively and openly in the creation of new stories, but they do have to agree that the scenarios they envision could actually happen.

Kahane explained that his methodology involves five simple steps:

1. An organizer convenes a team from across the whole system in question.

2. The team observes what is happening in the system.
3. The team constructs stories about what could happen.
4. The team discovers from these stories what can and must be done.
5. The team then takes action to transform the system.

Although simple, it is not easy, Kahane explained, because the actors typically have strong and opposing feelings, opinions and emotions. In addition, this kind of emergent process is unpredictable, uncontrollable or uncomfortable. Participants have to accept that some things will never change. This can be difficult. The first step is to just gather the actors together with a common goal, "not to take action, but to try to understand what is possible.... It's a much lower bar for participation."

How does Adam Kahane encourage people to work together? He believes that two things generate movement toward resolution: a feeling of frustration and a deep desire for change. "If I could get there alone, why would I bother to sit in long meetings with people I don't trust and don't agree with?" Is dialogue, by itself, sufficient? "The answer is sometimes yes but more often no. Dialogue alone does not advance a problematic situation because we need to change not only what we're saying but also what we're doing. That's a challenge for people who hope a pressing problem will go away by just talking about it. That's one reason why working in Canada can be so difficult: the status quo works just fine for most people and is a significant barrier to change." Whereas the advantage of working in South Africa, or Guatemala or India is "nobody has any illusion that things are just fine the way they are."

Kahane said the time limit associated with climate change is what makes it exceptional—and exceptionally difficult. We need creative work to get out of the climate change box because it is an extremely serious challenge; it has been the most clearly explained future crisis ever, and yet even that much information has failed to motivate people, he noted.

I suggested that industry and Harper's federal government might do a better job of managing their interests if they decided to be less combative and more constructive. He agreed and pointed out there are opportunities to be seized and costs to be lessened through engagement: "But there's a basic problem here that couldn't just be wished away through hand waving. What's surprising to me is that the dangers and costs of climate change are not taken more seriously by the population at large and by the representative government in particular." Yes, there are major costs associated with change, but the price of not changing is to live in an over-heated world: "I don't get why those slightly longer-term questions cannot be grasped." People tend to say, "Yeah, yeah, yeah. The world's burning, but...we're not going to fix this on the back of my stockholders, my employees, my tax bill." He is amazed that we have made so little progress, and in some areas are backsliding. "It's willful denial of the effects we're already feeling."

I asked if he believes Canada's federal government, under Harper, and industry have chosen this kind of combative style because the alternative is too damaging to business. Kahane agreed that it does seem that provincial and federal governments are saying the costs of addressing environmental concerns—not just for companies but also for tax revenues and national economic production—are too high. "We are simply not willing to sacrifice immediate benefits for an unpredictable future benefit. I don't think it's any more complicated than that."

Is Adam Kahane hopeful we can make progress on the climate file? Not until the cost of failing to engage with these issues and in collaborative action—for companies, governments, the voting public and consumers—is so high that ignoring it is no longer feasible.

Kahane explained one of the biggest, longest-standing and most successful multi-stakeholder, dialogue-in-action projects he has ever been involved with is the Sustainable Food Lab. He was the co-initiator of the project (with Hal Hamilton), and in

2004 during the first round of recruitment interviews, he had an interesting insight while meeting with the head of one NGO. Kahane's group listened very carefully during several days at the organizer's farm, but at the end of the meetings, the man stated flatly: "Look, it's very clear what you want to do, but I am actually not interested in entering into dialogue with these corporations until I'm stronger and they take me seriously."

Kahane suggested that this is why environmental activism is absolutely critical to advance dialogue, and may have to be scaled up tenfold before it has the necessary impact on businesses and governments. Even when dialogue does start, don't give up on mobilizing voters, consumers and protesters, he advised. You want to keep the pressure up because people are never keen to act against their immediate interests. We all hear statements like "Let's just put our interests and agendas aside and talk about what's best for the world." This is nonsensical, a ridiculous request of individuals, companies or governments. He noted it's equivalent to saying "Why don't you stop breathing while you're in this room?"

Kahane returned to his earlier theme about power and love: these two seemingly contradictory forces have much to teach us about the state of public discourse in the world today, whether a debate revolves around food security, judicial reform or climate change. Power helps us get the job done, achieve our ambitions. "Without it, nothing, literally nothing would happen in the world," Kahane said, adding that the ambition of politicians, oil companies and activists is all part of that power. Love becomes a critical counterbalance because power without love means everyone is doing their own thing, pushing for what they alone want. It's a scenario that's all about individual self-interest and ambition, without any recognition of the impact these might have on others, or society as a whole. Climate change is the ultimate example of this.

Kahane explained that pollution in the public square happens when one factor is applied without the tempering influence of the other: people exercise power without love by driving enormous cars or wasting resources in ways that are "ultimately destroying the conditions for life on the planet." But the opposite is equally important, perhaps more so. Love without power pays attention only to the good of the whole, what's best for humanity, and denies or ignores the interests and drives of the parts.

The best way to navigate is by paying attention to both power and love. It's like walking on two legs, he said, adding that without dynamically balancing and shifting from one to the other, we cannot propel ourselves and society forward—whether we're working with executives, political leaders, activists or guerillas.

Understanding the anatomy of a problem like climate change is helpful, and Kahane outlined three dimensions at play:

1. Dynamic Complexity—cause and effect are far apart in space and time, yet interdependent. For example, the coal we burned 50 years ago is influencing our climate today, or oil sands in Alberta are affecting rainfall in South Africa.
2. Social Complexity—the actors have fundamentally different perspectives, interests and worldviews.
3. Generative Complexity—situations are fundamentally unfamiliar and unpredictable. For instance, "We can't do what we did last time we heated up the planet like this."

For reasons that are pretty obvious when looking at these three dimensions, climate change is, in most respects, the most difficult problem in the world, Kahane said, and that's why, in spite of enormous, serious, intelligent, good-willed efforts, we are not making progress.

But by engaging with varied groups—people who are not like us, who operate in other parts of the system—we can begin to look at things differently. We can see things we may not have seen before, things we may not have wanted to see. It helps us overcome stereotypes and recognize how we might do things differently—although it doesn't always prompt us to do things differently. Studies have shown that the elites understand the climate change problem best, but that doesn't reduce their airplane trips to climate change conferences, or their overseas holidays. Which is why we need countervailing pressures.

High-quality communication is critical, and that springs from open-mindedness, self-awareness and good listening skills. Kahane said good communication is not simply downloading our own view. As long as we are stuck in downloading mode, we are impervious to change, he explained. The first step is to suspend our story, "to hang it on a string in front of us, put that little bit of distance between me and my story." This allows us to see it, question it, and maybe at the end of the conversation, take it back and say, "I think, that story is really not effective, or accurate or appropriate anymore."

The act of suspending says "I am open to the possibility of changing, but if others don't also take that step, we remain stuck parroting our set speeches to each other," which by the way, probably occupies 80 percent to 90 percent of usual discourse.

Kahane was working in Zimbabwe recently, in a highly charged, violently polarized political and social system, and the one thing that stuck with people at the end of the session was the word *suspending*; this pleased Kahane greatly because if you can only remember one word, that's the most important lesson from your experience. Suspending doesn't mean I'm rejecting my position or story, but I am making myself aware of it and making you aware of it, and giving us both permission to question it, to even attack it, without attacking me.

As powerful as dialogue is, Kahane said it would be a fundamental error to focus on that alone. "It's certainly part of the story, but dialogue is, above all, a love methodology, a love tool for uniting the separated. I'm all for love tools," but once again, love without power is dialogue without connection to action and implementation. "I have devoted my life to dialogue. I think there's a lot to be said for it, but the answer is not to scale up dialogue alone but to connect the dialogue with action to affect systemic change."

Kahane warned that love without power is more dangerous than power without love because it's hidden. "It produces perverted outcomes. Be careful of trying to walk on one leg."

I mentioned to Kahane that it's impossible to discount the persuasive power of some of the great leaders in history, who weren't involved in dialogue at all but single-mindedly focused on persuasion. He took that point further, explaining that the important dichotomy is not between dialogue and persuasion but between dialogue and unilateral action. Kahane argued both are required. Things change in the world when people see something that needs to be done and something that is, in some sense, in their interests. So they act accordingly. They may act insensitively, forcefully and in some cases even violently, but without that kind of drive, many things would not take shape.

The dangers involved in pure power without love, however, are rampant and are leading to the destruction of our planet, he said. "We mustn't let the pendulum swing to one side or the other."

No Fish? No Fish Sticks

with Peter Senge

Every single problem is a subset

of this mega problem of not being able

to understand the complexity that we have created.

Peter Senge

P ETER SENGE[1] is a world leader in systems thinking, and when helping students understand what he means by systems, Senge asks if they have ever seen how members of families sometimes produce unintentional consequences through their actions or feelings. This helps students step outside the world of theoretical jargon and into the reality that we all live in webs of interdependence. It's also a view of systems thinking that helps everyone gain a perspective on the "vexing, difficult and intransigent" problems we deal with, not to mention "some leverage and insight as to what we might do differently."[2]

I wanted to know why we are ignoring the alarm bells that scientists are ringing about environmental crises, and why we are bogged down by acrid debate. Senge is skeptical about debates in general and said universities are great places for people to argue round and round a topic, but these exercises usually achieve little. Senge explained a key reason why debate falls short in global warming discussions is that scientists are excellent at forming new questions and discovering new areas of uncertainty, but not particularly good at producing consensus around complex issues. Climate change is an iconic example of this failing, and "the climate science community has done a poor job of helping the public understand even the most basic ideas about which there is a very broad consensus."

For example, a simple basic of climate science is that greenhouse gas emissions accumulate in the atmosphere and that, consequently, reducing emissions will not reduce GHG concentration until emissions are reduced to below the rate at which GHG are removed from the atmosphere (e.g., via natural sequestration). Not understanding this rudimentary climate bathtub concept leads many laypeople to never intuitively understand why massive reductions (80 percent or more) in emissions will be needed—and that consequently we inevitably face long delays in solving this problem. Widespread misunderstanding of this basic concept also makes the "wait until we are all certain" strategy exactly the wrong strategy.

Science is basically organized around communities of enquiry that investigate smaller questions within much larger fields. Scientists typically produce deep knowledge about pieces, elements or aspects of a complex system such as climate change, but not Earth's climate system itself. So, when dealing with truly interdependent issues, mainstream science is often dysfunctional. Also, asking scientists what they all agree on is a waste of time because science never does, nor should, produce unanimity. Scientists are naturally focused on challenging existing ideas and sharpening debates that can illuminate future questions.

Society is faced with a twofold problem: Not only do scientists have difficulty communicating intuitively and effectively, but also the environmental community is "addicted to a fear-based strategy, hammering away at how awful everything is, so not surprisingly this leads a lot of people to just tune out."

We need to put the puzzle pieces together and look at group problem solving using systems thinking, Senge said flatly, because "reality is made up of circles, and we see straight lines."

A systems-thinking approach has three characteristics:

1. A deep and abiding commitment to real learning
2. An ability to admit that we too are part of the problem
3. The ability to triangulate, to gather different points of view from people in different parts of the system, so we can see something more holistically that is eluding us individually.

Senge also described the need for collective intelligence, not simply individual intelligence. When we pool our best ideas and work cooperatively, we end up with cities that operate differently, industrial sectors that value change and produce social, ecological and economic well-being.

Senge's fascination with systems began at a young age. Something he realized even before attending college was that the "level of interdependence mankind has created in the world has vastly outstripped our ability to manage and understand that interdependence." He sees this challenge in every large and stubborn problem we face today, from environmental issues to social concerns and global economics. "Every single problem is a subset of this mega problem of not being able to understand the complexity that we have created." Growing up in Los Angeles, Senge witnessed first-hand the completely out-of-control nature of urbanization: "[When I was] a child you could drive for miles and see nothing but orange and lemon groves, but within 10 years, they were gone, replaced by shopping malls and freeways. It was an astounding example of poorly considered sprawl, that created all kinds of unintended social, environmental, economic problems—and it had a big impact on me."

Senge saw the world around him as a total free-for-all where nothing was planned and everything was opportunistic. "It was driven by narrow economic interests and short-term thinking, with consequences that would last for lifetimes." He compared urban sprawl to cancer, a simple growth process which spirals out of control when cells lose their sense of interdependence. Similar patterns of unrestrained expansion are now being played out all around the world.

I asked Senge about change resistance and the self-activating, balancing forces within systems that sustain them. Are they preventing us from fixing environmental problems, and if so, how do we open up for change?

His answer was simple. On a biological level, one of the definitions of a living system is the ability to maintain balances crucial to survival. A living thing's first impulse is to maintain itself, and homoeostasis is the fundamental process creating that balance. In this sense, all systems resist change from the outside. If you push, the system will push back. We all know this at a personal level, Senge explained. "If someone says to you, 'Hey, Jim, be happy,' even though you might agree, you have a kind of a knee-jerk reaction to feel 'Who are you to tell me to be happy?' So going around the world telling people what to think is a particularly bad idea, a bad change strategy."

We often forget this human trait, naïvely believing that the truth and logic of our argument will convince people to take action, but instead we trigger tendencies to dig in. He said it is important to understand this. "If you really think deeply about why things are the way they are, you see the forces conserving balances, and this knowledge can help shape more effective strategies."

And so, in any kind of change process, Senge advised that the initial strategy should be to start with inquiry and focus on where things are already moving. "It's the first rule of all learning: All learners learn what learners want to learn." When people are pushy and force us to learn something, it's off-putting. But if someone politely asks if you want to learn something, you might consider it. One of the reasons we forget this basic fact is that we all have our own values; when something is really important to us, we think it will be important to others, that they should learn it. "We forget it's the learner's values that matter, not ours. So the first question always has to do with motivation. What will genuinely motivate another person, organization or society?"

The next step is learning how to "follow the energy. Put your focus where things are headed in the right direction, rather than trying to stop a river that has been flowing in a certain direction for a very long time. There's an old saying in traditional Chinese culture: 'You cannot move the river; dig a new channel instead, and the river will move itself eventually.'"

Senge pointed out that we must always remember the unprecedented nature of global warming. We are being asked by science to surmount all of our history, personally and as a species, and believe that something that has never happened is now happening. So, it is not hard to grasp why underlying disbelief exists, and this disbelief is exactly what misinformation campaigns exploit. If people were predisposed to accept what evidence is showing, misinformation would likely not have the same hold that it does. We must remember that people holding this disbelief are not crazy. Since human-induced global climate change has never happened before, it is in some sense quite reasonable to question whether it could be happening now. Deep beliefs don't change quickly or easily. So focusing on convincing people who are anchored as climate contrarians is a low-level strategy. Peter Senge articulated a transcendent understanding in systemic change: "People don't necessarily resist change—but they do resist being changed."

"That's why I think it's a total waste of time to try and shift the political climate in Washington. I don't think it's a coincidence that there's aggressive leadership on climate change in Beijing and little in Washington." When leaders in Washington get overwhelmed, they revert to what they're most comfortable with, "debating and acting lawyerly, because that's who they are." Most of the leaders in China, however, are engineers who want to get things done. Many understand the basic science of climate change, but of course they face their own very daunting problems, given the direction and inertia of the economic growth engine in China.[3]

Achieving change in the US will not be easy because entrenched interests are strong, whereas in China, people are discovering incentives to accelerate an energy transition. "I find it's tragic that so few people outside China sense the forces trying to move in a different direction there. It's real." The Chinese Communist Party has aggressive targets for carbon intensity reduction of 40 percent to 45 percent this decade. "That's a really, really big deal, and it's basically been ignored in the West. My personal feeling is that enough people in China, particularly in Beijing, have crossed the threshold...their mindset has shifted, and they are starting to believe that China can lead the energy transition, just as the West led the extraordinary shift to the fossil fuel economy. They have a different spirit and capability to confront really tough problems. It's state supported, and it's entrepreneurial."[4]

Senge believes the speed at which we are accomplishing change is woefully inadequate given the urgency of global climate change, but countries like Germany are also moving in the right direction, trying to accelerate decarbonization; other nations are strong on solar power. A major problem in the environmental movement in North America is the focus on convincing people of the problem and not accelerating entrepreneurial movement. Most large environmental NGOs are science-based and have spent way too much energy trying to convince people of the science rather than supporting more rapid deployment of non-fossil fuel energy; promoting new energy sources is both environmentally sound and sound for the economy by virtue of the enterprises and employment it can create. More NGOs are starting to see that "we need to find something that works, get out and do it. And do it again and again, and do it faster." We need to be more creative and proactive in scaling up much more rapidly. "We've got to make this feasible for millions and millions."

Senge suggested that North Americans are stuck in a chicken-and-egg situation: The present policy environment is shaped by the political power of the coal-oil-gas-utility lobby, but activists play into their hands by making the argument about the environment, which simply is not a top-level political issue in the US. However, economic revitalization and employment, technological leadership and national security are issues that can move political consensus. The movement will not be easy because the status quo lobbies are so powerful, but those urging protection of environments need a sound political strategy.

Senge emphasized that systems thinking is very pragmatic. It tells us that change is motivated not by fighting resistance but by going where things are already moving, by finding high-leverage changes which can create an environment that is drifting in the desired direction. "You don't grow anything, even a single tree, by standing over a seedling and saying 'It's a really good idea you should grow.' That's idiocy. You have to understand the water, nutrients and sunlight. You study the systems, the conditions, see where it is already growing and support that. If that innate growth process didn't exist, there would be nothing much you could do."

When applying this analogy to environmental advocacy, Senge said the first question is who is already trying to do something useful, and how do we support them? He believes fighting "wrongs" only gets us stuck in the past. We need to lean into the emerging future and work to accelerate positive efforts, and that means supporting companies that are aggressively doing the right things.

One example of potentially massive systems change thinking relates to the Internet, which currently consumes 8 percent to 10 percent of the world's electricity.[5] "That's a massive energy load, and it's been doubling worldwide every two or three years. Plus, people who see the Internet as pointing to our future believe technology is a key lever for change. Why not work toward a vision where the Internet is entirely based on alternative energy? You could start with huge server farms. Then concentrate on cell towers. Then, gradually build a consumer movement for non-fossil fuel-based electricity to power personal devices."

Senge suggested bringing two or three big device producers on board, and setting a goal to decarbonize the Internet in 20 years. "Hook up some of the biggest growth engines of electricity use to alternative energy, and then use them to pull the whole energy generation system." The key is getting the system moving. "It's a case of looking for places where massive change is already occurring, and then imagining how a large movement could really start to build." Even with massive changes, it will still take 50 to 100 years to slow and then gradually reverse the effects of climate change.

Senge referred to Australian environmentalist Paul Gilding's book *The Great Disruption* and his TED talk entitled "The Earth Is Full."[6] The former international president of Greenpeace has developed a crisis response strategy called The One Degree War Plan, which addresses the coming threat of global economic and geopolitical instability. Gilding believes climate change is a symptom of a growth mindset that has seen us expand our economies well beyond any material need. While there are many in the world with real material needs, they are not the ones driving this obscene growth.

Gilding has proposed reversing runaway climate change and starting to decarbonize, by digging a new channel rather than trying to move a river. Forget environmental arguments—forget climate change, species destruction and ocean acidification—because we now know these environmental crises only lead to polarized political debate. Instead, let's focus on economics, mobilizing people by talking about their pocketbooks. Add up all the different costs that climate destabilization generates—not in the future but right now—the droughts, floods, settlers' camps that are needed because of droughts and flooding, all the strange storms, the hurricane-strength winds in Washington DC that cut power to six million people in the summer of 2013. Gilding suggested that if we would only get serious about actually adding up all these very diverse economic costs of climate destabilization, we might see that they are already crippling our economies. We don't have to wait 10 years to see this.

Applied systems thinking can be summarized in one word: leverage. In the example of climate change, Senge said we have a challenge to get the energy economy system moving in a different direction, quickly. People's need to argue is "usually driven by ego needs to be right and prove somebody else wrong." So, let's let go of these ego drives and stop trying to force-feed people with opinions they cannot hold. Don't waste time talking to people who believe the world is so big and we are so small, we could not possibly alter global climate. "Go with people who are open-minded and are already predisposed to deep change...go to the young people."

He thinks young people will spearhead change and lead the energy revolution because they are the ones who will think it's crazy to have a car that gets less than 100 or 150 miles per gallon in the future, or will want fuel cell-powered motorcycles. Governments will follow with policy initiatives, and "it would have to be motivated or coordinated by a systems view so we don't waste time arguing."

Besides, who's future are we playing with anyway, he asked. We are gambling with young people's lives, which is why he suggests a strategy of bringing out the voices and encouraging the effective activism of people between 10 and 30 will pay dividends because their voices resonate. The voices of young people have an emotional quality that moves us. "When young people say 'You're gambling with my life,' it brings adults up short. You can argue there is uncertainty, or the needed changes are going to cost a lot, or I'm just one person, what can I achieve? But it always comes down to the fact that it's their lives we are playing with."

The common denominator underlying a lot of these problems—whether the environmental crisis, or social justice or the widening gap between rich and poor—is we don't seem able to develop wise, forward-thinking strategies, he said. Our society systematically undervalues the future and is strongly biased toward short term. This is deeply connected to the fact that the voices of children and young people simply don't exist in our society. The future is not emotionally real to us. "The future is a bunch of statistics and projections—but that would change if children and young people got involved."

Encouraging youth involvement also dovetails with his strategy of focusing where the movement is happening. He talked about schools that are establishing systems-thinking programs, with sustainability as a foundation. The Kid's Footprint Project shows high school students how to map energy footprints, starting with their own school buildings where they learn to analyze data and develop proposals for the return-on-investment of things like better lighting, better insulation, smart metering and other basic nuts and bolts. "It's a learning laboratory and the goal is to get them into their communities, working with small and medium-sized businesses that can't afford significant energy rises."

Nine times out of ten when you have a conversation with a daughter or a granddaughter, a younger person, you see a pattern arise: What will the world be like for them? Adults start to look in the mirror, and one day they say, "Shit. What am I doing here?" It's really a personal question. If you are stuck in your role as the CEO, it's very hard to get creative, or imagine a new perspective, Senge explained. "You can get so tied up in knots, trying to keep stakeholders and especially your shareholders happy. Your job depends upon your profit growth."

Senge said when an adult has this kind of epiphany, it's usually not because of any deep analysis. It's a realization, a kind of conviction in the heart that prompts them to suddenly say, "This is what I need to do." It becomes personal, matter-of-fact, and then they start thinking out of the box, looking at the larger system. "Unilever had a chairman who really got it personally. He was crystal clear. I remember him telling me, 'You know, I'm just trying to convince my people, if there's no fish, there's no fish sticks.'"

Change happens when something makes sense to you deeply, said Senge. So try to understand other people's logic, their reasoning, and gradually you will find a way to bring them along. "They may be keeping mum because their culture doesn't encourage it, or simply because they have not found what connects them to things they do care about."

You can think in terms of the classic bell curve. "There are people who are engaged. At the other end of the curve, you have people who are really opposed. Then there are people who are predisposed but aren't yet engaged because they don't know how to be engaged. You don't have to convince them. You need to help them see how to connect. Then there could be a large number in the middle, people on the fence, who just don't understand what it's all about, how they can do something about it, and why it would make a difference from a practical standpoint." So, you target a few key folks in the latter two groups and eventually find a way to reach them.

This is where you need skills in balancing advocacy and inquiry. For example, you would ask, how do you see this situation, and what are the questions that matter to you? Focus your communication on understanding where people are coming from and what truly matters to them. When appropriate ask their advice. "In short, create a real conversation, not a sales pitch. That's what an effective systems perspective looks like."

Listen Deeply

with Otto Scharmer

We go to the gym to train certain muscles,
and this is training the muscle of empathy,
getting out of old patterns.

Otto Scharmer

"The success of any intervention depends upon the interior condition of the intervener." This simple and perceptive statement summarizes what was an epiphany for Bill O'Brien, late CEO of Hanover Insurance and author of *Character at Work*.[1] He believed that the success of our actions does not depend so much on what we do, or how we do it, as it does on the inner place from which we operate.

Otto Scharmer often recounts this quote in the popular executive leadership workshops he facilitates around the world. The insight is central to Scharmer's work as a senior lecturer at MIT's Sloane School of Management. How can we access this inner source? What are the tools we need?

Scharmer's own first lesson in the connection of inner states with outer realities came when he was just 16 years old, and it has formed his work ever since. He grew up in northern Germany where his parents were pioneers in organic biodynamic farming. One day while at school in Hamburg, the principal came to Scharmer's class and said he should go home immediately. No one answered the phone at home when he called, nobody met him at the train; for the first time in his life, he took a taxi the final eight kilometers from the train station. Halfway home he could see the whole sky smudged with black, and dark smoke rising from the place where his family's farm had been.

The young Sharmer leapt from the car and ran past hundreds of onlookers and firefighters. "I was unable to believe what my eyes actually told me was true...that the whole world I had been living in up to that point no longer existed. I still remember time slowing down and almost breaking a surface level of my mind and slowly sinking into my deeper mind." Scharmer realized that something enormous had ended, but he also understood that something else was beginning. "I realized how much my identity was attached to all these things that no longer existed," and in that same instant of awareness, he suddenly recognized that the world that had vanished was not just outside him. He had lost something deep inside too, and with that realization came an intense experience of freedom. Scharmer was suddenly elevated, watching from above, and understood this loss went beyond the material dimension and had more to do with his essential self and the pure possibility of the future. "I had no idea that there was this other dimension that we can connect with under certain conditions."[2]

Scharmer has a PhD in economics and management, chairs the MIT Ideas program and is vice-chair of the World Economic Forum's Global Agenda Council on New Leadership. He founded the groundbreaking Presencing Institute which coaches people in how to learn from the "emerging future" and has authored the best-selling book *Theory U* and more recently *Leading from the Emerging Future: From Ego-System to Eco-System Economies*.[3]

When Scharmer joined the MIT Learning Center founded by Peter Senge, he focused on what they call learning from the emerging future as opposed to the past, "and only then did I start to tap into my best work." Scharmer believes a connection to this deeper level of awareness—"a state with an entirely different texture and feeling"—is not only prompted by great loss but can also be spurred by social movements or a mission that makes people question why they are here, who they really are and what kind of journey they're on.

Reflecting on his early life, Scharmer recalled the nascent peace movement, green movement and fledgling antinuclear movement that were starting to emerge in Central Europe. How were these mobilized? Certainly not through facts, he determined. "That's the big myth." The quest for a new reality is achieved by connecting with the realm of possibilities, which involves inspiring new ways of operating, communicating and co-creating. A second myth is that a movement can be mobilized by filling people with fear, an approach the environmental movement has often employed in the past. Like so many others I talked with, Scharmer believes trying to motivate people by frightening them—"It's even worse than you thought"—is no way to gain traction.

Scharmer believes we must open our minds, hearts and wills if we are to see our own blind spots, shift our awareness and connect with our best possible futures. And this is especially critical for leaders. Leadership training methodologies have long relied on historical lessons, but current challenges require new and different skills, an ability to let go of the past in order to connect, and learn from the *emerging future*—the land of possibilities. With that in mind, Scharmer developed the concept of *presencing*, a word he coined by blending the idea of "sensing," a feeling of the future possibilities, with "presence," which is the state of being in the now. Together the two refer to sensing and actualizing one's highest future possibility, "acting from the presence of what is wanting to emerge." It's the idea of diving deeply and opening up, of transforming our thinking and gaining new insights into what is true entrepreneurial spirit.

Presencing means moving beyond our ingrained default positions and deep-rooted habits, judgments and thoughts. Old style of communication often leads to denial, cynicism or depression as people try to cope, Scharmer said. Yet some people manage to sense another reality and are able to connect with the energy of a different future. That is the essence of all creativity and entrepreneurship, he stressed: "You operate from a sense of possibilities, something that isn't there yet, and you put your own journey into the service of making it all happen, bringing it into reality. You remove everything that's getting in the way."

How do we sidestep denial, depression and fear of the future? How do we help people and communities move from one state to another, and carry that message into social systems and global initiatives? Scharmer believes a big part of the answer involves learning how to move beyond fear and loss. Such deep "systems change" is wrought through human relationships, projects, networks and pulling together.

All this sounds a bit esoteric, but Scharmer makes the experience real for business students by taking them on *empathy immersion* journeys where they must confront extreme, raw, unfiltered situations. "In our world today, there is no more cynical place than business schools that prepare people to go to Wall Street. As a matter of principle, I don't download any of my values on these people because that's just the next straitjacket. I create high-quality environments that allow students to investigate their own levels of knowing and connection with relevant pockets of society."

He takes them into edgy situations where they identify with people who are politically, ideologically and socially at the extreme opposite of everything the students hold sacred. There, they are urged to experience another person's life, to totally empathize, become one with others for a period of time. When they connect on more authentic levels with people who are radically different and have no aspirations about careers on Wall Street, the students cultivate new capacities and begin to operate from a deeper entrepreneurial impulse. Empathy immersion also helps people identify their true missions in life, rather than again downloading old models and operating on the basis of dusty frameworks.

Scharmer believes profound change and true leadership can evolve by moving through the deepening process he calls the *Theory U* which happens on three levels:

1. The level of the mind, which involves suspending old habits of judgment
2. Opening the heart and beginning to see problems through the eyes of other stakeholders, walking in others' shoes
3. Gaining the capacity to let go and let come

In the business realm, Scharmer explained that the latter is a key element. "The issue here is fear and holding on: fear of losing staff, of not making it, of failure, of being excluded from the community if you're not successful." He has never seen this kind of fear in any start-up innovator "because as an innovator you challenge the assumptions of your professional community."

Scharmer explained that the English root for the word *leadership* means "to go forth, to cross the threshold." But he also traced the word through its Indo-European roots in a different translation and found it literally also means "to die." Essentially leadership is the ultimate process of letting go and letting come. "It's letting go of one world that we know very well and stepping into the territory of the unknown. This is the quality that experienced entrepreneurial leaders have, and it's the collective first-person experience we have as a global community today vis-à-vis challenges in climate change.... That is the capacity to deal with issues around which there is fear."

The three-part process of Theory U can broaden and deepen our view of a situation. Next, we should seek to connect all that we observe and experience together with deep reflection, contemplative practices that move people into intentional stillness. "Basically you give everyone, as an individual and as a community, quality time to focus on what matters most...what is it that, for me, and my own journey is most essential? Basically it is letting go of all the noise that is nothing."

Scharmer believes the environmental movement has missed out on this deeper awareness dimension and advises creating "high-quality reflection spaces for groups and individuals, with different stakeholders going on that journey together, where there really is a possibility for the system to see itself." Scharner's definition of dialogue is not two or three people talking to each other. It is the capacity of people to reflect on and to see themselves as part of a larger ecosystem, to recognize how their own behaviors and assumptions shape what's going on. "It's like switching on an awareness outside of myself."

Scharmer told me that moving through the Theory U process can lead to elegant results. A system that was previously bogged down by people working from ego, seeking to optimize their own careers or blindly following institutional interests or agendas, can begin to change. Individuals can start the process of co-creation as they move from ego-system awareness to ecosystem awareness.

How exactly does this wisdom help us deal with the change resistance problems we face in the world today?

When people connect intensely with others who are different from them, they begin to operate from a more profound entrepreneurial impulse. "You begin to experience yourself in a deeper way, to sense a possibility in yourself that you weren't aware of before. That deeper level of awareness is already there. We just need to remove the rubble, all the noise that keeps us from attending to that." He said that the process builds confidence and greater creativity, better problem solving ideas.

How do we open our minds and hearts so we can connect on deeper levels?

"It's an improvisation," Scharmer responded, but on a practical level, it starts with genuine conversation and relationship building. Fifty percent of his classwork is about listening, helping people move from judgmental listening, where you just pay attention to what you already know, to factual listening, which is when you begin to see something new. This leads to empathetic listening where people begin to see a situation in the eyes of another, and finally to what he calls generative listening. This is listening in a way that allows something new to happen, something that hasn't quite manifested yet. The process requires people to open their minds and suspend rigid and narrow former habits; open their hearts and begin to see through the lens of other stakeholders, to walk in other's shoes, particularly those of the most marginalized; and thirdly, to "open the will" to let go and let come.

Listening becomes "effective" and is actually a kind of birthing process because it leads to something that did not exist before, Scharmer explained. In this sense, it is co-creative. Generative listening can give voice to what is about to happen, what is about to emerge. It is a kind of event in the making.

Scharmer believes listening is foundational, not only for leadership but for mastery in any kind of profession. In all creative projects and applications, it is the most important and relevant of skills. You will know you have achieved something if you leave a conversation with far more energy than you entered it. After truly generative interaction with another person, you are no longer the same. You're closer to who you really are. "There is a subtle letting go of the 'old me' and a keener connection to Self (with a capital 'S') which is my highest future possibility." When we lose track of who we are, we become exhausted, burned out, depressed. Reconnection to the authentic self switches on high energy. "So you practice, practice, practice. It may sound a bit abstract, and it's not something you can perfect in ten minutes," he warned, but mastering generative dialogue is as satisfying as learning to play a musical instrument.

Scharmer said this kind of listening skill is important whenever there is a culture clash or divide where social or economic systems are breaking down. He emphasized that generative listening is definitely not focused on fixing anything or problem solving: "That's the big inhibitor of change, and another big myth." He called the urge to fix "the problem of problem solving." Empathetic listening does not mean offering palliative statements such as "Hey, I know exactly what you're talking about and here's what you need to do." Instead, Scharmer suggested that the goal is to mobilize energy around creating something successful, perhaps in a community context or as a collective function. "It's a more subtle dimension of leadership, and one which has been largely ignored in the past."

Listening in such dialogue would be useful in the environmental movement where much of the talk in past years has centered on sustainability, doing things less badly. A more inspiring and successful viewpoint would be to envision a future that is worth committing to, that features a series of reframed economic activities around what matters in life, such as happiness and well-being. Such a focus would encourage the dimension of mindfulness in a very natural way, Scharmer said.

He advised the environmental movement should not be about forcing something down the throat of anyone, which leads invariably to resistance and people getting stuck in their own positions. It should focus instead on people who are ready to participate, willing to take action. "Go where the change is already taking place," he said, echoing the words of Peter Senge.

Scharmer's goal is to help people find and identify conditions that allow small, incremental changes. Institutions need to look for the cracks too, gateways or openings that are made critical and timely because old behaviors and routines no longer create results. Institutions can become willing to put their attention here, and commit resources to trying out new ways of operating and collaborating.

The way to leverage change is to shift the inner place from which we operate. When we deepen our own listening, we engage in a conversation that affects people differently. We shift the quality of awareness and attention away from resistance interaction and resistance intervention. This new field is where the greatest potential impact for change lies, and where we need to place our attention. It's the blind spot in all leadership. "This is where—

through small experiments—we have found a whole bunch of very usable methods and tools that we can make accessible to people."

In a paper prepared for the 2010 World Economic Forum, Scharmer talked about this blind spot in institutional leadership.[4] He said today's leaders and change makers are caught between two worlds: They are confronting unprecedented 21st-century challenges, with inadequate 20th-century management tools. They are struggling to bridge the gap, but he said the biggest problem is a lack of collective leadership "to draw together all key stakeholders and involve them in a process that begins with uncovering common intention and ends with collectively creating profound innovation."

Scharmer called this missing capacity the scarcest resource in society today. It is a quality that is not being nurtured, and little focus is given to its development anywhere in our system of higher education. Business schools focus on leadership, public policy and the social sector, but nowhere do all these intersect. We need all three if we are to address and solve the pressing challenges of our time, and without them we will continue to produce results that nobody wants: poverty, pollution and institutional paralysis.

The Mighty Tool of Public Narrative

What Are They Thinking?

with Anthony Leiserowitz *and* Ed Maibach

We now have great data to support the formula
that simple, clear messages, repeated often by trusted sources
are effective.... The big lie has been incredibly effective,
and scientists need to take the science, simplify it
and then just keep saying it over and over and over again.

Ed Maibach

SEVERAL YEARS AGO, I received an email from Kate Moran, an American oceanographer, who was seconded to the White House as assistant director in the Office of Science and Technology Policy, where she focused on the response to British Petroleum's Deepwater Horizon oil spill. Having read *Climate Cover-Up* and given it to her boss, who circulated it around her office, she wrote to ask if I would meet with them to talk about climate change communications next time I was in Washington. At the bottom of her email, I noticed it said the Office of Science and Technology Policy of the President. I thought this can't mean *the* President, but sure enough it did, so I put together a small group of experts and we made a presentation to about fifteen White House scientists and communications people in the Obama administration. The renowned Moran later became a professor at the University of Victoria, where she was director of the NEPTUNE Project and president and CEO of Ocean Networks Canada.

Being both honored and cautious about American public opinion, I decided to invite Anthony Leiserowitz and Ed Maibach to
help with the presentation, as they are two of the most knowledge-
able people in the US on this subject.

That White House meeting, and our strategic recommendations, became part of the then president Obama's behind-the-
scenes work on public education about climate change in the US,
and it also gave me the chance to learn more about the work of
Leiserowitz and Maibach. These two social scientists are principal investigators with the Climate Change in the American Mind
survey, experts in the field of American public opinion on climate
change.[1] In this continuing study of global warming beliefs, they
analyze what people are thinking and why they think that way,
so I decided to speak with both of them again when writing
this book.[2]

Leiserowitz is director of the Yale Project on Climate Change
Communication and a prominent scientist at that university's
School of Forestry and Environmental Studies. He is widely respected for his research into the psychological, cultural, political
and geographic factors that motivate public environmental perceptions. He was the first to undertake an empirical assessment of
worldwide public values, attitudes and behaviors regarding global
sustainability, environmental protection and economic growth.
Maibach, who is with George Mason University Center for
Climate Change Communication, is an authority in the uses of
strategic communications and social marketing to address climate
change and related public health challenges.

The survey questionnaire looks at measures of the public's
climate change beliefs, attitudes, risk perceptions, motivations,
values, policy preferences, behaviors and underlying barriers to
action. When the study began in 2008, the team identified six distinct groups, Global Warming's Six Americas, which each respond
to the issues in a distinct way. Since then researchers have tracked
the evolution of these six unique audiences—the Alarmed, Con-

cerned, Cautious, Disengaged, Doubtful and Dismissive groups—and while they saw a sharp decline in public engagement between late 2008 and early 2010, a gradual rebound has happened since.

The Yale Project's March 2018 report showed a rising trend in American adults' concern about global warming and a growing certainty that global warming not only is happening but also is harming people. It found 7 out of 10 Americans think global warming is occurring, a number that has remained steady since March 2016. Fewer than 1 in 10 believe it is not happening. More than half of those surveyed think global warming is primarily due to human activities, especially the burning of fossil fuels, and only 3 in 10 say it is mostly due to natural changes in the environment—the lowest level since the surveys began.

A follow up poll conducted just a few months later, in November and December of 2018, found surprisingly higher numbers. Leiserowitz said he had never seen such jumps in key indicators. That told him a wide majority of Americans no longer see climate change as hypothetical. That survey found 69 percent of Americans were "worried" about warming, an eight-point increase since March, and 28 percent see it is harming people, which is an increase of nine percentage points.

"People are beginning to understand that climate change is here in the United States, here in my state, in my community, affecting the people and places I care about, and now," Leiserowitz said. "This isn't happening in 50 years, 100 years from now."

But it is troubling to learn that only 1 in 7 knows that nearly all climate scientists (more than 97 percent) have concluded that global warming is happening. Even Americans who are highly concerned about climate change drastically underestimate the scientific consensus.

Leiserowitz's work with the Yale study has made it clear there is no single public. There are multiple publics, all with different levels of knowledge, gaps in their knowledge, fundamental misunderstandings and different values which predispose them to interpret information in very different ways. They have different politics. They trust different messengers and don't trust certain messengers. They get their news and information from different sources.

This is why any message using a one-size-fits-all approach will fail. He stresses these six different audiences mean we have to be more sophisticated in recognizing the need for different engagement strategies.

Leiserowitz used the example of himself, a disciplined researcher who trained as a scientist and responds to empirical data, analysis and results: "If you want to convince me, you need to show me the data. That's my culture, my worldview." And that's why when someone disagrees with him his first reaction is to say, give me your evidence, show me a scientific report. A conspiracy theorist on the other hand has a very different thought process: "For them the bigger the evidence you show them, the bigger they believe the conspiracy is, so our default approach (of showing the data) isn't an effective way to engage with people who don't trust us in the first place."

Much of this comes down to who we trust as an information source, and Leiserowitz believes this highlights the damage done by two well-publicized mistakes in the 2010 report by the UN's Intergovernmental Panel on Climate Change (IPCC). Those who are predisposed to skepticism become even more dubious and less trusting of the scientific community after these events. And once trust is lost, it's very hard to regain. You have to earn it in person, through hard work and trust building. You can't just say, "Oh, look, I've got another set of papers that show I was right," because now people won't even engage with the data.

He said climate change deniers have taken advantage of the economy and people's fears about potential impacts on jobs, as well as scandals around Climategate—a 2009 controversy over emails that falsely claimed global warming was a scientific conspiracy and that scientists manipulated data—and IPCC mistakes.

Climategate was later utterly rejected as untrue, but following the story, about 12 percent of those surveyed said they had less belief in climate change and more importantly were less trustful of scientists in general. That's a significant proportion, and the greatest impact was concentrated among those ideologically predisposed to being most skeptical in the first place. "So that's really where the denial movement has had its greatest success, in increasing the number of Dismissives," said the researcher. Denial organizers used these episodes to solidify their base and intensify hostility.

Leiserowitz suggests it is time for new frames. Scientists and environmentalists, who have been the primary messengers on this issue until now, have been incredibly successful in that everyone has heard of the issues and the question of global warming has risen to the highest levels of geopolitical decision-making. These early advocates deserve credit for this but should no longer lead the charge. The challenge now is to come up with version 2.0—which requires broader involvement, greater engagement and a bipartisan approach across non-environmentalist sectors.

He explains why in a vivid example drawn from his Six Americas research. The environmentally alarmed individual cares deeply about polar bears and other species, and is willing to get active, but this message backlashed among other groups whose members responded by saying they don't care about polar bears, they care about people. "If I saw a polar bear, he would try to eat me," is their comment. So this approach is no longer effective. It resonated with the right people and did its work, but it's time to break out of that frame and move on to another.

For example, his data shows virtually nobody understands the human health consequences of climate change, because people in the States don't connect the dots. This is a potentially important new issue to frame. When asked about the likelihood of having to abandon major cities on the Atlantic coast because of rising sea levels, everyone has an opinion, but ask them if there will be serious human health implications and half the population has no opinion at all and won't even hazard a guess. The other half will estimate by an order of magnitude: "Oh, by 2050, a few thousand people will be harmed, not millions." When given information about health implications, they become more interested and suddenly see that one of their core values is at stake.

Leiserowitz stressed the new frames should target issues we all have a stake in rather than narrower messages about polar bears on ice floes thousands of miles away, or specific groups who live in threatened areas. Those previous frames kept climate change at a distance for many: "It's happening, but not in my state, or my city, or to people I love." It's time to bring the message home and key into the faith dimension, national security issues and business sector, by outlining both risks and opportunities.

He applauds the hundreds of eco-conscious organizations and thousands of individuals who have been working to raise the profile and motivate action on global warming, but adds they have been disorganized. By contrast, a small set of climate deniers has been super organized: "This is not an accidental metaphor, but it's like the difference between an incandescent light bulb and a laser: same amount of energy, completely different result. And we're the dim bulbs. People are working at cross purposes, contradicting one another and not building in synergies and so on."

He said all aspects of global warming have been trapped for the past 20 years in one of three frames: In the climate science frame, we hear endless debate about whether it's human caused or not. We will never reach consensus on this, and that's backed up by his Six Americas research that shows how we are divided into different groups. Second, the message has been trapped in the environment box where it's about polar bears not people. It will impact other species, not us. And third is the political frame: If you're left wing, a good Democrat, you believe in global warming, and if you're on the right, you don't. "From a climate scientist perspective, this stuff makes us tear our hair out because the climate system doesn't care whether you're a Democrat or a Republican," said Leiserowitz, who has served as a consultant to the John F. Kennedy School of Government at Harvard, the UN Development Program, Gallup World Poll, the Global Roundtable on Climate Change and the World Economic Forum.

Climate change is far too big to be solved by a group of lawyers and environmental lobbyists in Washington, which has been the dominant strategy so far. Why? Because this fight affects us all and because the primary cause of our problem is also the lifeblood of our civilization—fossil fuels. It's in our clothes, our food, in the way we get around. It's embedded in everything we do. "So we have a problem of unprecedented scope that will require changes that affect everyone in a fundamental way. It cannot be dealt with through a bunch of expert policy tweaks in Washington. These are issues that have to be rooted in democracy."

So why are we stalling, I asked, and how do we get moving?

Leiserowitz believes people need to recognize their personal stake in all of this. Water resource managers should realize it's their issue. Public health officials and communities should know this would have dramatic implications for local, state and national health. The military already sees it as an important national security threat; businesses are viewing it as a liability, a potential legal risk, even a reputational risk. Faith communities can be more involved, when people see how it touches their core values.

Another crucial strategy is to involve the silent majority. Seventy-five percent of the public may not have been out marching in the streets during the tumultuous civil rights times, but the issue was out in the streets and that shifted the views of the silent majority. So these are the two vital elements: an issue that is demanding change and the silent majority "giving permission."

Leiserowitz said an adequate response to both the mitigation side and the protection side will require decisions at every level of society including cities, states and countries. He warned the number of decisions is almost incalculable because climate change is an incredibly decentralized decision-making problem. The fact that city governments and municipalities seem to be more progressive than upper levels of government ties in with his research on the Six Americas which shows some populations are more disposed to believe in climate change, for instance, those who live closest to where there may be rising sea levels or rising temperatures.

Increasingly severe weather incidents have put climate change back in the spotlight, but this doesn't affect the Alarmed segment, which is already firmly convinced it's happening. Nor does it affect Dismissives, whose members are convinced it's not happening. It's the people in the middle who are the most likely to be swayed.

The researcher said many forces are converging now, and they will fundamentally change our worldview. Power is being diffused and decentralized throughout the globe. Evolutions in economics, science, politics, communications and values are accelerating and creating both anxieties and excitement. "So buckle up and get ready for the grand roller-coaster ride" because we are entering turbulent times. Leiserowitz sees much to be hopeful about and cited the Earth Charter as a wonderful example of a conscious effort to establish and articulate our core values, the United Nations' Millennium Development Goals for taking concrete steps toward progress in line with our essential beliefs, and the National Academy of Science for funding a project that has led to the Great Transition Initiative.

Now more than ever, it is important not to let anger cloud our effectiveness. While anger is an incredibly powerful, motivating force when channeled appropriately, it has a dark side that can spin out of control, be manipulated and exploited to accomplish others' political goals. Leiserowitz added when trying to reach out to concerned groups it doesn't help if we come across as outraged or we seek to make others feel guilty. Today's effective spokespeople are "happy warriors" willing to engage in a fight, but with a smile, so their message doesn't turn into a moral crusade where people point fingers or condemn each other. Think of the stance of a great competitor, he said, a sportsman who appreciates and even celebrates his opponents while trying to beat them. A dour, moralizing, overly serious activist is always a turnoff and fundamentally ineffective.

"Yes, we have serious problems, but we can solve them if we get people of different backgrounds, values and perspectives to come together. Right now, our consciousness is typically formed by a cookie-cutter, nation states identity—'I'm American, I'm Canadian, I'm Japanese'—and we have to realize we are citizens of Earth and our destiny is inextricably bound up with everyone on the planet. More than 80 percent of us have cellphones, and through the Internet we are connected in ways that can bring about greater global consciousness."

The American government is a prime example of people not coming together, of polarization and gridlock, Leiserowitz said. The country's internal divide is so serious in terms of power that it doesn't matter whether Republicans propose something or Democrats do. No one will agree. "We've been talking for decades about long-term collective problems such as the climate, environment, debt, social security, health care," and both sides are dug in. "They believe anything they give up will be seen as a win by the other side."

In the US today, an incredibly tense and polarized environment has been created by hyper-partisan elected representatives, said Ed Maibach, Leiserowitz's colleague in the Global Warming's Six Americas study. "They can't even genuinely have a conversation about the nature of the problem because they have such diametrically opposed definitions of what the problem is, and understanding of what is driving those problems."

Maibach also believes most members of the public are more interested in being nostalgic about yesteryear than they are in being cognizant of what tomorrow will look like. "Most people don't really want the truth. They simply want things to continue being okay." Finding out why is one of the questions that drives these two communications experts.

Over the last two decades, much has been learned about the state of the world's oceans, species destruction, desertification, melting ice caps and rising sea levels. But only recently have researchers like Leiserowitz and Maibach started to collect the critical collateral data that tells us what human beings think about it. We all have different belief systems, concerns and psychological characteristics that affect how we absorb information or make judgments, said Maibach. Understanding these differences is vital if we want to connect with people and encourage positive steps toward saving not only energy but also our planet and ourselves.

Maibach, who has a doctorate in communication research from Stanford and a master's in health promotion from San Diego State University, explained his research focuses on how to expand and enhance public engagement in climate change. He has received grants from the National Science Foundation, NASA and more, while also publishing more than 100 peer-reviewed journal articles.

His own interest in the field was ignited when he started investigating public understanding of these climate issues and was looking around for opinion polls. "I discovered there weren't a lot, which is really surprising" especially when compared with the mountains of information on climate change itself, said the scientist who joined George Mason University faculty in 2007 to create the Centre for Climate Change Communication, and in 2010 was given that institution's highest honor. He was named Distinguished University Professor.

So Maibach and Leiserowitz began digging. Their research shows the Alarmed group of Americans, about 21 percent, is "apoplectically concerned" about what tomorrow will bring as a result of climate change. They are developing a state of helplessness because they look at the very people who should be making better decisions and see they're not even having the conversation about options. We've got this one-issue public that cares deeply but is becoming helpless, and losing their sense of agency and collective efficacy, said Maibach.

However, the Six Americas research also looked at perceptions of extreme weather and found the public is beginning to connect the dots when it comes to worsening weather systems. He believes fluctuations in public opinion are lessening as we all start to grasp the local ramifications of climate change as opposed to some sort of global apocalyptic vision: "These changes we're seeing in perceptions of extreme weather are an exciting lead indicator of enhanced public understanding." The public is now seeing the issue personally, through the lens of extreme weather, and this will likely lead to a more stable understanding as well as a deeper state of engagement.

Maibach said a majority of the two largest segments of Americans—the Cautious and the Concerned—mistakenly believe there is still a lot of disagreement among climate change scientists, and he credited my book *Climate Cover-Up* for exposing this fiction. He calls this misconception "the perfect killer app" because it was designed to kill our curiosity about whether or not climate change is even real: "If I believe the experts are still debating whether or not it's real, what possible motivation do I have as a layman to try to understand the issue? It's a perfect excuse for me to watch *American Idol.*"

His research shows that the manufactured belief about disagreement is a "gateway belief," in other words, it is an underpinning of concern about the threat of climate change that leads to the conviction about whether or not society ought to respond to it. He said the issue involves four key beliefs: that climate change is real, human caused, bad for people and solvable. Those who believe there is disagreement among the experts are less likely to believe in any of the other four. And so the essential job is to find a way to debunk that manufactured myth.

"It is the single most pressing climate communication challenge we face"—and it became the inspiration for six different experiments that Leiserowitz and Maibach conducted in late 2013. Each one sought to answer the question: How can we explode this "gateway belief" and realign people's thinking so they understand there is actually a state of scientific consensus among more than

97 percent of climate experts, that human-caused climate change is happening? In fact, Maibach said reviews of the literature, published in the fall of 2012, showed the consensus is closer to 99.9 percent. Tens of thousands of papers support human-caused climate change, and only a handful disagree.

The experiments showed several simple ways to debunk the myth. First, it's important to make a quantified, not a qualified, statement about the consensus. They were shocked to find a qualitative statement like "an overwhelming majority of the experts agree" doesn't change public understanding. But a quantified statement, "97 percent of climate scientists are now convinced that human-caused climate change is happening," moved public understanding upward by about 15 percentage points. "That's a whopping difference from a single exposure to a message." When the statement was modified slightly and "primed for scientific reasoning" by adding four words at the beginning, "based on the evidence," researchers saw an additional bump of 2 to 3 percent.

This was consistent across the whole series of different studies, so it is considered a robust finding. They then tested whether or not they could get an additional incremental bump by introducing an appropriate metaphor, so they asked: If 97 percent of the doctors in your community told you your child was sick, what would you think or do? Curiously, this diminished the effectiveness of the basic statement by 2 or 3 percentage points, perhaps because people understood already and didn't need or want any elaboration.

Pie charts were also tested as graphic representations. They showed a tiny slice of dissenters and a large piece representing convinced experts. That didn't harm the effectiveness of the basic message, but it didn't help either. It was irrelevant. What did help was another strategic move. Before people were shown anything, the researchers asked test subjects to estimate the percentage of climate experts who are convinced that human-caused climate change is occurring. This led to an additional bump of about

3 or 4 percent and showed that "when you get people to go on record with their belief, then give them surprising information that conflicts with that, it forces them to come to terms with the discrepancy."

This took people's understanding up a total of about 20 percent. So on average, they were moving it from 60 to 62 percent up to 80, 82 and 85 percent. This significant result got the communications experts excited about tactical implications. Namely, if you want to communicate the consensus, work hard to make people write on paper, or say out loud in front of others, what they believe the current state of consensus is—before shattering the myth. Forcing them to face the reality that they totally misunderstood this important piece of information helped solidify their new opinion.

In another experiment, the study presented de-biasing statements along with photos of prominent climate scientists, using taglines such as: "To learn more about what he's learning about climate change in the Chesapeake Bay region, click here." Researchers theorized that, by linking a statement with a local expert everyone knows and reveres, they could personalize an abstract statement. And they did. Subjects were de-biased by another couple of percentage points.

"We now have great data to support the formula that simple, clear messages, repeated often by trusted sources are effective," said Maibach. He also believes, since these trusted sources in the climate science community are the ones who've been maligned, they are the ones who should explode the myth: "The big lie has been incredibly effective, and scientists need to take the science, simplify it and then just keep saying it over and over and over again." (This is the same advice I heard from the Dalai Lama who said the messages from scientists should be clear, concise and expressed again and again. Like the Tibetan saying encourages: "Nine times failure, and then nine times effort.")

Maibach pointed out the head of communications and marketing for every fossil fuel company on the planet already understands

this very well, which is why we constantly see greenwashing campaigns and full-page ads in every major newspaper in the world,
"explaining they are good corporate citizens, they care about the
environment and don't worry you can sleep well tonight because
we are on the job." They understand the power of repetition.

I asked if the medical metaphor failed because it was oversell-
ing. Maibach said he is currently looking at why some analogies
and metaphors work to make information more accessible and
some don't. He has found that metaphors are primarily of value
when the information being explained is very dense and convo-
luted. The more complicated the information, the more potential
value a simplifying metaphor has. In the case of this study, the
consensus message was not complicated, "So it's like, Okay. We all
understand what 97 percent means."

Note: Although this Six Americas research is about climate change, it
is an excellent example of what I see as best practices in public communication strategy. What Leiserowitz and Maibach are doing is the
epitome of the best: excellent research, evaluation and analysis of communication challenges, which then leads to the development of effective
strategies, messages and narratives for a public education campaign. It
is professional in every sense of the word.

The Myth of Apathy

with Renee Lertzman

What if we presume that people do care,

very deeply, and about many of the

same things we care about?

Renee Lertzman

B EING GREEN is attractive, desirable and profitable, said environmental communications specialist Renee Lertzman. But
it is also potentially frightening because it threatens what many
of us hold dear, what is central to how we construct meaning in
our lives. So being green creates anxiety. Lertzman has studied the
deep, psychological dimensions of sustainability, and we discussed
why people fail to take action on severe environmental threats,
why no nation has managed to adequately reduce carbon emissions and why instead we see international and national indifference and lack of knowledge.

Change resistance is complicated, explained Lertzman, who
has a master's in communication studies from the University of
North Carolina and a doctorate in social sciences from Cardiff
University in Wales. She said the current shortage of engagement,
activation or inspiration is typically framed in terms that reflect a
lack of something, the idea that people don't care enough about
what's happening. She disagrees with this diagnosis, and has
blamed the situation on what she calls the *Myth of Apathy*. It's a

concept that arose during her doctoral research, which took her to a "very degraded" and industrial part of Wisconsin. Her study was conducted in the Great Lakes region where she recorded a high level of frustration among activists who felt people were not sufficiently mobilized or engaged when addressing serious threats to the lakes. She surveyed thousands of people in Green Bay and followed up with in-depth interviews with those who knew something about what was going on, but were not particularly engaged. Her work has been featured in the *New York Times*, Dot Earth, KBOO Radio and *The Ecologist*, and she has been a visiting fellow at the Portland Center for Public Humanities. Lertzman also serves on the editorial board of *Ecopsychology*.[1]

Renee Lertzman did not set out to explore the values, belief systems or opinions of Wisconsin residents but rather their actual experience about where they lived, their water, their air quality. Her study, however, led to revelations about all kinds of "complex, contradictory, messy experiences, feelings and perceptions" that suddenly made it obvious there was no clear apathy. What she discovered instead was a huge amount of concern about what was going on with the Great Lakes, with the water, with the environment, and a perplexing mood of loss—a sense of mourning, melancholy and nostalgia. Lertzman found a lot of tension too. People loved the lakes, wanted to fish there and wanted them to be clean, but were caught in a dilemma because many a family member worked in the paper mill that was destroying the water quality. The mill gave them their livelihood.

And so a premise about the Myth of Apathy began to take shape. Lertzman has come to believe that apathy is constructed and perceived as an "enemy" or dragon that must be slain. "It's like we have to fight our way through this pervasive apathy in order to get people to care," and yet her research found the opposite. She now poses the question: "What if we presume that people do care, very deeply, and about many of the same things we care about?"[2] This new train of thought explains why current narratives fail:

They are based on a misguided perception that apathy is a serious hurdle.

Lertzman urged us all to ask, What if the lack of involvement in climate change has come about because this care and concern is not expressed or acknowledged? If we presume there is a surplus of care and concern and a desire to make things right, how does that change the way environmental advocates conduct our communication strategy? "It becomes more about how can we support, invite, cultivate and channel rather than this impossible task of getting people to care."

Lertzman suggested that branding people as apathetic is not only erroneous but also disrespectful and patronizing. It's a lazy approach because such an assessment is rooted in our tendency to make snap judgments; it also assumes that people do and say what they actually want. "I know this might sound strange, but that's just not the case." Why we do what we do is complicated, so really, the Myth of Apathy is about reframing the question of care. What would happen if we started to act on the assumption that there is a surplus of concern, an overabundance of energy to be tapped into and an earnest desire to make things right—not a lack? Lertzman believes this different point of view could create a tectonic shift in our communications strategy.

Of course, there is such a thing as apathy, and Lertzman mentioned the work of American psychiatrist Harold Searles, one of the first clinicians to talk about how the ecological crisis deeply affects people. Influential papers that he wrote in 1972 described how some humans are hampered by a sense of apathy, but Searles saw that as a symptom, a defense mechanism just like projection. "If we recognize apathy as a symptom, this is another piece of the picture," said Lertzman, who added there is much to learn about people's conflicts and tensions.[3] "It is easy to blame others and say something is all their fault," but in the case of climate denial, she said, there is real hatred circulating and being projected onto others, and this can lead to apathy in some people.

Lertzman suggested that these insights help expand our thinking and spirit of enquiry. What would our world look like if we were curious about what people actually deeply feel? Most of us don't even know what's going on in our own minds, let alone others' minds, and are completely unaware of our unconscious wellsprings of inner conflicts and tensions. Are people feeling sad, or anxious, or angry—and how do we determine that?

We can begin by drawing out people's stories and narratives, Lertzman said, using this new understanding to change the tone and language of our approach. We can do this on a societal level, too, by translating our tone into something more invitational, truth-eliciting and acknowledging. Lertzman is not opposed to incentives like taxes and other external prods, but she believes they are superficial compared to this kind of deeper work. "I'm talking about going to a more fundamental level of what constitutes be-havior in the first place, which is how we construct and produce meaning in our lives."

For instance, how do we encourage people in a building to use less electricity, less water and recycle more? Of course we can try to tweak behavior through external stimuli or prods, but we are more effective when we bring deep meaning into the process. This approach would look at the narrative of a building, its story and history, what it feels like to live there and be part of that commu-nity. "This is tapping into meaning, and it can become something that really makes sense because I am part of the building. I am wearing this relationship."

Real and lasting change is not imposed. It emerges, said Renee Lertzman. "And it's not about lack, it's about what we create. It's a very positive, generative narrative that taps into our innate de-sire to be part of something bigger than us." We don't generate meaning on our own, or in a vacuum. We create it together, in relationships, in interactions. Meaning is co-constructed and pro-duces a sense of connection, cohesion and validation because we feel part of something larger. We connect with people better when we communicate at a deeper level, when we are meaning centered.

I asked Renee Lertzman if outing climate change deniers is a good tactic, and she advised it has its place, when done with compassion. "Compassion is the only way to adequately and effectively engage with ignorance—because that's what we're talking about here, in a spiritual sense, not a literal one. This is ignorance of who we are and the reality of our connection to everything." That kind of ignorance can lead to tremendous destruction. There's something very violent about climate denial, and it almost certainly arises from fear and anxiety, Lertzman suggested. As Bryant Welch noted in his book, *State of Confusion*, hatred can be a defense against feeling confused.

This is very sensitive territory, Lertzman warned. If you push on a defense such as this, it will push back. We always resist change, even positive change that brings growth and development, because we try to valiantly protect what we think needs protecting or we feel is at stake. Yet criticizing climate change deniers is a crucial function, just as it was when people spoke the truth about the Holocaust. Lertzman referred to eminent British psychoanalyst Hanna Segal who said silence is the real crime.[4] But Lertzman suggested that we should speak in a way that is compassionate, while not letting people off the hook. As the Dalai Lama says, "compassion can be very fierce." We need to practice compassion for ourselves too, and be concerned about our own anger or impatience, she said.

Compassion helps us understand what's really causing the inaction—the fact that we're caught up in a series of complicated dilemmas and tensions, contradictory drives and anxieties that we are unable to sort out or negotiate. "We need to begin to recognize what's being asked of us in terms of how we manage and negotiate these tensions, which are very deep in our identity and part of who we are as human beings."

Such inner drives are not rational, and they go far beyond surface emotions, to a less conscious level. "We are dealing with any
number of ecological threats that are deeply anxiety producing.
It seems totally obvious to say that, but it's as if this piece has
been completely overlooked." We consistently focus on tuning into
people's rationality or their knowledge, or we try and appeal to
their self-interest, to basically manipulate and engage behavior.
We're not actually appreciating with compassion what we're really
talking about. "We're skipping over that experience of fear."

Lertzman explained that psychoanalysis's concept of *splitting*
is useful when thinking about sustainability. Splitting describes
how we tend to split off anxiety, emotional loss, feelings that are
scary. For example, environmentalists tend to see things in terms
of black and white, good versus evil, "so they can sidestep dealing
with the really messy reality of sorting through difficult change."

Lertzman reiterated all change can provoke anxiety, even if it's
positive or productive, like moving into a nicer house or taking a
better job. All change involves anxiety and loss, as well as gains in
opportunity or growth. And the shifts involving climate change
are ultimately much more worrying because they require some
recognition that humanity has done wrong. For some, there could
be an intolerable sense of guilt, "the fact we've really effed up."

And so Lertzman suggested that the issue of climate change is
both psychological and social. This change is immensely anxiety
producing—"It is almost in a class of its own" because we're talking
about change in response to human-generated circumstances that
we know are life-destroying. Asking people to confront that and
deal with it is asking them to take some responsibility for what's
happened. "I don't think we see much capacity for that socially,
culturally, individually" because people find it too overwhelming.
So, there is guilt and impotence, combined with a lack of political
will and inaction among government and business leaders. "It's a
protective strategy to distance oneself from that which causes this
sense of powerlessness."

Self-protection can manifest in denial, projection and splitting, Lertzman said, which are all defensive mechanisms and strategies. Sociologist Kari Norgaard described these strategies as not being just our own individual psychology, but aspects that are performed socially, organizationally and politically. In other words, we need each other to collude in our denial, to help manage our anxiety, said Lertzman. Norgaard also said silence on the subject of climate change should not be interpreted as disinterest, but rather as something people find too painful to acknowledge because of their role in causing it.[5]

I asked what happens if people can't avoid these feelings? How can people, groups and organizations feel safe enough to tolerate and face up to tough environmental issues? She said this is where clinical psychology and new clinically inspired research offers insights and "potent tenets," many of which she has written about in *The Ecologist*.[6]

What does a therapist do when working one-on-one with a client who brings harmful, self-protective attitudes into a session? They do three things, Lertzman explained:

1. acknowledge
2. encourage the truth
3. support and mobilize

Acknowledgment involves saying, "I hear you, I see you, and I reflect back to you what I think you're feeling." That simple act is powerful in helping disarm defense mechanisms. When we feel heard and supported, we soften a bit, we become a little more receptive, have a little more access to what our own experience is, rather than feeling we have to defend. Related to acknowledgment is the second tenet, which is the need to uncover the truth. The therapist supports a person as they speak the truth, and provides a sense of "working through this together." And finally, a therapist demonstrates leadership and strength, and as an example, Lertzman recalled Winston Churchill's famous "We shall fight on the beaches" speech. Here Churchill talked about a military disaster and warned of possible invasion by the Germans, yet spoke magnificently about defending "our island home and riding out the storm of war." Lertzman said the statesman did not cover up recent losses and defeats or deny the reality of the situation, but painted a picture of heroism and strength in moving forward.

So this technique involves revealing the truth, no matter how dire, acknowledging it and tapping into proactive solutions. She said it's important to focus on possibilities, on what can be done. "It's like being the rah-rah cheerleader. There has to be some element of truth telling, an acknowledgment of the reality of the situation and that other piece of moving forward. One without the other is incomplete and limited. We point out innovations, possibilities, potentials and say: Let's move forward. Let's be champions."

Psychic Numbing

with Paul Slovic

There is the drop-in-the-bucket effect:

The problem is so big, and I'm so small.

It won't make much difference, no matter what I do.

So, why don't I just do whatever is comfortable.

Paul Slovic

PAUL SLOVIC is an expert in human judgment and decision-making. He is president of Decision Research, has been president of the Society for Risk Analysis and is a professor of psychology at University of Oregon.[1] Slovic's research looks at how the general public and experts perceive perils and threats very differently, and offers critical lessons for those involved in risk perception and communication, including insights into why we fail to respond to large-scale international tragedies. His most recent work looks at what he calls *psychic numbing*; according to Slovic, psychic numbing helps explain why we fail to respond to mass atrocities and crises like climate change.

I asked Slovic why are we glued to our television sets, cells and tablets when a small child is trapped in a well for 58 hours, yet yawn and switch channels when more than 500,000 are slaughtered in Rwanda over the course of 100 days? What is the role of emotions and cognition when it comes to our conceptions of danger and problems that are enormous in scope, and how has his work concerning biotechnology, prescription drugs, terrorism, nanotechnology and more guided his own thinking?

Slovic said there are many large-scale, worldwide problems that affect us both close to home and abroad, and that we tune out. There is no single reason why. "We're talking about an under-reaction to problems that are large in scope,"[2] and this is starkly different from what happens at a community level where we typically have a strong and immediate reaction to violence, after a murder for instance. "We've got a system of law enforcement that tracks down perpetrators and brings them to justice. We've got laws and institutions that are very strong and aggressive at the local level. But we have little or nothing like that at the international level." Slovic believes this has contributed to a string of genocides dating back to 1915.

Slovic argues the "psychic numbing" phenomenon, the difficulty we have with emotionally connecting to problems that are large in scale, is highly relevant to species extinction too. Do we really have to wait until we are looking at the world's last polar bear standing on a small piece of ice, before we'll take seriously the extinction possibility for these animals? Why don't we act when the problem is still in the thousands? Again, it relates to his premise that we react strongly to individuals in distress, but don't take action when problems exist for thousands.

There is no simple reason for this indifference, although Slovic believes that numbers alone, "dry statistics," do little to communicate the true meaning of atrocities. They don't spark emotion or feeling and thus fail to motivate action.

We need strong guidelines and laws, Slovic suggested, because it's not a question of not wanting to do the right thing or not valuing people. We value people very highly in some cases, "but despite the high value we place on individuals, we don't seem able to act, to ramp that up in scale." When numbers soar, our consistency with basic values and concerns collapses. Most people are caring and highly responsive when they hear of an individual's desperate plight, yet are numbly indifferent when one person becomes many. Slovic explained that this was evident in the Darfur region of western Sudan, when more than 200,000 people were murdered by government-sponsored militias.[3]

One of the obvious barriers to involvement and decisive action is what Slovic refers to as the drop-in-the-bucket effect. "The problem is so big, and I'm so small. It won't make much difference, no matter what I do." He sees this response every day in the work he does around global violence and believes this attitude may affect response to climate change and other large-scale environmental problems.

It may even be easy for those of us in the West to be numbed relating to climate change and other global environmental problems because we are not feeling physical effects in any immediate or distinct way. It's easier to see soaring temperatures as extremes of natural variation, rather than significant developments worldwide. "There's a great temptation to view it [any incident] in a way that's most comfortable for us, so we say nothing's really changed." That way we don't have to sacrifice anything that we like doing. A lot of people feel their interests will be threatened if we get tough on pollution, restrict activities or change technologies out of concern for the planet's environment. "Powerful people would be hurt economically, their industries would be hurt. So, it's a battle."

Slovic co-authored a paper with Elke Weber regarding risk perception, and I asked him to describe the difference between how an expert evaluates risk and how a layperson perceives it.[4] "On issues like cigarette smoking, the public and the experts were pretty much on the same page, but issues involving radiation, chemicals and biotech revealed strong differences." He found that whether people are exposed voluntarily or not to a hazard will affect their attitudes, as will the potential outcome and whether it is catastrophic or just affects a few individuals.

"A lot of specific qualities of a hazard are important to the public and less important to the experts." For instance, experts tend to concentrate on probabilities that something will go wrong, the size of consequences, mortality, morbidity and anticipated losses. They are very calculating in their approach and focus on a small number of factors. But riskiness means a lot more to people than mere statistics. The public is sensitive to issues such as personal control. They want to know if they are deriving any benefit from an activity that puts them at risk. They want to know if they bear the risk while someone else is getting the benefit. Qualitative factors of personal benefit and fairness influence public perception and acceptance of risk too.

When Slovic and Weber looked at qualities of hazards that influence perception and acceptance, one thing that stood out was the element of dread, which he found is one of the best predictors of the perception and acceptance of risk. Over time, he came to appreciate more and more how important this was. He began studying perception of risk in the late 1970s, and by the 1990s was focusing not only on dread but also on broader concepts that resulted in his book, *The Feeling of Risk*.[5] Here Slovic explored the interaction of emotion and cognition relative to risk perception. He found elements of knowledge, cognitive skill and communication are necessary when making good decisions in the face of risk—but he underscored it is almost impossible to understand risk without taking emotional components into account.

The statistics in climate change discussion, besides being confusing, lack emotion. Few people grasp the impact of global atmospheric concentrations of carbon dioxide passing 400 parts per million—but tell them about greater glacier melt, rising sea levels, more droughts and hurricanes, more mosquitos spreading malaria and dengue fever, and the true meaning of the crisis hits home. Emotion can motivate people to take action, and hopefully prevent even greater disasters.

"What has become clear over years of work is the importance of emotion and feeling—this is where risk resides in us most of the time," said Slovic. We rarely do mental calculations of risk. We rely instead on a gut feeling whether it's safe to overtake a car on the highway or eat that food which has been in the refrigerator too long. We use our senses and our feelings, and that skill stretches far back in the evolution of the human species. It's how evolving humans judged risk for millions of years. "Our brain evolved a way of processing information via feelings that is quite sophisticated and effective in many cases. But over time, we also evolved the capability of thinking about and dealing with risk in a more analytical way." We developed probability theory, mathematics, symbolic reasoning. And that led to risk assessment as an analytic domain, and then toxicology, epidemiology, environmental science. So our brain now operates using both of these remarkable qualities; scientific knowledge and method function alongside structures that allow us to make judgments based on feeling. Analysis and calculation can take us to the Moon or Mars. That's not done with feeling. That's science, Slovic said.

Most of the time we judge risk in our personal lives with our gut—but science is vital too, Slovic stressed. He illustrated his point by explaining human vision is a very sophisticated capability, and most of the time it is very accurate and rational. However, in some situations, there are visual patterns that deceive the eye. "You look at something and you think that A is bigger than B, when in fact B is bigger than A because of the context; the visual system can be misled…. Our emotional system, for reacting to people in need—which is primarily tuned to protecting people around us—breaks down in the context of distant, large-scale, anonymous suffering. Just like a visual illusion, it's kind of a moral illusion." We can hear about things, watch the news broadcast and then turn our backs and deal with our concerns. We forget about the bigger picture especially if there's nothing immediate we can do. It's like a moral illusion that everything is okay, when in fact it's not.

When it comes to climate change, Slovic sees a future that is so problematic we should start taking action now. He believes problems of global warming, species extinction and pollution require slow, deliberate, analytical thinking, not fast gut reactions which tend to be so much easier for us and are typically delivered with great confidence. Slovic recommended Daniel Kahneman's bestseller, *Thinking, Fast and Slow*,[6] which described how we often process information: quickly and intuitively, versus slowly and thoughtfully. Kahneman's research demonstrated the differences between these methods and some of the problems inherent in fast thinking. Slovic and Kahneman edited a book with Amos Tversky called *Judgment under Uncertainty: Heuristics and Biases*.[7]

To the extent that people will continue to rely on feelings emanating from fast thinking, Slovic believes we need to make climate data more emotionally gripping. Cold facts and statistics need to be wrapped in individual stories, personal accounts, emotional images that have the power to "penetrate and impact the fast system." He's not suggesting that people ignore the numbers, "but don't make them salient." You have to make them personal to convey feeling. When you see a number, it has to have a tinge of emotion behind it that tells you this number is either "something very good or something very bad." If a number doesn't carry feeling, we don't really understand it, and we won't act on it.

The element of strong emotion is also what makes humans experience dread, said Slovic. We spend a lot more money to study and prevent cancer than we do to prevent certain types of accidents, which are just as deadly and horrific, because cancer has more "dread quality." While studying terrorism, he found an anthrax attack is more "dreadful" for people than a bomb because anthrax is invisible, and its scope is unknown, whereas a bomb is more contained. "Some things are more dreaded than others because they carry stronger feelings, relating to how much work we have to do to prevent them."

So Slovic urged sensitive communicators to present information in a way that touches emotions, and makes things imaginable—for example, the dreadfulness of a world that is dangerously polluted. "We see things happening now with drought in the US. But again, a drought is something that many of us still feel pretty distant from, although certainly not the people who are experiencing it. There are two ways to go: one is to focus on sensitizing fast-thinking people, also called System One thinkers. We can speak to them through vivid images, emotion, stories and narratives. The other is to approach the problem with System Two thinkers, the scientific deliberators, where we step back and say, 'Let's think more carefully about this problem, and bring science into the picture and analysis.'"

Clearly we need both fast and slow thinking, emotional and analytical skills, to address major problems, but it is important to understand that fast thinking lulls us into complacency. If we take the time to sit down and do some careful, slow thinking, we could expand laws and institutions that would aggressively pursue problems, and we wouldn't have to always be emotionally reactive. If you have created a system of laws and institutions based on thoughtful evaluation of what your values are for certain outcomes, then they take over and run day and night, regardless of how you're feeling.

"I argue in the violence area that we don't have such effective laws and institutions at the international level," he said. "We thought we had it in the United Nations as an institution, and it's basically impotent. We thought we had it in the Genocide Convention as a rule of law, and that's been found to be impotent. So we're leaving it to our feelings, and basically our feelings are worrying more about the Olympics or whatever than about what's going on in Syria."

Slovic suggested that we need laws and institutions in the environmental arena for the same reason. We need people around the table who think slowly and deliberately about where we're headed in this world, what kind of future we're creating for our descendants and what kind of laws and institutions we need to make this future less ominous, rather than depending on fickle feelings of the moment, which are very distracting.

"We need the analytic structure of laws and institutions," he said flatly, offering another analogy: We know taxes are important for the functioning of government so we don't leave it to individual feelings. We have a very quantitative, calculated, analytic system that tells each of us, based on our income, what we are obligated to pay. And then, it's backed up by the force of law—not that there aren't loopholes—but that's the idea. You don't leave it to feelings. It's done through analysis and supported by legal institutions.

I noted that in *Climate Cover-Up* and DeSmogBlog we tell stories that aren't just about big environmental problems. They are about gaming the system, about being manipulated and hoodwinked. I asked if this is an easier issue to get people concerned about than climate change?

"Yes, because what you're doing is providing information that, if people are paying attention, should make them angry, and anger is a powerful emotion." Those manipulating information are putting their self-interest ahead of you and your family, your children, your grandchildren. Something that makes people angry is a motivator for action, for fighting back in some way. So that's important. "We see this in the tobacco area where I think one of the factors that tipped the balance in the last 20-something years was the finding that secondhand smoke is harmful, so it's no longer just the smokers harming themselves, but they are exporting the risk to nonsmokers, which is unfair. You get this element of unfairness, which is again part of the risk related to acceptable risk."

After a long career studying human nature and risk, is Slovic hopeful that we can deal with these issues eventually? What he is finding and documenting is a complexity of issues involving risk, uncertainty and high stakes. If we don't understand that complexity and how it works, we are going to be buffeted by things we can't control. "That is very worrisome. But as we understand more, we gain the ability to potentially manage this important domain of risk and complexity. It doesn't guarantee that we're going to do it, but through greater understanding we have a better chance of shaping the future in a better way."

21

Sometimes David Wins

with Marshall Ganz

If you are in public life,

you must learn to tell your own story.

If you don't, others will, and you'll turn over authorship of

your story to others whose interests may differ from your own.

Marshall Ganz

LONG AGO, on the steep shores of an ancient valley called Elah, in what is now Israel, the Philistine army was assembled and preparing to do battle. Their greatest warrior, a nine-foot giant called Goliath, was hurling insults at the Israelites, taunting them to come out and fight, but his opponents were cowering in terror, frozen with dread. Young David, a shepherd who had come to bring lunch to his warrior brothers, was outraged by the abuse and decided to act. He volunteered to fight the giant, and although King Saul had some doubts, he agreed to let the youth fight if he used the king's own armor. David dutifully put on the king's helmet and breastplate, picked up his shield and heavy sword, but found he couldn't move. That's when he noticed five smooth stones at his feet. He remembered who he was, a shepherd not a soldier, who had learned to defend his flock against wolf and bear with stones and a sling. He took off the armor, picked up the stones and turned to face Goliath. In his arrogance, Goliath began to laugh—"You send a boy with a stick to face me"—but his laughter was cut short by a stone in the forehead. David then grasped the giant's own sword and sliced off his head.

This is a favorite story of renowned social justice advocate Marshall Ganz, the brilliant community organizer whose framework was the basis of President Obama's winning ground game campaigns of 2007–8 and who has contributed to many other movements in the United States and around the world. Why does Ganz choose this particular story when teaching a class on leadership, organizing and action at Harvard's Kennedy School of Government? Because it shows how resourcefulness—fueled by courage, commitment and imagination—can overcome nominally powerful resources, as well as the arrogance that often goes with them.

"The fact is, David sometimes wins,"[1] said Ganz, adding that the young hero of this tale did not have a plan all figured out at the beginning, but he emerged victorious because he found his authentic self and shed the borrowed weaponry. David was skilled in the use of a slingshot, and because he was a shepherd, not a soldier, he saw the battlefield through different eyes. He knew what he was doing, was prepared for it, strategically creative in his use of power and found resources in a few stones: "David's heart enabled him to devise a strategy that worked, and he had the skilled hands to carry it out. Without the strategy, the story wouldn't be enough."

Ganz believes it is through narratives such as this one that people learn to access the moral and emotional resources we need to act with agency in the face of danger, challenge and threat. Those resources can be found in our own lived experience, in how we have dealt with our own pain and where we have found hope. Such narratives describe how we become inspired leaders in the face of uncertainty. They are gateways through which we learn about courage and hope, about what we stand for, who we really are and why we should take action. "They are the portals on the transcendent."

Ganz's theory of public narrative is one of the most important lessons set out in *I'm Right*, and is a mighty tool for leadership and change. An urgent need to improve narrative skills is painfully clear after looking at all the barriers to communication and action I have described. Weak storytelling skills and mistaken ideas about the power of facts not only leave the public unmoved, but they can also trigger antagonism and contribute to polarization and ineffective advocacy. Strong narrative skills can, however, not only deliver an inspiring message for change but also counteract PR and disinformation. We have a better chance of sidestepping the advocacy trap and avoiding the triggering of psychological barriers if we stay strongly rooted in the values that emerge from our own story.

I sought out Ganz to ask how we can better connect with people in difficult conversations. His initial response was not what I expected. It was rooted in his own story and his exposure to many inspiring messages at a young age. Born in 1943 in Bay City, Michigan, Ganz's family lived in Germany for three years after the World War II. His father was a rabbi and an army chaplain who worked with Holocaust survivors, "and as a child, I met people whose lives had been destroyed, who were looking for some way to find enough hope to restore them." One of his first memories was of his fifth birthday in a camp for people who had been displaced, amid many other youngsters. Ganz did not realize until much later why there were no parents present.

After graduating from high school in Bakersfield, California, where his family moved when he was eight, Ganz won a scholarship to Harvard in 1960, the same year John Kennedy was elected President of the US. Ganz was captivated by the President's rousing message about a new generation of leadership. Stirred by the 1963 March on Washington, the Battle of Birmingham, the murder of civil rights leader Medgar Evers and, finally, the assassination of the young Kennedy, Ganz was drawn into the Civil

Rights Movement, in part because his parents had interpreted the Holocaust to him not simply as a form of anti-Semitism but from the broader perspective that racism kills. "It's not a very complex idea but it's a very true one—and the Civil Rights Movement was, of course, challenging institutionalized racism in this country," said Ganz. "So that was a no-brainer."

As a youth, Ganz grew up hearing the story of Exodus told every Passover, and came to understand that this journey from slavery to freedom was not simply an account of one time, one place or one people, but a story that has been retold and reenacted from generation to generation. The US Civil Rights Movement spoke to the nation in the language of Exodus.

Marshall Ganz volunteered for the 1964 Mississippi Summer Project, leaving university a year before graduation. He began working in civil rights where he learned the difference between charity and justice, that power without love is never just, and that likewise, any love that doesn't take power seriously can never achieve justice. He became part of a movement in which power mattered, and realized nothing would change unless something was done about the basic political, economic and cultural power-lessness of the black community.

Through the Bus Boycott, a social protest campaign led by Martin Luther King who was just 25 at the time, Ganz gleaned a fundamental insight into collective power. Ganz realized that if people used their feet to get on a bus, they empowered a bus com-pany, whereas if they used their feet to stay off the bus and walk to work, they empowered themselves. "Things begin to change when people find a way to use their resources to shift, to turn their dependency into interdependence." This is a craft that can bring communities together and empower people to begin solving their own problems.

In 1991 Ganz went back to university, finished his senior year in history and government, wrote his thesis and graduated at age 49. Now bitten by the education bug, he followed up with a master's at Kennedy School, then a PhD in sociology at Harvard, where he ended up joining the faculty. He has been teaching ever since, first developing courses on leadership, organizing and action and more recently on the unique role of narrative.

Immersed in the study of what motivates people, in what are the primary drivers of social movements, and having been steeped in the Exodus story, Ganz put together a class on public narrative and hoped a few students would register. When 35 showed up for the first class, he realized he had touched a nerve. "I was onto something, and then the Obama campaign came along—and it was a great way to figure out how you get lots of people to understand how to use narrative." In the fall of 2015, 130 students, from 31 different countries, enrolled in this course.

Narrative is a form of empowering discourse through which we learn to exercise agency itself. It is a mindful response to a challenge, as opposed to a fearful one. A public story can help create collective agency by linking together the speaker's story of self, the community's story of us and the challenge's story of now. Such public narrative starts with a story of self because, Ganz stressed, "if you are in public life you must learn to tell your own story. If you don't, others will, and you'll turn over authorship of your story to others whose interests may differ from your own." As illustrated by his own story in this chapter, a *story of self* communicates the values that call an individual to action. It should speak to the heart and describe our unique experience: the challenges we have faced, the choices we've made and the outcomes that unfolded during our journey through life. This story of self explains not only why we are called to our work but also how we see ourselves connecting to it, which in turn enables others to connect with it through us.

Next, in the *story of us*, a group can animate the values shared by our constituency. Through stories of joint experience, that everyone recognizes, this narrative creates a sense of the values we share, that are common to our community. It explains how we are connected to each other. As in the story of self, the idea is to tell a specific tale of challenge, of choice, and outcome with rich details of specific people, time and place that bring attention to common values.

And finally, a *story of now* turns the present moment into a narrative moment where "we are confronted by a challenge and must find sources of hope and the courage to act." The challenge creates anxiety, tension and the question is do we react with fear, isolation and self-doubt, or find the wherewithal to respond with hope, empathy and self-worth that enables a mindful, intentional and strategic response? In the story of now, the group is the protagonist, the one who enters the conflict and faces up to a test or task.

Ganz explained the challenge for any organizer or leader who wants to initiate change is to break through the "inertia of habit" and get people to pay attention, to motivate them to risk doing something new and uncertain. An urgent need, outrage or a sense of injustice can propel a breakthrough: "It's the contradiction between the world as it is and the world as it ought to be. Our experience of that tension can break through inertia and apathy."

When I asked Ganz why the climate change narrative failed, he explained that campaigners should always create a powerful sense of injustice, a need for immediate change, or as Dr. King described it, "the fierce urgency of now." But for urgent action to become real, the sense of challenge must be combined with a sense of hope by describing a plausible pathway to action, a credible path forward that makes strategic sense. When Ganz talks of hope, he is not referring to some abstract dream of a better day. The goal needs to be specific and particular.

For instance, when he was trying to help farm workers years ago, Ganz spoke about justice for farm workers and the need for a farm workers' union, but since getting the employers to recognize such a union required boycotting their product (in this case grapes), achieving justice for farm workers boiled down to "don't eat a grape, don't buy a grape, get those grapes out of the stores." That was strategic and symbolic, and people made the connection.

It was what Gandhi did in his Salt March through India. Martin Luther King did the same thing with bus seats, and the American Revolution of the 18th century used tea. But the end of Al Gore's film *An Inconvenient Truth* offered 53 things that you could do. Too much information "trivialized the message." And none seemed linked to a focused strategy that offered a plausible pathway to success.

The emotional dissonance that arises from awareness of an injustice can motivate people to act, but not if it is linked with despair. "When anxiety hits and you're down in despair, then fear hits. You withdraw or strike out, neither of which helps to deal with the problem. But if you're up in hope or enthusiasm, you're more likely to ask questions and learn what you need to learn to deal with the unexpected," Ganz warned. "Leaders and organizers grapple all the time with how to create the tension to inspire a recognition of the need for change, which may incite anger, but also enough hope, empathy and self-worth so that the need for change translates into mindful action and not just reaction."

Ganz explained a good story can help us not only understand the plot's lesson in our head but feel it in our heart. When a story communicates courage, fear, hope, anxiety or exhilaration, we can feel it and understand the lesson not just conceptually. We grasp it emotionally, and the story's moral teaching, both cognitive and emotional, helps equip us to deal with our own challenging choices. Faith traditions, family traditions, cultural traditions are best taught through stories, he said, "This is a critical form of empowering discourse. It's how we learn to be change agents."

He stressed that relationships are built through narratives and shared commitments, but if a leader only creates anxiety, in an effort to communicate urgency and break through inertia, the result can be some form of despair or fear that doesn't spark action at all. So when telling a story of injustice or crisis, a leader must also weave a message of hope, evoke an experience of possibility, of empathy, and one's own self-worth. Hope allows us to be creative problem solvers, and it helps to counterbalance anxiety. "It is one of the most precious gifts we can give each other and the people we work with."

Ganz told me that a challenge and quest for hope and courage is found in the celebrated Saint Crispin's Day speech in Shakespeare's play *Henry V*. Here the young king is motivating his troops before the Battle of Agincourt. His army is grossly outnumbered and exhausted; the odds are fearful, and their opponents are fresh. Henry explains that anyone who wants to leave can go, he would not die in that man's company, but for those who stay—"We few, we happy few, we band of brothers"—the king promises an opportunity for immortality. Ganz loves this speech because King Henry never talks about victory and never even mentions the French. His call to arms is purely about who we are and what our values call us to do. It's about possibilities. "It is a moment when we can grasp the meaning of our lives and our deaths," said Ganz, who adds its brilliance also lies in the way Shakespeare showed us how to restore agency and value to people who are utterly despairing. It's a prototypical locker-room speech that doesn't demonize opponents or even mention victory, yet it speaks to the core of its audience and explains what gives meaning to their lives.

A public narrative is a call to action. Its story is built around a shared challenge, the choice that must be made in response to that threat, and an outcome that conveys a moral. Ganz offered a simple and contemporary analogy: Being asked to change one wasteful light bulb is one thing, "but ask me to help persuade all of the Kennedy School to change all of its light bulbs by signing a student petition, joining a delegation to the dean and adding my name to a public list of students committed to changing the light bulbs where they live," now that's a call to arms. Even if the possibility of success seems remote, this is a story that offers a credible path and specific action.

Stories not only teach us how to act, they also inspire us to take action, and Ganz detailed how a compelling narrative is crafted with three essential elements: plot, character and moral. *Plot* engages us, captures our interest and moves us toward a goal. It becomes exciting when there are unexpected twists and turns. We listen with greater attention to the storyteller when something surprises us, when the unknown intervenes. It doesn't have to be a gut-wrenching calamity or a dangerous predicament, but when a suspenseful challenge looms, we are intrigued.

This is where the protagonist must figure out what to do, and we become engrossed and involved in their *character* as he or she makes a critical choice. For the story to have power, it must draw us in emotionally, so we can identify empathetically with the characters, so we feel and see through his or her eyes. Up until this point, the story maybe had been boring, but suddenly we all lean forward, we're all ears. Why do we care? Because we have all had to face the unknown and make choices, and at the core of the human condition—ours and the character's—is agency and choice.

The story's conclusion needs to have a *moral* that brings us greater understanding, something to live by, a lesson of the heart as well as the head, Ganz said. The memory of a favorite book or film stays with us for years or decades because we can still feel the pull of emotion and the moral universe that created it. "We experience the emotional content, not just the intellectual takeaway. A story teaches us a moral. How did the protagonist access those emotional resources? How did he or she find courage? How did they find hope? It turns out we're incredibly curious about that."

Stories also show us how to manage our lives, face difficulties and rise above stressful situations in unfamiliar circumstances, and while outcomes may be uncertain, we gain strength and hope from watching a hero face those challenges and navigate through rough waters. Dealing with fear is a central moral question, as is the question of how to learn through empathy. This shared wisdom, and uplifting of positive values, is what makes a ripping biography so difficult to put down, and it is achieved through the language of emotion, not through vague, intellectual abstractions.

People are often reluctant to share their stories because they think their own experiences are too trivial or don't matter, but that is not true, especially in the public domain. Everyone has a story, "and you have a responsibility to offer a public account of who you are, why you do what you do, and where you hope to lead." Ganz referred to a Yiddish riddle that asks who discovered water. The answer is I don't know, but it wasn't a fish. The point is, we are all fish in our own experience, and we can't see beyond our own little ponds.

Whenever Ganz coaches people in developing their stories, the first thing they usually say is nothing dramatic ever happened to them. So he asks: Have you experienced pain or loss? Did you ever find hope? When you start digging, you find the experiential foundation that enables a person to communicate something real about themselves, Ganz said.

The Harvard expert said such stories are never trivial, never irrelevant, which is why parents of small children spend a lot of time telling stories. Are they doing this simply to entertain them? No. Storytelling sessions are instructions in agency, in how to access the emotional resources we will all need later in life, to make the right choices. It's value teaching, and children crave this.

Narratives provide information that both children and adults need in order to make judgments. "We're just beginning to actually understand these processes that have been known to religious leaders for thousands of years," said Ganz. So let's build hope instead of fear, empathy instead of alienation, people's sense of self-worth rather than their sense of inadequacy. The current oversupply of scientific information often increases that sense of inadequacy: "Economists do that very successfully. They've mystified the whole debate about economics."

Good leaders understand a story must always be very specific and evoke a particular time and mood. It should be framed in a vibrant setting, with bright color, flavor and gritty texture. The more detail the teller paints into a picture, the more effectively the canvas communicates feelings, values and morals. Paradoxically, Ganz pointed out that the more specific and detailed a story, the more universal it becomes and the greater its connection to us all.

Skilled public narrative is an essential element in leadership, especially when the public square is filled with PR, mistrust and disinterest. As we have seen all through this book, presenting people with a barrage of facts and evidence that stirs up feelings of guilt and fear is not enough. Virtually everyone I interviewed had concerns about the poor quality of environmental narrative and how a lack of storytelling facility leads to greater public anxiety and inaction.

Marshall Ganz brilliantly details how to craft a public story that can deliver really bad news about a problem while it offers a level of hopefulness that rises above any anxiety created by a deeper understanding of a problem. Such a story becomes an emotional dialogue that speaks about deeply held values, about an inspired future that is hopeful and steeped in those values.

From the Heart

22

The Golden Rule

with Karen Armstrong

Look into your own heart, discover what gives you pain,
then refuse under any circumstances whatsoever
to inflict that pain on anybody else. Never treat others
as you would not like to be treated yourself.

Karen Armstrong

PRIZE-WINNING British scholar Karen Armstrong has spent most of her life delving into the history and mystery of the world's great religions. In 1984 she was assigned to write and present a television documentary focusing on the life of Saint Paul, and while retracing his steps in the Holy Land, Armstrong's own life found a new direction. Absorbed in discovering similarities and connections between religions, she began delving into the history of such traditions, and made history herself by winning the TED prize in 2008. TED Talks—a lecture series named for Technology, Entertainment and Design—named her as its most exceptional speaker that year, and she used her $100,000 award to spearhead the creation of a Charter for Compassion.[1]

"When you win the TED prize, they give you a wish for a better world, which they then try to make happen. I felt that what was needed from my field was a greater emphasis on compassion," Karen Armstrong explained.[2] This is what all the great world traditions insist is at the center of the religious life, and compassion is the test of true spirituality. We rarely hear about it yet our "paramount duty" is to respect our fellow human beings. Compassion is a virtuous cycle, and practicing the Golden Rule yields an expanded sense of self, which yields ever more compassionate behavior.

Armstrong's research has shown that although ancient sages, philosophers and religious leaders such as Confucius, Socrates and Buddha may have come from different traditions, they all advanced a practical message for everyday life. The Chinese philosopher Confucius, who lived from 551 to 479 BCE, is said to have been the first person to formulate the Golden Rule: Do not do to others that which we do not want them to do to us. The book of Leviticus, written circa 1400 BCE, said, "Love thy neighbor as thyself." Similar statements are found in Taoism, Buddhism, Hinduism and many other religions and philosophies.

Religious knowledge is meant to be practical, Armstrong stressed, although in the West and in this modern era, people get hung up on doctrines and beliefs that become a kind of "head trip." Traditionally, religion is about changing behavior in a way that changes an individual at a profound level. One of the chief obstacles to enlightenment is selfishness and egotism, and compassion is the surest way to move beyond the ego. "You have to dethrone yourself from the center of your world and put another there." When the disciples of Confucius asked which of his teachings could be put into practice all day, every day, his answer was simple: *shu*. This means to "look into your own heart, discover what gives you pain, then refuse under any circumstances whatsoever to inflict that pain on anybody else."

Confucius said that practicing this all day, every day—not just when you feel like it—leads to an ecstasy of stepping outside the self, and gradually this becomes the path to enlightenment and enhancement of being. When asked how to apply this in political life, Confucius said that when among the common people, you must behave as though you were in the presence of an important guest. If you seek to establish yourself politically and economically, then seek to establish others. In Buddhist terminology, this means taking responsibility for the pain you see in the world, not dismissing it or thinking it is not your concern. It means active concern for others.

I told Karen Armstrong that people in Canada's environmental community are angry about the lack of action on climate change and frustrated by the resistance of governments and business leaders. It appears activists are unreceptive to the message of compassion, because it seems passive and they have made a moral choice not to be bystanders.

Armstrong said compassion may seem like an idealistic pursuit, far removed from the realities of life today, but she was quick to explain that the great sages who preached compassion didn't live in caves. They lived in extremely violent societies, like our own, where "aggression had reached an unprecedented crescendo." During the era of Confucius, for instance, all the Chinese states embarked upon a fight that lasted two centuries, until only one was left and became the Chinese Empire. "The loss of life, destruction of property and the environment was absolutely appalling."

Ours is an equally threatened world in many ways, and if we persist along our present course, we may not survive. The most important path to change is to treat one another with absolute respect. The historian went on to say it is important to speak out against injustice, "but to be effective, you must ask yourself, are your actions about your ego and punishing your opponent or are they about real change?" If you come from an antagonistic, egotistical position, people will double down and resist what you are trying to achieve. This is why advocates and other public figures need to develop self-discipline and self-awareness. "They need to realize that the pain and fear motivating their anger is the same pain and fear motivating their opponents to deny this horrendous scenario."

Gandhi is an obvious example of someone who was working in an extremely difficult environment, but he refused to condemn the British. He was not averse to speaking out, but he urged his followers to always ask themselves whether they were speaking out to punish rather than to ameliorate the situation.

Armstrong is fond of quoting Saint Paul, who included a hymn to charity in his letter to the Corinthians: "Charity is patient, is kind. It is not puffed up." He also noted, "Charity takes no delight in the wrongdoing of others."[3] Very often when people are protesting against an injustice, they become puffed up with self-righteous indignation. This will get you nowhere. Armstrong admonished us to always ask ourselves, Are you seeking to make a difference? Or do you simply want to let off steam?

Armstrong's work often deals with acrimonious individuals, and in her studies of fundamentalist religions, she has found that every militant religious movement has a profound fear of annihilation in its origins. "They believe, even in the United States, that modern, liberal or secular ideologues want to wipe them out." When people feel their backs are to the wall, they lash out violently. If any movement is attacked aggressively, their members invariably become more extreme.

When it comes to the environment, Armstrong suggested that much of the denial that results from public debate is rooted in fear and dread, because change means doing away with a lot of material comforts on which people have come to depend. We, especially in the Western world, have become "absolutely spoiled and selfish," and people in a materialistic culture cling to their possessions because they have no psychological resources to deal with scarcity. The idea of giving things up, of not having a warm house or not being able to jump into our cars every time we need to, bewilders and paralyzes people. "The scale of what is required if we are to meet this challenge is monumental, and so some people say it isn't happening, it's all nonsense." Instead of yelling at people and being inimical, which simply makes them more paralyzed, Armstrong suggested that activists must try to gently guide one another out of that paralysis. Our best hope is to share each other's pain, dial down the heated discussions so we can all realize we are on the brink of situations that are unprecedented in human history.

How do we achieve a sustainable environment? This is something none of us have a full answer to, yet. If we think we have all the answers, we are deceiving ourselves. The situation is exacerbated by a plethora of social and political problems. People in developing countries ask why they should hold back on industrial growth and continue living in poverty when those in the West enjoy much better living conditions. We've got to sit down quietly together, face the problems, find solutions and learn to live with a new reality, said Armstrong.

And what is required of us all—whether we are trying to decrease the threat of terrorism or create a viable environment—is a spiritual revival. That doesn't mean we should all go off and say our prayers, Armstrong commented. People who think that have adopted the modern, reductive way of thinking about religion. Instead, spiritual revival "means that we have to do a lot of work on our own internal selves, so that we are ready to make sacrifices, to give up comforts, to cut down on our travel."

This asks an awful lot from people. It's asking them to make massive sacrifices, and not everyone can do that just by thinking about it rationally. "You need to dissuade these fears and not present people with a world of stark terror, which makes them batten down the hatches. Do it in a way that allows them to start thinking: How am I going to live without my motor car?"

During the financial crisis in 2008, many business people gazed into an abyss and realized what can happen when greed takes over. Greed is helping to destroy our environment, through our lust for material consumption, our desire for luxury, warmth and travel—doing whatever we like without being accountable. But it's not too late. People such as Buddha and Confucius are remembered to this day because they changed the world by changing the way people thought and acted. Kings and important businesspeople who were alive at that time are long forgotten, but the Buddha founded one of the oldest and most enduring institutions in all of world history.

23

Tending Our Inner Ecology

with Joan Halifax

Don't deny the sense of despair or jam it down inside you.
Despair is important. It can paralyze you
but it can also humanize you.

Roshi Joan Halifax

A MERICAN ZEN BUDDHIST Joan Halifax says we are ignoring the looming juggernaut of climate change—everything
from ocean acidification to ecosystem destruction—because our
society is utterly self-absorbed and egocentric. People are not
thinking clearly about consequences and have forgotten that all
things are interconnected.

"With greater consciousness comes greater responsibility,"[1]
said the anthropologist, ecologist, civil rights activist and author, during an interview in a traditional adobe building at her
beautiful Upaya Zen Center near Santa Fe. I first met Halifax in.
Dharamsala during one of my trips to see the Dalai Lama, and was
immediately fascinated by her powerful spirit and poetic language.

During our conversation, she explained the lack of responsibility and connection we witness today stems from "a race of the
ego" and is rooted in a sense of deep insufficiency. His Holiness
the Dalai Lama often describes what's missing as the connection
that exists between a parent and child, in family systems, in neigh-

216

borhoods or communities where there is a "fundamental sense of respect and affection woven into the psychosocial fabric."

Halifax said we're in a peculiar time of global crisis that has environmental, economic and psychological implications. To overcome this sensibility of the individual as a separate self, we have to step out of the rat race and understand the profound value of an inner life. Our identity should not be predicated on how much we have or what we consume because it will never be enough. It will never actualize our basic humanity and good hearts.

I mentioned that research shows most people do actually recognize they are helping destroy the planet, but don't do anything about it. Why are they unwilling to change?

It's the magnitude of the issue. People feel helpless in the face of this "Goliath of a tragedy," and that leads to anger, despair and moral outrage. It's natural to go into states characterized by intense suffering, including denial. As Buddha said, "My Dharma is swimming against the stream," and it takes tremendous commitment not to buy into the prevailing view of self-centeredness. It is a characteristic not only of Western culture but of global culture as well, Halifax said.

Just as greater consumption won't solve inner emptiness, more facts won't help turn things around. People don't practice meditation or take part in social activism or environmental activism because of data. Many of us live in an incredibly privileged way, jetting around the world, turning on air conditioners and heaters whenever it suits us, consuming incredible amounts of goods wrapped in plastic containers. "It's really amazing how we are fouling our own nest." She described the comment of a man from Nanjing, capital of Jiangsu Province in China, after she told him about the stunning skies in New Mexico: "I've lived here my whole life, and never seen a blue sky," he told her.

Halifax lives high in the mountains of New Mexico, off the grid, in a room that measures eight by ten feet. "It's like living in the century before last. I come down and teach here at the Zen

Center, and then I go back to my retreat. I choose to live like a so-called poor person because the natural world gives me life." The natural world energizes her, "and then I can do the work I do with a perspective that is more spacious, and also more patient and determined; two qualities that you find in the natural world."

Halifax, who was 70 at the time of our conversation, told me how she had driven across the Sahara Desert half a century earlier. Many parts of the world were undiscovered and inaccessible then, but today tourists scour the planet for new thrills. They leave no rock unturned. They are absorbed in the mystery of outer space and travel to exotic lands, yet seem uninterested in the mystery of the present moment, here and now, inside. This is why spiritual practice is important. If you see clearly, "you will not only want to cultivate your capacity for discernment, but you will also want to engage morally and instrumentally in transforming the psychosocial fabric of the world we find ourselves in."

She noted that suffering is not always a bad thing. Sometimes it opens a doorway or leads to a eureka moment. An environmental activist, for instance, may suffer deeply when learning about the loss of another species, or seeing another swath of Amazon rain forest going up in smoke, but that can spur effort. Hopelessness can fuel a passion that may stimulate individuals to dedicate themselves to a cause, or inspire them to work for the common good.

When Halifax goes out into the urban world, she is often struck by the idea of how it must have looked centuries ago. "The Island of Manhattan, London, Los Angeles...I go into those worlds and bear witness to the outcome of civilization and delusion." While she sees a metropolis for the incredible organism it is, she says those cities don't necessarily become more beautiful as they age, unlike an old forest or a wetland. One of her concerns is what's happening in the lives of children today and how many can only glimpse nature on a computer screen. They look at a nature channel and think that's the real thing. "But what really renews this body and mind, of course, is to be awake and alive in an actual natural setting. It's not going to happen virtually."

I asked her about despair, something I am acutely conscious of when I talk to climate scientists, environmentalists, conservationists and others who wish they didn't know what they know. How do we process the grim news and not sink into despair?

She used the analogy of a driver turning into a skid on an icy road, to regain control of their car. "Don't deny the sense of despair or jam it down inside you. Despair is important. It can paralyze you, but it can also humanize you." Feeling intense grief over loss of habitat or the demise of a species can encourage a deep sense of responsibility. It can lead to reduced consumption and propel action, whether it's taking one teaspoon of water back to the ocean or "a vast gift such as liberating a river from its dam. We only can do our best. Our own life cycle is a perfect example of our finiteness. We're all going to die. Species will die, evolution will happen, the Earth is a self-organizing system."

Halifax explained she lives in a valley that has unquestionably been getting warmer, and as a result, a pond in the area developed a thick algae growth. "But this year I looked in the pond and saw enormous salamanders eating the algae. I haven't seen a salamander there for years. So there is this regulatory process. We don't understand biological systems sufficiently to create a global system that is any greater than the one we already have."

The Zen priest has faith in human beings, as well as nature, and ironically it became most clear when she worked on death row, in maximum-security prisons. "I worked with some of the most difficult beings imaginable, and there was always a moment when we saw through clearly, eye-to-eye into a place of basic goodness.... These people had done really bad things but somehow touched a place inside themselves that was deeper than their suffering." We're so smart as Westerners. We're so prescriptive. We want to control everything. But the most important thing is to open up into a kind of beginner's mind, to look through all the neurosis, selfishness and self-centeredness of the human beings and see ourselves.

Rather than being immobilized by despair, she advises bringing curiosity into that anguish or helplessness. This happened at Bearing Witness Retreats where survivors of Auschwitz came together with people who served in SS military units, as well as children of the SS, children of survivors, Jews, Palestinians: "You would think this would be a recipe for disaster, but human beings in the right circumstances have the capacity to be truly noble, to truly meet this moment." There are pieces of our history that are so horrendous it is hard to be reconciled, whether it is Auschwitz or Rwanda, and these events are not unlike what we're doing to the environment. We have objectified the natural world by not realizing it is *us*. As a result of that dissociation, there's a reconciliation process that must happen between the natural world and us.

A sense of moral outrage can be debilitating and give rise to a lot of suffering if taken to the extreme. It can be incapacitating, just as anger is incapacitating. But that's not to say we shouldn't have a profound moral and ethical perspective, and she believes the "raw energy of anger" is characterized by an ability to see things much more clearly. When an individual moves out of the reactive phase and into the plain energy of anger, it produces tremendous discernment: "So I personally find anger generative."

It becomes dangerous when we get caught up in the story of anger, in a hard, polarized position where you say others are wrong and you start to blame. We're all responsible for this mess, one way or another. So it's about taking responsibility, staying above the line in communication.

"A few elections back, we had a vice president, and I really thought this is fascinating, because I felt a lot of polarization and aversion. It was exactly what I felt in the 1960s when I was in the anti-war movement, the civil rights movement, and thought we were right and they were wrong. And, yes, I think we *were* right they *were* wrong...but blaming never produces a helpful outcome." The problem with polarization is one side hardens, and then the other side hardens. When we are seeking social justice and environmental justice, a wise person understands this strategy is ineffective.

She admires the work of American environmentalist and journalist Bill McKibben, but explains he is "prescriptive and prophetic." He's got the data and he lays it out. He carries a critical piece in the whole puzzle, and we need somebody to do that, but if everybody did that, people would be in a state of absolute despair and helplessness because from his point of view we've gone past the tipping point, and there's no way back.

Halifax believes that's not a good outlook: "When I first went into the prison system, I had a lot of ideas and lots of data, but as soon as I went through the doors of that system, I had to put everything aside and really sit with not knowing." It's the same with sitting with dying people, said Halifax, who is renowned for her hospice work. "I had to put everything I knew aside and be a kind of open slave. I had to simply bear witness and not let my prejudice and opinions interfere with more immediate perception."

She said there is no single solution to global warming. We don't know how systems operate when their territory is so profoundly threatened, and the more fear we spread in our gullible and global culture, the more consumerism there's going to be. People will want more and more, in order to cover up their sense of helplessness, their fear. Scaring people with facts will not work; blaming them will not help our environment. The answers lie on a much deeper level of human consciousness, in inner transformation.

She said three helpful tenets in the Zen Peacemaker Order are helpful: not knowing, bearing witness and loving actions toward our self and others. The first refers to the ability to be a beginner, to maintain an open mind, to realize that all the science we have today won't look anything like this in 50 years. Very few scientific principles have been sustained over hundreds or thousands of years, since the Arabs and other primitive scientists came on the scene. So the first tenet involves opening up to a bigger view of "not knowing." Vimalakirti calls it a tolerance for the inconceivable, and Halifax points to an example of this being the satellite dish in her remote wilderness valley that allows her to receive emails at 9,400 feet above sea level. "Back in the 1960s, I couldn't have imagined that, or thought of an iPhone, or an iPad or an Android." The connectivity we experience today is extraordinary, and wouldn't it be a miracle if that same kind of interconnection could somehow be mirrored in our relationship with the natural world and our relationship with our own psychological processes, she added.

Bearing witness is the second tenet, and it refers to presence, to the capacity of being mindful of what is happening and able to see both the joy and suffering of the world. It includes the idea of not letting our prejudices and opinions interfere with more immediate perceptions. The third tenet involves compassionate or loving action toward ourselves and others. It means responding to the world from a basic view of compassion and love. It requires a sense of moral responsibility, social and environmental engagement that springs from a much deeper base than panic.

I asked Halifax how we can develop compassion, in a world awash with worry, and in the face of intentional wrongdoing by people whose actions could have huge consequences? How can people find compassion in an atmosphere of such emotional and physical pollution?

Compassion can't be found, she said simply, "but it is possible to train in the processes that precede compassion, that actually prime compassion." For example, compassion is not possible without the capacity for balanced attention. Positive regard is also critical. Other precursors include intention and unselfish motivation: "How can I serve here? What needs to happen? What will reduce suffering?"—that's not just intention, she stressed, it's also insight. And if you tend to be a reactive person, you can start to see and feel your own reactivity when it arises and turn that dial down. Ask yourself the question: "Can I know myself well enough?"

Other aspects include cultivating a moral and ethical sensitivity so that we operate responsibly in the world around us, and are not attached to any outcome. She acknowledges this is difficult for Westerners. "I know from working with dying people, the outcome is going to be death in most instances, and if I try to manipulate the dying individual so they die a so-called good death, it often interferes with their experience. My job is to constantly enquire and look at what really serves this individual."

Halifax concluded that the final set of qualities that give rise to compassion are related to our somatic capacities. People often ask her why she lives in such minimal circumstances, and she explains it is good to chop wood and carry water, to be part of the natural world. It produces more vitality and embodiment. She believes embodiment is a pillar that supports compassion. An individual who is cut off from their own body is unable to sense their own somatic experience, and unable to empathize, which is a vital feature of compassion. She sees compassion as an emerging process within a context of features and processes that pave the way. "Attention training, affect training, insight training and embodiment are basically the four domains—and they are what meditation practice is about."

24

Speak the Truth, But Not to Punish

with Thich Nhat Hanh

There is suffering, fear, and anger inside of us,

and when we take care of it,

we are taking care of the world.

Thich Nhat Hanh

A COUPLE OF YEARS AGO, my wife Enid and I participated in a five-day program at the University of British Columbia with the renowned Vietnamese monk Thich Nhat Hanh.

"As activists we want to do something to help the world to suffer less," Thich Nhat Hanh said, but when we're not peaceful, when we don't have enough compassion in us, we are unable to do much to help the world. "Peace, love and happiness must always begin in us, with ourselves first. There is suffering, fear and anger inside of us, and when we take care of it, we are taking care of the world."[1]

Thich Nhat Hanh used the example of a pine tree and suggested, what if that tree asked us what it could do to help the world? Our answer would be very clear: "You should be a beautiful, healthy pine tree. You help the world by being your best." That is true for humans also. The most basic thing we can do to help the world is to be healthy, solid, loving and gentle to ourselves. Then when people look at us, they will gain confidence and say, If he or she can do that, I can too. So anything you do for yourself, you do for the world, he said. "Don't think that you and the world are two separate things. When you breathe in mindfully and gently, when you feel the wonder of being alive, remember that you're also doing this for the world. Practicing with that kind of insight, you will succeed in helping the world. You don't have to wait until tomorrow. You can do it right now."

During the retreat, lectures invariably touched on the subject of anger, and I listened as he encouraged me to examine the anger I felt toward special interests that mislead the public about the environmental challenges we face. One day Thich Nhat Hanh told us Buddha's story of the second arrow: When an arrow strikes you there is pain, but if a second arrow drives into the same spot, the pain is excruciating, much worse. The Buddha advised when you have pain in your body or your mind, breathe in and out and recognize the significance of the pain but don't exaggerate its importance. If you are full of anger, worry and fear over the pain, you magnify the suffering. This is the second arrow—and it is directed from within.

The Buddha proposed many ways to practice reducing pain in our bodies and in our emotions, to become reconciled within ourselves. Pain increases as tension increases, and it can be reduced when we release the tension. The monk said that this can be done while lying, sitting or walking. "Walk like a free person.... The skill we need is how to lay down our burden in order to be light. The Buddha said that you shouldn't amplify your pain by exaggerating the situation.... So when you experience pain, whether physical or mental, you have to recognize it just as it is and not exaggerate it... when you can make peace with it, you won't suffer as much." When we get angry and revolt against something, when we worry too much and imagine we are going to die soon, our pain is multiplied 100 times. "That is the second arrow."

If we want to help the environment suffer less, we have to reduce the suffering in ourselves, Thich Nhat Hanh explained simply. "Be loving, and gentle to yourself." Avoid the second arrow.

He talked about a heart of understanding that is beyond intellect, that is discovered by looking so deeply we touch the seed of understanding and compassion within. Compassion can neutralize anger and hate, and meditation can burn away afflictions such as fear, despair and delusion. "Deep meditation helps us transcend the notion of being and non-being. Nirvana is not a place we will arrive at in the future, but the nature of reality."

He suggested we should listen more deeply, and allow others to speak as this helps to reduce their suffering. "Water the seeds of compassion; don't water the seeds of anger and hatred." Use non-accusatory language so it is easier for others to hear our message. Effective listening does not involve hearing something and comparing that information with our own views. We learn nothing from such an exchange.

Grassroots success is only effective and possible if activists and leaders first deal with their own anger and fear. Spiritual practice is needed to transform society, and give courage to leaders so they will speak out. He said a mother would die for her children because of her great love, and similarly, if a person has great compassion, they will not fear being ostracized or ridiculed if they decide to challenge the status quo.

I had been asked to moderate a conversation between David Suzuki and Thich Nhat Hanh, and the day of our taped interview, following the five-day course at UBC, started with an extraordinary experience. Thich Nhat Hanh arrived at the pre-arranged location while David Suzuki and I were in another part of the building, so someone quickly found us and explained the famous monk had gone for a walk in the garden. We rushed to catch up with his small group and strolled about 20 paces behind. Walking in this peaceful space, he touched some of the flowers with great tenderness, and as I watched, the garden became intensely green. As the monk was appreciating each flower, petal and leaf, Suzuki leaned over and said softly: "Do you know what I see? I see photosynthesis: The sun pouring down, creating energy, turning it into all this green, all these plants that allow us to breathe."

The conversation began when I asked for Thich Nhat Hanh's reaction to a 1930 statement made by a Wall Street banker: "People need to be trained to desire, to want new things, even before the old things have been entirely consumed. Man's desires must overshadow his needs."[2]

I was expecting an answer about consumerism and the destructiveness of clinging, but he gently turned the conversation in an unexpected direction by saying how the desire for more can be a deep and noble desire in each human being. "Like the desire to love, to protect, to help, to serve, the desire to be loved, to understand, to learn. These are very deep desires in each human being, in every one of us, and you cannot set a limit on that kind of desire.... You can continue to learn, to understand more about yourself, about the world outside you. You can continue to develop your love into the infinite. In Buddhism we say that love is something that has no frontiers."

I asked how we can bring about the collective awakening needed to stop destroying our planet, and Thich Nhat Hanh told the story of a similar longing for change in a five- or six-year-old child who stood up in front of a large audience in Plum Village (the spiritual community he founded in France) and asked why his father continued to smoke, knowing it was not good for him. "That [wanting change] is a theme, a subject of meditation, and I think if we can answer that question, we will have a lot of insight about how to handle the situation of our planet. It's very difficult to offer an answer to the child if you do not have the time to look deeply into the situation." But Thich Nhat Hanh told the child that in order to stop smoking the father must feel his child's love: "Your love will be an important force in order to help him to stop."

During our UBC interview, Thich Nhat Hanh said we must build communities that model how to live sustainably, and that requires inspirational, confident leadership. Vancouver mayor Gregor Robertson said it was a compelling concept, but the challenge is how to reach consensus for a higher-level commitment in a city that is a very culturally and politically diverse community. He added that politicians are often criticized for trying to set big goals, such as ending homelessness or becoming the greenest city in the world. Robertson said many citizens are disillusioned with issues of climate change and poverty.

The monk explained people should remind each other that this is the way of life that guarantees a future. Senior members of the community—the mayor, city council, people in government—should set an example and show people "that they are abiding by the spirit and the way. I think it's very important." He said citizens should only vote for those who adopt the kind of lifestyle that sets an example to inspire hope and confidence. Leaders should be people who not only have the talent to run the country's business, but also represent our global ethics.

Feelings of despair must be dealt with because they overwhelm and paralyze people, said Thich Nhat Hanh; he added that this is a key reason why people do not respond to the threat of global warming, despite mounting and devastating evidence. They cannot raise themselves out of the pit of despair, let alone save the world. "Despair is growing in our society, and because of that, we feel helpless. We don't believe that we can do anything to reverse the situation. Again, I think community building is very important, to show people that living simply and happily is possible." When we understand the interconnectedness of all life, when we recognize we are not separate, we can expand our compassion and ourselves so that we embrace Earth and protect it.

The monk said that people are deluded into thinking fame, power, wealth or sex will bring them happiness, and these become refuges from the truth and challenges facing Mother Earth. Today's addiction to consumerism and a frantic lifestyle is a mask behind which people hide their emotional and spiritual wounds.

It provides only a temporary respite from fear and unhappiness: "They suffer deeply even if they have a lot of these kinds of things. Many of them commit suicide." Without love, brotherhood and sisterhood, people destroy themselves, and Thich Nhat Hanh urged people to step onto the path of love and understanding if they want to find the strength to let go of the mask and awaken to reality.

A life of consumerism is not life. "We have to help people learn how to live again. We just sit down and breathe and enjoy each other." He said this is one of the best moments of a retreat: when people don't consume anything, don't have music, don't have sound, don't have alcohol, don't have anything but a chance to sit and enjoy each other's presence. He said everyone knows how to breathe, to appreciate they are alive on this beautiful planet, and that can bring joy. "So we have to educate our citizens to see that happiness does not lie in consumption but lies in the fact that you are free enough: you have enough time to enjoy yourself, to enjoy each other, to enjoy the environment."

The simple acts of life are treasures, and we should savor them, knowing everything we need to be happy is right here, right now. "In the Buddhist tradition, we have a practice like a tea ceremony. We just have one cup of tea, but we spend one hour and a half together. Why do we need one hour and a half in order to enjoy a cup of tea? Because the tea ceremony is an art. If you know how to sit, how to breathe, how to look, how to listen and how to be together, that ceremony can bring a lot of joy. And you don't consume much, one cup only. We have lost our capacity of being happy, because we are so busy. And busy in what? Busy trying to cover up the suffering inside."

I mentioned that there are climate scientists and political leaders who want to do something positive about climate change but have a difficult time because so many people stir up mischief about these issues. When the public is misinformed and unaware that a problem exists, it's very difficult for leaders to lead, I said, and while I understood what he said about community building and agreed that is the solution, I explained I still worry about taking our eyes off the people who are up to mischief on larger levels.

This took us directly back to the issue of despair, and Thich Nhat Hanh said if we don't deal with despair, the situation will get worse. "We have to accept this civilization can be destroyed, not by something outside, but by ourselves. Many civilizations have been destroyed in the past, and to accept that can only be helpful, and it may give us a sense of peace so we can become a better worker for the environment." He said that many people know what is happening but do nothing because they are just trying to survive. "If you help them to sort out the inside, you can help them to have hope, to have peace in themselves, and suddenly they have the strength to come back to themselves...and that person could be an instrument for the protection of the environment."

During our interview, David Suzuki asked if accepting the reality that this could all end disastrously means we retreat into passivity.

Thich Nhat Hanh said a century or two is nothing in geological terms. "This civilization might be destroyed, and it may take a billion years more in order to have another civilization. That already happened in the past. We have to accept reality, and acceptance like that can bring us peace. And with that kind of peace, we have force and it can flow, and it can reverse the situation. Meditation plays a role." He said that to meditate means to look deeply, and by looking deeply, we have insight, which frees us from despair and anger. This allows us to become a better worker for the environment.

Suzuki added that he understood the cycles of extinction of species, as a natural part of evolution. Species become extinct as conditions change, and new species evolve, "but many of us have children and grandchildren who are precious, and when we see the approaching calamity, it is difficult to accept." Again Thich Nhat Hanh stressed the importance of building community and living in a way that can become a model for others. "If everyone can live like that, truly there will be a future for our children. Our society needs a lot of healing, and this is not possible without a good environment. That's why, when building a community, you build also an environment where you can see hope, brotherhood, sisterhood and a future."

He said we should bring a spiritual dimension to the work of protecting the environment. "The role of meditation, the role of community building, the role of healing and transforming in our daily life is crucial for the environment. You cannot just have projects and initiatives without taking care of the suffering inside." At the end of our interview, I was worried that Thich Nhat Hanh had been saying that we should simply withdraw and meditate, so I mentioned that one of his monks had told me his Bay Nha monastery in the central highlands of Vietnam had placed pictures on its website of bad police who were abusing monks and nuns. I pointed out that this seemed like the strategy of activists. Was he saying we should not be activists?

He looked at me in a quiet, piercing way that stopped my breath, and said slowly: "Speak the truth, but not to punish." It took me some time to realize that I had been given a Zen koan[3] by one of the most important Zen masters of our generation. I've been thinking about it ever since. It was the most profound moment of this entire three-year journey of research and writing, the seminal moment, because it gathered together the deepest voices and most profound threads of this long book into one elegant sentence.

Understanding this koan is a work in progress for me, but the more I ponder it, the more it seems to be about balance, speaking up against injustice with courage and passion but with greater awareness of the dangers in becoming overly adversarial and treating those who disagree as foes.

It is important to educate the public about the PR campaigns written about earlier in this book, but it is equally important to ensure, as Rabbi Hillel encouraged, that our argument is for the sake of heaven. We must be willing to stand in the shoes of others, if we are to debate controversial issues with equanimity and avoid gridlock.

Thich Nhat Hanh's koan brought me back to his advice to hold our anger with an energy of mindfulness, like the sun shining upon a flower, penetrating deeply until the petals open. Anger can give us the mettle to speak with courage and conviction, but also the venom that blinds us to the views of others.

25

We Need Warmheartedness

with The 14th Dalai Lama

I think you acknowledge sometimes the Western brain
looks more sophisticated, but in Tibet we operate
from the heart and this is very strong.
So combine these two, Asian heart and Western mind,
and then we will have real success. Real success.

The 14th Dalai Lama

THE TIBETAN PLATEAU has often been referred to as the roof of the world because it stretches over a vast area with an elevation averaging more than three miles above sea level. This magnificent region—larger than France, Spain, Germany and Italy combined—brings life-giving nourishment to almost 40 percent of the world's population.

Its glaciers, located northeast of the Himalayas, have been described as the water tower of India and China because this icy realm holds the third-largest reservoir of freshwater on Earth, outside the North and South Poles. The Tibetan plateau, of which the autonomous region of Tibet covers about half, is the birthplace of four of the world's great rivers—the Yangtze, Mekong, Yellow and Brahmaputra—and many others including the Indus and Salween.

Climate change is visible to the naked eye in Tibet. "Temperatures are rising four times faster than elsewhere in China, and the

Tibetan glaciers are retreating at a higher speed than in any other part of the world," said glaciologist Qin Dahe, former head of the China Meteorological Administration. He said this catastrophe is causing floods and mudflows in the short term, and in the long term the melting will affect vital Asian lifelines such as the Indus and Ganges. "Once they vanish, water supplies in those regions will be in peril."[1]

Recent research by experts at NASA and the Chinese Academy of Sciences shows the black carbon being deposited on these glaciers, generated from industrial production in South Asia, is accelerating shrinking. Soot absorbs incoming solar radiation and speeds melting, and it's helping to turn the world's largest non-polar ice masses into what has been described as a climate change hot spot.[2]

I first travelled to Tibet in 2003. Our group, including former Canadian cabinet minister Flora MacDonald, toured for two weeks with naturalists, community organizers and one of the world's leading ornithologists. We were looking into primary health care and environmental sustainability projects being led by Future Generations in villages across Tibet, and our host was the founder of that group, Daniel Taylor. He had invited the David Suzuki Foundation to become involved in Future Generations' Four Great Rivers Project in eastern Tibet.[3]

Future Generations was promoting community-led development and helping create a conservation zone in the southeastern part of Tibet, to protect 46 million acres of biodiversity. The Chinese government had started to reevaluate the massive amount of trees being cut down in what is now designated the Four Great Rivers Protection Area, and we were helping them better understand sustainable land-use planning and resource management.

I learned how deforestation in Tibet was affecting the Yangtze River region, an area that suffered some of the worst flooding in half a century during a disastrous 1998 event that resulted in 15 million homeless and an economic loss of $26 billion.[4]

Our trip to Tibet was capped off with a drive down the treacherous Friendship Highway to Kathmandu. We passed many beautiful sites, and a mixture of fear and weather—starting with a snowfall on an 18,000-foot mountain pass—sometimes deterred us from seeing all the sacred sites we would have liked. But on our descent, we managed to visit a cave of revered Tibetan saint Milarapa, who is said to have concentrated so intensely one day that he levitated its massive stone roof. We also visited Rombuk Monastery, the highest monastery in the world at 16,300 feet (near the base of Mt. Everest), and because we were with Flora, we privately toured the Jokhang Temple in Lhasa, the holiest site in Tibetan Buddhism.

I visited Tibet again in 2006, to evaluate and report on the progress of our joint conservation project.

Important work continued for about five years in this botanical treasure trove which boasts some of the world's deepest, steepest river valleys (such as the Brahmaputra gorge—four times deeper than the Grand Canyon) and features climate zones ranging from tropical to polar. We were training villagers as caregivers in health and hygiene, developing leaders in ecosystem-based land-use planning. It is the kind of environmental work that is bottom-up, not paternalistic in the sense of being directed from the top down or from outside the region.

Back in Tibet, we toured the Four Great Rivers area and drove for five days off-road to the base of Mt. Kailash, which we circumnavigated on foot. Here I saw the spirituality of the people but also how little Tibetans have, how rudimentary their lives are, how arid the landscape is—and how perilously close they live to the edge.

At one point we stopped for a break under some trees, and I saw a young boy selling some dismal-looking apples. The Good Samaritan in me said I should buy all his apples for far more than he was asking. As I walked back to the car, feeling very content and thinking he would be shocked at what he received for his apples, my wife Enid was yelling out the window, "Give him back his bowl, give him back his bowl." Turning around, I saw a woeful look on his face and rushed to return his precious bowl. Suddenly his face lit up in a huge smile as happiness was restored. I don't know exactly how many bowls I have in my house, but obviously far more than I need. That was a big lesson for me, from a small boy, and my wife.

We have such abundance in Canada, yet everything at this high elevation in Tibet seemed brighter, more saturated with color, more vividly intense. The sky was bluer, the snow is whiter, and the feeling of connection was stronger too. Gazing at the peak of Mt. Everest, you see it pierce the jet stream's river of wind that streaks around the globe at high speed, and you see how it stitches together Earth and sky.

Once, on our way to hike around Mt. Kailash, when we were days away from any town or sustained light, I stepped outside the little pup tent in the middle of the night. Everything around me was pitch black, but it seemed the stars were right beside me, not just above. I could see the depth of the Milky Way, almost touch the constellations, and everything was so close I felt completely connected with the stars.

Tibet offers an acute lesson in interconnectedness that is hard to miss when you're there. Tibet showed me precisely how an area can suffer when climate change is on fast-forward. I also realized how vulnerable its people are. Sometimes we would pass through a village where everyone was outside trying to plant trees in what looked like desert to us. Travelling to Tibet was like visiting a canary in a coal mine, tracking a sensitive indicator that's issuing an early warning of great danger.

In 2011 I travelled to Dharamsala—home of the 14th Dalai Lama and headquarters of the Tibetan government in exile—for the 23rd Mind and Life Conference,[5] a five-day discussion about the environmental crisis, ecology and ethics of climate change. Meetings were held in the Dalai Lama's house, and speakers included people like Sallie McFague, Elke Weber, Joan Halifax and psychologist Daniel Goleman.

During this conference, I spoke with His Holiness privately, and that intensely moving interview was one of the first I did for this book. Although our conversation took place years ago, I believe the Dalai Lama's thoughts and words are most fitting at the end of this long project. The journey reminds me of T.S. Eliot's lines in *Four Quartets*:

> We shall not cease from exploration
> And the end of all our exploring
> Will be to arrive where we started
> And know the place for the first time.[6]

His Holiness said, "The environment issue is most serious, the topmost importance. Billions of lives depend on the major rivers, which ultimately come from the Tibetan plateau. So it is very, very serious."[7] He made a surprisingly strong suggestion about Beijing, noting the political agendas revolving around Tibet should be shelved for the time being so that the international community can focus on the impact of climate change on the plateau.

"If the Chinese leaders could look at the Tibet issue more realistically, then within a few days we can solve. But once environmental damage is done, it is impossible to change. Damage has already been done there. The repercussions will remain for decades, and in some cases cannot be reversed. So the political problem can wait another five years, 10 years, 50 years. We can wait. But the environment issue can't wait. Every month some more damage is done due to mining or deforestation. It has already happened like that."

His Holiness said it is our responsibility to raise awareness in people's minds because everyone should know of this crisis, and that people are suffering. Corruption is at the root of the issue: "It is like a new disease, a cancer on the whole planet, the whole humanity. What is wrong? Not a lack of judicial system, police force or government organization, but ultimately a lack of ethics and self-discipline. We should be thinking: I am a human being. I should not do this, for my own reputation, for my own interest, my own health, my family's well-being. We have a moral responsibility to make this known."

The spiritual and secular leader talked about communicating the information frequently and clearly, saying that for 40 years he has been repeating his message of compassion. "Since 1973. I would repeat this a thousand times, seeing some affect. Whether people listen seriously or not, I continuously repeat that."

So I asked, do we simply ignore the propaganda and repeat the message? "Oh yes. Yes. Talk continuously," he said with a smile. "That is the main thing. I am always mentioning a Tibetan saying: Nine times failure, then nine times effort. This means effort, fail, again effort, again fail, again effort." He said people today want immediate results, and if we fail, they give up and stop trying, "That's wrong. That is defeat."

He punctuated his remark by pointing a finger at my forehead, almost touching my brow. And then came one of the most profound moments for me through this entire journey, through all the interviews I have subsequently done for this book. It was the emotional, straight-to-the-heart message that spun me around and sent me down a different path of understanding, connecting and communicating.

The Dalai Lama said, "I think you acknowledge sometimes the Western brain looks more sophisticated, but in Tibet we operate from the heart and this is very strong. So combine these two, Asian heart and Western mind, and then we will have real success. Real success."

His Holiness planted the seed for a different kind of book, one that would look at the causes of miscommunication, mistrust and propaganda, but also look at educating the heart. He explained that warmheartedness extends to us all, to the planet, the ecology and is at the root of solving this ethical problem. Rather than anger, fear, suspicion and distrust, we need warmheartedness.

During one of the sessions in Dharamsala, His Holiness said that warmheartedness comes from the genuine practice of love, genuine compassion, genuine friendship and a genuine concern for the well-being of others. "We must respect all different forms of life, with less concern for getting something back." Genuine friendship is not based on money, education or knowledge, and "because of human intelligence we understand the deeper meaning of reality, beyond biological factors."

The Dalai Lama's message connects with the comments of cognitive scientist George Lakoff (that facts don't change minds) and with the emotional dialogue lessons of Marshall Ganz. A search for answers in this new direction led me to interview Joel Bakan (who discussed the human impact of unfettered capitalism) and Dan Kahan (who explained how trust networks inform public opinion).

Writing *I'm Right* led to a much larger consideration about why we feel disconnected, disengaged, hopeless or frightened. Why are we gullible, and why do we fail to act? The Dalai Lama has said we are raising a generation of passive bystanders, but why is that? These questions led me to interview people such as Carol Tavris, Jason Stanley and French philosopher Bruno Latour.

"When I came from Tibet in 1959, I had a shock," the Dalai Lama told our group at the outset of the Mind and Life conference. "In Tibet, everywhere there is very clean water, clean and pure. You can drink, enjoy. Only after I came outside Tibet, was the first time I heard 'this water you cannot drink.' And I was very surprised. In Tibet, there was no such thing." He said we are all aware of issues such as this now, and we should be deeply concerned because "it is a question of survival, not of me, not of 200 people, but of nearly seven billion people."

For this reason, he said it is time to bring out the Western scientists, people with open, unbiased minds. He spoke of scientists as gurus because they occupy a position of great authority in his view. "Through awareness, not meditation, we are learning. Through the help of scientists." And he stressed their message must be constant and clear, which led me to interview experts in deep listening skills such as Otto Scharmer, social scientist Daniel Yankelovich and scenario planning guru Adam Kahane.

When the Dalai Lama explained that our problem with climate change is about ethics, I started to ponder the moral imperative: It's one thing to unknowingly harm someone, but another altogether to cause harm once you know damage is being done. There is an obligation to stop. The great tragedy of climate change is that those who will be harmed most are not those who are causing the problem.

During one of the sessions at the Dalai Lama's house, theologian Sallie McFague said consumerism is going global, becoming a major problem everywhere because of overconsumption and greed. "We pretend we can hoard and gather more and more for ourselves, never worrying about the rest. Science tells us we are interdependent and interrelated whether we like it or not, but our culture fails to accept this." She explained that happiness is found in self-emptying, not filling up with material goods, but those of us who are well-off and have benefited tremendously from market capitalism don't want to give up our privilege, "our exceptionalism."[8]

His Holiness emphasized the real enemies are ignorance, greed and lack of inner peace. "Physical things provide only physical comfort. Inner peace never comes from things. It comes from a peaceful mind, a happy marriage, a healthy family and a warm heart. These are key values. Taking care of physical comfort is just half."

He pointed out that we human beings have been blessed with a keen brain that allows us to learn from the past and anticipate the future. "Animals are just day by day, but we have this marvelous brain that thinks in 10 years, 100 years, maybe 1,000 years. We human beings have the ability to develop visions, and think long into the future, this is our special quality, a gift from God, so we must use it. If we are like animals, then there is no hope.

"We also have a wonderful memory so we can record what happened. Only human beings know how to do this, maybe angels know that too. We have the capacity, the ability, to look back several centuries, and also think into the long future. With that ability we have to make a proper plan. Make constant tireless effort."

During my time in Tibet, I realized that I have been answering David's question: I have explained how to improve communications on crucial current issues; why people are not hearing the messages; why they actively deny what they hear. On another level, I have been forced into some serious self-examination.

My work takes place in the public square and involves interaction with lots of folks around the world with whom I consult, lecture and lead projects. During the journey of writing *I'm Right*, I free-dived deeper than ever before into the realm of communication and came up almost breathless with new understandings about speaking from the heart. It's not good enough to be passionate about a subject, to feel strongly and speak loudly about it. To create powerful, persuasive narratives, our starting point must be rooted in an attitude of empathy and compassion.

We are not going to change the world by yelling at people and telling them what to do—and that doesn't mean having to compromise on what we feel is right. We can make terrible errors if we assume people just don't understand, don't have all the facts or are being apathetic; we need to recognize we can cause terrible damage and add to the confusion if we hold fast to these attitudes. We become better ambassadors for the environment, or any cause, by putting ourselves in others' shoes. The lessons in this book are about the fundamentals of human relations—rooted in strength and compassion—or as Adam Kahane said, power and love.

Toward the end of this journey, I talked to Peter Senge about the idea of keeping an open mind and an open heart. We discussed how an open will is fundamental to human communications and human interaction. We spoke about cleaning up the inner ecology along with the outer, especially as it relates to how we collaborate on problems in the environment and pollution in the public square.

Senge is an expert on social systems dynamics who understands the undercurrents at play in all of us when we push our own ideas, try to win an argument or convince somebody about something. This usually involves a pretty strong ego drive, and the ego is very sophisticated. It can disguise itself and convince us that the reason we're acting like a zealot is because we're right, we have the evidence, and we are trying to save the world. But he said we become self-aware by asking ourselves from time to time, "Am I being effective in this situation? Are my inner needs getting in the way?"

All we really ever have is our own awareness, our own experience, and we all know that we're not as effective as we could or should be because our anger sometimes gets in the way. But if we become more disciplined in developing our awareness and compassion, we are able to operate in a state of harmony, alignment and ultimately become more effective communicators.

Peter Senge illustrated his point with an artistic metaphor. "I think all great artists have a deep understanding that they're on a very personal journey, and that, paradoxically, it has nothing to do with them. Whether it's music, poetry or visual art doesn't matter. It comes through them. It doesn't come from them. There's a larger force or a larger reality that they're plugged into that is enabling their art to manifest. Artists understand that to be aware gives them a kind of a doorway into the larger reality."[9]

This paradox is very alive in a project like this book. Researching and writing it has been a deeply personal exploration, and yet the larger reality has little to do with me. When we are working with all our hearts for a cause, we are in a state of connection to something far beyond ourselves—like that night I stood on a dark Tibetan plateau and felt the stars shimmering all around me.

"The inner and the outer are dissolving, the inner and the outer start to dance," is how Senge described it. "Let's just say the boundary between the self and the larger world, the universe, has become more permeable." People talk about a calling—something you find you've just got to do—and perhaps this kind of passion shows up in our awareness when we are more connected, more in tune with some larger reality, and when we manage to connect the Western brain with the Asian heart.

Epilogue:
Hope, Compassion, and Courage

PUBLIC DISCOURSE in democracies around the world—in the United States, the United Kingdom, even Canada— have been polluted by the politics of us versus them. And as the forces of tribalism contaminate the commons, fair-minded public thinking seems to be drawing its last gasp, while respect for facts and evidence fades and the impulse to lie explodes without consequence.

Much of this is intentional. Toxic manipulation is designed by consultants, ideologues and bad actors whose strategy is simple: to divide. Propaganda campaigns described in the early chapters of this book began as backroom schemes to stir up fear, anger and division, but eventually this attack on reason took on a life of its own, fueled by the dark forces of in-group, out-group psychology that people bought into.

The democratic right to have honest, public conversations about our collective concerns is a precious gift, and the quality of public discourse matters. But the warlike approach of some has damaged that ability and polluted the commons with unyielding one-sidedness and demonization of opposing views. Collective problems seem unsolvable when they are defined by these extreme polarized points of view. The broader public disengages.

When we started DeSmogBlog in 2005, I was naïve about the scope and nature of propaganda. I thought of disinformation campaigns as being intentionally crafted to persuade the public that climate change was a hoax.

It's true, of course, that propaganda spreads lies and disinformation, but persuasion is not its real power. Back then I didn't fully understand the central, corrosive role of ideology and the psychology of teams. Over the last decade, I've learned that campaigns such as Foreign Funded Radicals and Ethical Oil were designed to create discord and confusion by creating division. Disinformation was merely the nudge and the self-justification.

Although the scale and content are different, the same holds true of the Brexit and Trump presidential campaign strategies, which share age-old propaganda techniques of relentless ad hominem attacks on out-groups, attacks that deepen fear, anger and division. Whether we're talking about foreign funded radicals, asylum seekers from Central America or people fleeing the drought and violence of North Africa—it's the same. Bad actors stir up fake threats and ugly feelings so voters will support flawed public policy decisions, and to create scapegoats of groups that deserve our support, not demonization.

Loss of faith in public discourse is the outcome. Misinformation is not at the toxic heart of propaganda. Tribalism is. It results in that deep us-versus-them divide that inoculates people against any evidence that challenges the beliefs of their team. Objective facts and collective reasoning vanish in a social pathology that predisposes us to being misled.

Genuine democratic discourse requires engagement in a healthy public square, and for that we need to defuse polarizing propaganda and create conditions that allow reasonable conversations, whether about the environment or social justice. We need to become savvier about how propaganda works, not only because we don't want to become its victim, but also because we don't want to inadvertently contribute to its dark divisive purpose, which hot-headed, knee-jerk response risks doing.

It's painful to watch propaganda derail efforts to address important environmental or social justice issues and hard not to get riled up. When we become angry about this sleight of hand, we get motivated, which is good. But the goal should be a proper sense of public outrage without stirring up a more toxic and hyper-polarized ruckus that amplifies public division and drives us into gridlock.

It reminds me of George Bernard Shaw's advice about never wrestling with a pig. George Orwell thought the same: "One defeats the fanatic precisely by not being a fanatic oneself."

I believe we put fair-mindedness and understanding at risk if we ignore this advice.

My education regarding polluted public discourse didn't stop after this book's release in 2016, and I anticipate it will be a lifelong exploration. Since the book came out, I have done countless media interviews and lectures, which raised many more questions.

How we find the balance between advocacy and collaboration is a complicated undertaking. When we look at existential crises such as climate change, it is clear we need more people paying attention and demanding change. For that to occur, we need advocacy, strong advocacy. But if we want sustainable change, we also need to steer clear of the gridlock of tribalism.

At every talk, people were deeply touched by the advice in the book, and I was constantly reminded of Karen Armstrong's statement about the golden rule: "Look into your own heart, discover what gives you pain, and refuse under any circumstances whatsoever to inflict that pain on anyone else. Never treat others as you would not like to be treated yourself."

We must speak up against injustice but not in a way that causes more hatred, "and to be effective you must ask yourself, are your actions about your ego and punishing your opponent or are they about real change?"

I would mention how Jason Stanley warned that we too could

unknowingly be under the influence of bias, but most importantly that we need to heed the advice of Thich Nhat Hạnh to "speak the truth, but not to punish" and the Dalai Lama's guidance about the need for compassion.

The audience was often divided on this advice as well as the causes of the problem. Some saw this as well-meaning but ultimately a risky strategy that would undermine efforts to change our environmentally destructive ways. Some suggested it's not polarization, it's corruption; some believe it's not polarization, it's indifference, and we need more polarization to get public attention. Still others felt the problem is not outrage, but a lack of outrage.

One exchange went something like this, when I said: "It seemed to work for Martin Luther King," the response was: "It likely wouldn't have worked without the militant threat of Malcom X lurking in the background."

There is no straightforward answer to how we raise our voice in the exercise our democratic responsibilities.

My Breakfast with Alex and Miles

In June 2017, I had breakfast with friends Alex Himelfarb and Miles Richardson in Toronto before a David Suzuki Foundation Board meeting.[1] The conversation started with a discussion of my book and the idea that we should tread lightly around polarization because if we don't, we risk inadvertently energizing opposition from the other side and muddying the story we are trying to tell.

Miles questioned this saying there is evil in the world, hate and corruption so deep and toxic that some people cannot be reached. Alex concurred and added we cannot be looking for some middle-ground with people who are burning crosses or painting swastikas on mosques. He said flatly: "In our attempt to be fair-minded and reasonable, we shouldn't do anything that normalizes the abnormal or validates hate."

Alex and I have discussed this point since I was on a Chicago NPR show. He said the problem, as my interviewer implied, runs deep. All around the globe, we are seeing the rise of demagogues who divide us into tribes: Christians versus Muslims, hardworking families versus self-serving elites, white versus black. When leadership should be about bringing people together, they seek to win by exploiting our fears and turning one against the other, often scapegoating the most vulnerable. They attack the institutions that promote any sense of common citizenship. Indeed, they attack reality itself, obliterating the distinction between fact and fiction. There are no more lies, just alternative facts. We are seeing all this play out now, in real time, yet again, unleashing very dark forces of hate in its various guises: white supremacy, racism, sexism, religious bigotry, fear of immigrants and refugees, contempt for the poor.

Alex said there is no common cause to be found with divisiveness, hate and scapegoating. These must be met with unequivocal opposition. At the same time, we cannot define ourselves solely in terms of opposition. Rather, we need to offer a progressive alternative that unites, that enables a "movement" of movements. We need a new common sense that recognizes that competition does not automatically trump cooperation, that private doesn't trump public, that extreme individualism and consumerism provides only the illusion of freedom, that we are stronger together.

The priority must be to build a movement not only to fight the forces of darkness, but also to reshape politics and influence governments to take steps necessary to rebuild trust, to fight inequality, attack climate change, reverse the decline in nature and enhance democracy, he continued.

Alex and I strongly agree about not wasting time trying to find common ground with extremists.

We also agree we must defend the institutions that work to mediate competing versions of the truth—through science, universities, the media, courts and the arts—and we need to help people better understand the techniques of propaganda and media manipulation so they are equipped to handle the rise of demagogues.

Miles went on to caution against overstating the negative role of tribalism. He said we need to recognize what we have in common—we are all human, we are all social beings—and that bonding with each other is a social good. We have differences in beliefs and values, but we should celebrate those differences.

Controversy and differences are inevitable, and we should embrace them. First Nations communities, for instance, take the edge off political acrimony by holding ceremonies that remind people we are all in this together.

Miles spoke about the importance of these values in Canada and referred me to a speech given by Rosalie Abella who sits on the Supreme Court of Canada. She said: "Integration based on difference, equality based on inclusion despite difference, and compassion based on respect and fairness: These are the principles that now form the moral core of Canadian national values, the values that have made us the most successful practitioners of multiculturalism in the world, and the values that make our national justice context democratically vibrant and principled."[2]

This conversation with Alex and Miles, and others like it, made me realize I needed to do a better job of explaining the need for balance between advocacy and collaboration.

I learned from David Suzuki never to be afraid of controversy when speaking the truth, or fighting injustice. We need more passionate public debate, not less, and the truth on its own can be polarizing for groups on the wrong side of an issue.

As Marshall Ganz explained, taking a conciliatory stance in the face of injustice compromises the "adversarial mechanisms" that citizens rely on to find truth. We live in a democracy where public figures are expected to raise the level of debate in search of truth, but not to crush or demonize someone who disagrees with them.

When I chaired the David Suzuki Foundation, I asked Adam Kahane[3] to speak to our retreat at Brew Creek Centre in Whistler. During his talk to our board, he got into a brief but heated disagreement with David Suzuki who argued that in some cases dialogue is a waste of time. David spoke about the CEO of a consortium of companies who wanted to discuss international criticism of the Alberta oil sands regarding its environmental performance.

David said he would be willing to work with the CEO if he would first agree to certain basic principles: that we are all animals and that we need clean air, clean water, clean soil, clean energy and biodiversity. The CEO declined. Adam challenged Suzuki on this, saying that seeking such an agreement in advance of a dialogue was unreasonable and unproductive.

Adam recently told me this exchange had a big impact on him. Initially, he couldn't make this new idea fit into his frame of collaboration so it stayed with him as an unresolved tension. He didn't dismiss the argument because he holds David in such high esteem.

And gradually this principle seemed more important and altered Adam's thinking about how to approach advocacy, conflict and dialogue, and this exchange became an important section of his new book, *Collaborating with the Enemy: How to Work with People You Don't Agree with or Like or Trust.*[4]

Adam writes: "I could now see that engaging and asserting were complementary rather than opposing ways to make progress on complex challenges, and that both were legitimate and necessary."

If we suppress assertion and advocacy, in an effort to engage with an opponent, "we will suffocate the social system we are working with," and we end up with feeble collaboration. He is now convinced that healthy collaboration needs to include "vigorous fighting."

Rather than focusing on finding harmony when dealing with people who hold radically conflicting opinions, we can embrace both conflict and connection, he said. "If we stretch beyond our conventional, comfortable, habitual approach to collaboration we can be more successful more often, and don't have to default to polarization, and worsen the situation."

He recently told me it's wrong to think we can only collaborate successfully by first forging harmonious teams that have reached agreement on where they're going, how to get there, or who needs to do what.

This discussion got me thinking about how my own attitudes have evolved while searching for better ways to deal with antagonists of all kinds, including the anti-climate science crowd. Adam's new book reinforces my belief that influencing public opinion and public policy requires both advocacy and collaboration—although I've learned that both have their limits.

Advocates tend to overplay their hands and unintentionally strengthen the resistance they work so hard to overcome. Collaboration, on the other hand, can create a false equivalence that undermines concerns that arise from real science, when an opposing viewpoint that's often ideological is presented as alternative science when clearly it is not.

A perfect example of this is the decades-old debate between genuine climate scientists and climate change deniers working for industry-funded, right wing think tanks. Any advocacy to counteract alarming environmental problems such as climate change, marine ecosystem destruction or species extinction is by its nature difficult and adversarial.

I told Adam it's hard to collaborate with someone who says climate scientists have a political agenda or it is a hoax perpetrated by the Chinese, because engaging in such a specious argument only drags the conversation down to a ludicrous level. I also said when it comes to climate change, dialogue often fails, but lessons from the civil rights movement give us hope. They tell us that people who meet with resistance can eventually see results if they keep demanding it and never give up. On the other hand, I believe our social capacity for pluralism and diversity will either empower or prevent us from emerging from the climate crisis.

Let's face it, we are not going to solve environmental crises like climate change if sensible public policies are repealed every time a right wing government is elected. Being right on the science or righteous on the issues is not enough. We need to develop our ability to work with the enemy.

We should strive to be as good at respectful collaboration as we are at advocacy, and give 100 percent effort to both speaking the truth and respecting others, even when we feel they don't deserve it. And this is true in personal relationships too.

When Thich Nhat Hanh advised me to "Speak the truth, but not to punish," he wasn't saying be polite and courteous. His advice was much more than that. He challenged me to take responsibility, share the true facts, but when I do, even in the face of willful ignorance and corruption, not to satisfy my anger but rather shed light and show a way out of a bad situation.

Right-minded people get angry at the wrongdoing and environmental destruction they see around us, and rightly so. When I see industry front groups and ideologues pushing campaigns designed to dupe the public about environmental destruction, it makes me furious. I'm a bit reactive, but I've learned that being furious is not a great communications strategy. Of course, we never want to meet dead wrong or evil halfway, just to get along with people. Facts, science and what's right do matter even if some people strongly disagree.

Much of the advice in this book is about opening up public spaces that have been closed by fear, anger and propaganda. If we don't sharpen our empathy, we won't reopen these spaces and we will be waiting a long time to deal with problems like climate change. I assume this is why the Dalai Lama nudges us towards warmheartedness. Without compassion and deep listening, we will have no change. So it's our choice. It's not easy to treat an idiot, or someone whose views we consider vile, with compassion, but it is certainly doable. Speak the truth, but not to punish is advice for opening up public spaces to frank and passionate public conversations.

On Deep Listening

When I was on a panel of authors at the Wordfest writers' conference in Calgary, a young woman asked me a sensitive personal question. She had just received her PhD in marine biology and as an environmental scientist was concerned about climate change. Her mother, also a scientist, was owner of a large environmental consulting company in Alberta. The two were at loggerheads because her mother was a climate change denier.

The mother-daughter relationship deteriorated to the point where the young woman said they could barely speak to each other. She couldn't believe her mother could hold such anti-science views, and that she should know better.

I remember feeling the weight of her question, the responsibility, as it was so personal and important to her peace of mind. I gave her my best answer, but I have continued to think about it ever since. I believe the Dalai Lama has the best solution. He believes the real troublemakers are our destructive emotions, and we have to deal with these emotions if we are to come to grips with a dilemma like this.

How do we do this? Through warmheartedness. This wisdom nudges us toward understanding how communication works in the midst of conflict.

During an intense conflict, if we try to convince people to think like we do, if we imply we are right and they are wrong, or worse, that we are right and they are idiots, they aren't likely to change their minds. They will dig in deeper, regardless of the facts. Sustainable change happens when both sides see some benefit from the outcome and feel they have been treated with respect.

In highly polarized public discourse, direct attacks on an opponent's point of view are often ineffective. It paints people into a corner. It is usually better to explore ways to drain some of the emotion and passion in the conversation.

Real communication starts when we stop talking and start listening. Not long after I met Thich Nhat Hanh, I heard him interviewed by Oprah, and he explained the goal of deep listening is to relieve another's suffering, anxiety, anger and despair. He advised us to listen with one purpose: to help the other person empty their heart.

If the other person says things that are mistaken or bitter, don't react. Wait for another time to correct misperceptions. Deep listening can transform and heal broken relationships because fear, anger and despair frequently spring from our mistaken perceptions of others and us. This is often the foundation of conflict. When practicing deep listening, you tell the person you know they are not happy with you; that you haven't understood their concerns or point of view; you haven't listened, and that's not your intention now, because you want to understand.

If they believe you are sincere, they may open up and tell you what's on their mind. And then you listen, just listen. During this process, we can learn about our own perception as well as the perceptions of others, said the monk, and we can remove conflict and discord. This is where real communication begins.

From the Heart

I recently spent a day with Paul Slovic,[5] who echoed the advice of Thich Nhat Hanh on deep listening, which is a central theme of this book. Slovic reminded me of another theme: That when having public conversations about environmental risk, we need to speak to people's feelings.

A lot of the environmental problems we face today require us to influence or change people, and facts alone won't do this. Public figures need to participate in emotional dialogue if they want to touch people. By telling stories from the heart, stories about values that embrace diversity and pluralism, stories about us, we find common ground. We add feeling and deeper meaning to public conversations.

Misreading public emotions intensifies the conflict and miscommunication we witness in so many public disputes. It pollutes the public square. It's difficult to be seen as authentic in an argument if you don't appreciate what Slovic calls the "whisper of emotion," which is the good or bad feeling, the gut instinct that helps people make decisions.

The emotional dialogue that is taking place around today's risk issues—such as climate change or immigration—is often unconscious. We need to be more conscious of these feelings, bring them to the surface so narratives of fear, anger and intolerance are replaced by stories of hope, compassion and courage. There is nothing wrong with a hard-hitting fight against corruption, but communication will fail unless we have a two-way process: a dialogue of the heart where both sides have something worthwhile to contribute, each side respects the other's views in a story of us that as Alex Himelfarb says, "puts people and the planet first."

Notes

Prologue: A Beginner's Mind

1. Shunryu Suzuki. *Zen Mind, Beginner's Mind*. New York: Weatherhill, 1970.
2. Michael Lewis. *The Undoing Project: A Friendship That Changed Our Minds*. W. W. Norton, 2016.
3. Otto Scharmer, personal communication.
4. Dan Kahan, personal communication.
5. *DeSmog Blog*. desmogblog.com.
6. James Hoggan and Richard Littlemore. *Climate Cover-Up: The Crusade to Deny Global Warming*. Greystone, 2009.
7. Deborah Tannen, personal communication.
8. "Basques Mourn Symbolic Oak Tree." *BBC News*, April 22, 2004. [online.] [cited: December 16, 2015.] news.bbc.co.uk/2/hi/europe/3649397.stm.

Chapter 1: Like Ships in the Night

1. Viewpoint Learning. "About Us: Daniel Yankelovich." [online]. [cited October 7, 2015]. viewpointlearning.com/about-us/who-we-are/daniel-yankelovich/.
2. Viewpoint Learning. "About Us: Steven Rosell." [online]. [cited October 7, 2015]. viewpointlearning.com/about-us/who-we-are/steven-rosell/.
3. James Hoggan and Richard Littlemore. *Climate Cover-Up: The Crusade to Deny Global Warming*. Greystone, 2009.
4. Source for quotations from Steve Rosell and Daniel Yankelovich, personal communication.
5. Daniel Yankelovich. "Across the Red-blue Divide: How to Start a Conversation." *Christian Science Monitor*, October 15, 2004. [online]. [cited October 8, 2015]. csmonitor.com/2004/1015/p10s02-coop.html.

Chapter 2: The Advocacy Trap

1. Source for all quotations from Roger Conner, personal communication.
2. Roger Conner. "Strategy and Stance: A Framework for Understanding Public Advocacy." *SSRN Electronic Journal* #11 (2005). [online]. [cited October 20, 2015]. researchgate.net/publication/228195710 _Strategy_and_Stance_A_Framework_for_Understanding_Public _Advocacy.

Chapter 3: Mistakes Were Made (But Not by Me)

1. David Brooks. *The Social Animal: The Hidden Sources of Love, Character, and Achievement*. Random House, 2012.
2. Carol Tavris and Elliot Aronson. *Mistakes Were Made (But Not by Me): Why We Justify Foolish Beliefs, Bad Decisions and Hurtful Acts*, 2nd rev. ed. Pinter & Martin, 2013.
3. Source for quotations from Carol Tavris, personal communication.
4. Ifat Maoz, Andrew Ward, Michael Katz and Lee Ross. "Reactive Devaluation of an 'Israeli' vs. 'Palestinian' Peace Proposal." *Journal of Conflict Resolution*, 46 (4) (2002), pp. 515-546. [online]. [cited: November 28, 2015]. jcr.sagepub.com/content/46/4/515.

Chapter 4: Morality Binds and Blinds

1. Source for all quotations from Jonathan Haidt, personal communication.
2. Jesse Graham, Brian A. Nosek and Jonathan Haidt. "The Moral Stereotypes of Liberals and Conservatives: Exaggeration of Differences across the Political Spectrum." *PLoS ONE*, 7 (12) (2012). [online]. [cited: November 28, 2015]. doi:10.1371/journal.pone.0050092; journals.plos.org/plosone/article?id=10.1371/journal.pone.0050092. You can participate in their research and find out more about your own moral foundations at: yourmorals.org.
3. Jonathan Haidt. "The Moral Roots of Liberals and Conservatives." TED talk, March 2008. [online]. [cited October 14, 2015]. ted.com /talks/jonathan_haidt_on_the_moral_mind.
4. Jonathan Haidt. *The Righteous Mind: Why Good People Are Divided by Politics and Religion*. Vintage, 2013.
5. Gary Marcus. *The Birth of the Mind: How a Tiny Number of Genes Creates the Complexity of Human Thought*. Basic Books, 2004, p. 34.
6. Jesse Graham et al. "Moral Foundations Theory: The Pragmatic Validity of Moral Pluralism." Advances in Experimental Social Psychology,

47 (2013), pp. 55–130. [online]. [cited: November 28, 2015]. bcf.usc.edu
/~jessegra/papers/GHKMIWD.inpress.MFT.AESP.pdf.

7. Matthew 7:3-5, Luke 6:41-42.

Chapter 5: Why We Want to Be Misled

1. Dan M. Kahan, Hank Jenkins-Smith and Donald Braman. "Cultural
   Cognition of Scientific Consensus." *Journal of Risk Research*, 14 (2)
   (2011), pp. 147–174. [online]. [cited November 29, 2015]. dx.doi.org/10
   .2139/ssrn.1549444.

2. Source for quotations from Dan Kahan, personal communication.

3. Dan M. Kahan, Ellen Peters, Erica Dawson and Paul Slovic. "Motivated Numeracy and Enlightened Self-Government." Yale Law
   School, Public Law Working Paper #307, September 3, 2013. [online].
   [cited October 15, 2015]. culturalcognition.net/browse-papers
   /motivated-numeracy-and-enlightened-self-government.html.

4. Dan M. Kahan et al. "Biased Assimilation, Polarization, and Cultural
   Credibility: An Experimental Study of Nanotechnology Risk Perceptions." *Harvard Law School Program* on *Risk Regulation*, Research
   Paper #08-25 (2008). [online.] [cited: November 30, 2015.] dx.doi.org
   /10.2139/ssrn.1090044.

5. Dan M. Kahan et al. "The Polarizing Impact of Science Literacy
   and Numeracy on Perceived Climate Change Risks." *Nature Climate
   Change*, 2 (2012), pp. 732–735. [online]. [cited October 15, 2015].
   nature.com/nclimate/journal/v2/n10/full/nclimate1547.html.

6. Dan M. Kahan, Hank Jenkins-Smith and Donald Braman. "Cultural
   Cognition of Scientific Consensus." *Journal of Risk Research*, 14 (2)
   (2011), pp. 147–174. [online]. [cited November 29, 2015]. dx.doi.org/10
   .2139/ssrn.1549444.

Chapter 6: Facts Are Not Enough

1. Source for quotations from George Lakoff, personal communication.

2. John Harding. "10 Million Scallops Are Dead: Qualicum Company
   Lays Off Staff." *Parksville Qualicum Beach News*, February 25, 2014.
   [online]. [cited October 15, 2015]. pqbnews.com/news/247092381.html
   ?mobile=true.

3. Damian Carrington. "Q&A: Climategate." *The Guardian*, November 22, 2011. [online]. [cited October 15, 2015]. theguardian.com
   /environment/2010/jul/07/climate-emails-question-answer.

4. George Lakoff. *Don't Think of an Elephant! Know Your Values and
   Frame the Debate*. Chelsea Green, 2004, p. 19.

5. George Lakoff. *Whose Freedom?: The Battle Over America's Most Important Idea*. Picador, 2007, p. 16.

Chapter 7: Matters of Concern

1. Source for quotations from Bruno Latour, personal communication.
2. Bruno Latour: *Pandora's Hope: Essays on the Reality of Science Studies*. Harvard, 1999; *We Have Never Been Modern*. Harvard, 1993; *Science in Action: How to Follow Scientists and Engineers Through Society*. Harvard, 1988; *Politics of Nature: How to Bring the Sciences into Democracy*. Harvard, 2004; Bruno Latour and Steve Woolgar. *Laboratory Life: The Construction of Scientific Facts*. Princeton, 1986;
3. Holberg Prize website. *Bruno Latour Wins the 2013 Holberg Prize*. [online]. [cited October 16, 2015]. holbergprisen.no/en/holberg-prize-2013.html.
4. Bruno Latour. "From Realpolitik to Dingpolitik: An Introduction to Making Things Public." *Pavilion Journal for Politics and Culture*, no. 15 (2010), [online]. [cited October 16, 2015]. pavilionmagazine.org/bruno-latour-from-realpolitik-to-dingpolitik-or-how-to-make-things-public/.
5. Ibid.
6. Clive Hamilton. *Requiem for a Species: Why We Resist the Truth About Climate Change*. Earthscan, 2010.
7. Walter Lippmann. *The Phantom Public*. Transaction, 1993.
8. Robert Proctor and Londa Schiebinger, eds. *Agnotology: The Making and Unmaking of Ignorance*. Stanford, 2008.

Chapter 8: The Self-regulating Psychopath

1. Joel Bakan. *The Corporation: The Pathological Pursuit of Profit and Power*. Free Press, 2005.
2. *The Corporation*, directed by Mark Achbar and Jennifer Abbott. Zeitgeist Films, 2005, DVD.
3. Source for quotations from Joel Bakan and Noam Chomsky, personal communication.
4. Leo E. Strine Jr. "The Dangers of Denial: The Need for a Clear-eyed Understanding of the Power and Accountability Structure Established by the Delaware General Corporation Law." *Wake Forest Law Review*. Inst for Law & Econ Research Paper #15-08 (2015). [online]. [cited December 3, 2015]. ssrn.com/abstract=2576389.
5. Judith Lavoie. "Enbridge Depiction of Clear Tanker Route Sparks

Outrage." Canadian Press, August 15, 2012. [online]. [cited October 20, 2015]. bc.ctvnews.ca/enbridge-depiction-of-clear-tanker-route-sparks-outrage-1.916234; Carol Linnitt. "LEAKED: Enbridge's New Northern Gateway Pipeline Ad Campaign 'Open to Better.'" *DeSmogBlog*, October 1, 2013. [online]. [cited October 20, 2015]. desmog.ca/2013/10/01/leaked-enbridge-s-new-northern-gateway-pipeline-ad-campaign-open-better.

6. American Legislative Exchange Council website. [online]. [cited October 20, 2015]. alec.org/.

Chapter 9: Steve Bannon's Full-service Propaganda Machine

1. Carole Cadwalladr. "Google Is Not 'Just' a Platform. It Frames, Shapes and Distorts How We See the World." *The Guardian*, December 11, 2016. theguardian.com/commentisfree/2016/dec/11/google-frames-shapes-and-distorts-how-we-see-world.

2. Elizabeth Denham, *Democracy Disrupted? Personal Information and Political Influence*. Information Commissioner's Office, London, July 11, 2018. ico.org.uk/media/action-weve-taken/2259369/democracy-disrupted-110718.pdf.

3. Carole Cadwalladr, "Elizabeth Denham: 'Data Crimes Are Real Crimes'"; Interview, *The Guardian*, July 15, 2018.

4. *Findings, Recommendations and Actions from ICO Investigation into Data Analytics in Political Campaigns*, July 10, 2018. ico.org.uk/about-the-ico/news-and-events/news-and-blogs/2018/07/findings-recommendations-and-actions-from-ico-investigation-into-data-analytics-in-political-campaigns/.

5. Elizabeth Denham, *Investigation into the Use of Data Analytics in Political Campaigns: A Report to Parliament*. Information Commissioner's Office, London, November 6, 2018, p. 4. ico.org.uk/media/action-weve-taken/2260271/investigation-into-the-use-of-data-analytics-in-political-campaigns-final-20181105.pdf.

6. Ibid.

7. Ibid., p. 19.

8. Ibid., p. 6.

9. Ibid.

10. Carole Cadwalladr, "The Cambridge Analytica Files: I Made Steve Bannon's Psychological Warfare Tool, Meet the Data War Whistleblower." Interview with Christopher Wylie. *The Guardian*, March 18,

2018. theguardian.com/news/2018/mar/17/data-war-whistleblower
-christopher-wylie-facebook-nix-bannon-trump.

11. Ibid.

12. Emma Briant, "I've Seen Inside the Digital Propaganda Machine.
And It's Dark in There." *The Guardian*, April 20, 2018. theguardian
.com/commentisfree/2018/apr/20/cambridge-analytica-propaganda
-machine.

13. Carole Cadwalladr. *The Guardian*, November 26, 2018.

14. *BBC News*, March 18, 2018, p. 106. The info was taken from a series of
meetings filmed at London hotels over four months, between November 2017 and January 2018, by an undercover reporter for Channel 4
News who posed as a fixer for a wealthy client hoping to get candidates elected in Sri Lanka.

15. Jaron Lanier. *Ten Arguments for Deleting Your Social Media Accounts
Right Now*. Henry Holt, 2018.

16. Carole Cadwalladr. "Google, Democracy and the Truth About
Internet Search." *The Guardian*, December 4, 2016.

17. Jaron Lanier. *Ten Arguments for Deleting Your Social Media Accounts
Right Now*. Henry Holt, 2018.

18. All quotes by Zeynep Tufekci are from "YouTube, the Great Radical-
izer." *New York Times*, March 10, 2018 and a TED talk on October 27,
2017.

19. Jack Nicas. "How YouTube Drives People to the Internet's Darkest
Corners." *Wall Street Journal*, February 7, 2018.

20. Karsten Müller and Carlo Schwarz, "Fanning the Flames of Hate:
Social Media and Hate Crime." University of Warwick study, *Social
Science Research Network* (SSRN). November 30 2018.

21. "Facebook Hate Speech Spiked in Myanmar During Rohingya Crisis."
The Guardian, online, April 3, 2018. bgr.in/news/facebook-hate-speech
-spiked-in-myanmar-during-rohingya-crisis/.

Chapter 10: A Case Study: Foreign-funded Radicals

1. World Meteorological Organization. "WMO: 2015 Likely to be
Warmest on Record, 2011-2015 Warmest Five-Year Period." Press
Release, November 25, 2015. [online]. [cited January 6, 2016].
wmo.int/media/content/wmo-2015-likely-be-warmest-record-2011
-2015-warmest-five-year-period.

2. Chris Cesare. "California Snowpack Lowest in Past 500 Years."
Nature News, 2015. [online]. [cited January 6, 2016]. nature.com/news
/california-snowpack-lowest-in-past-500-years-1.18345.

3. Rohit Inani. "More Than 2,300 People Have Now Died in India's Heat Wave." *Time*, June 2, 2015. [online]. [cited January 6, 2016]. time.com/3904590/india-heatwave-monsoon-delayed-weather -climate-change.

4. Kamran Haider and Khurrum Anis. "Heat Wave Death Toll Rises to 2,000 in Pakistan's Financial Hub." *Bloomberg*, June 23, 2015. [online]. [cited January 6, 2016]. bloomberg.com/news/articles/2015-06-24 /heat-wave-death-toll-rises-to-2-000-in-pakistan-s-financial-hub.

5. NOAA National Centers for Environmental Information. "NOAA National Centers for Environmental Information, Global Analysis for November 2015." December 2015. [online]. [cited January 6, 2016]. ncdc.noaa.gov/sotc/global/201511.

6. World Meteorological Organization. "Hurricane Patricia Is Strongest Recorded in Eastern North Pacific." *WMO News*, October 23, 2015. [online]. [cited January 6, 2016]. wmo.int/media/content/hurricane -patricia-strongest-recorded-eastern-north-pacific.

7. Alexandra Witze. "Corals Worldwide Hit by Bleaching." *Nature News*, October 8, 2015. [online]. [cited January 6, 2016]. nature.com/news /corals-worldwide-hit-by-bleaching-1.18527.

8. *Wildfire Today*, October 26, 2018.

9. CBC's *Power & Politics with Evan Solomon*, January 11, 2012. "Pipeline Debate Heats Up." (2012) [online.] [cited December 29, 2015.] cbc.ca /player/play/2186004232.

10. *CTV's Question Period*, January 8, 2012. "Kathryn Marshall Debates Northern Gateway." [online]. [cited December 29, 2015]. youtu.be /KvIx_wimOlI.

11. Debates of the Senate, 41st Parl, 1st Sess, 148 (54) (February 28, 2012) at 1710 (Nicole Eaton). [online]. [cited October 27, 2015]. parl.gc.ca /Content/Sen/Chamber/411/Debates/054db_2012-02-28-e.htm#70.

12. Canadian Press. "Environmental Charities Don't Top List of Foreign-funded Groups." *CBC News*, May 10, 2012. [online]. [cited October 20, 2015]. cbc.ca/news/politics/environmental-charities-don-t-top-list-of -foreign-funded-groups-1.1247417.

13. Canadian Press. "Canadian Charities in Limbo as Tax Audits Widen to New Groups." *CBC News*, July 10, 2014. [online]. [cited October 20, 2015]. cbc.ca/news/politics/canadian-charities-in-limbo-as-tax-audits -widen-to-new-groups-1.2703177.

14. *Ottawa Citizen*, March 14, 2012. o.canada.com/news/senators-call -foundations-anti-canadian-question-if-environmental-groups-could -take-money-from-terrorists.

15. *The Big Chill: Silencing Public Interest Science, A Survey*. Professional Institute of the Public Service of Canada, n.d. [online]. [cited October 20, 2015]. bigchill.en.pdf.

16. The author's Sustainability Research Initiative surveyed 10,000 Canadians on their opinions. Eighty percent rated environmental sustainability as a top or high priority. Hoggan website. "Sustainability Research." [online]. [cited December 28, 2015]. hoggan.com /Sustainability-Research.

17. Joanne Richard. "Pumping Up the Volume: Sun News Presents Ezra Levant." *Calgary Sun*, December 26, 2011. Republished by ezralevant .com. [online]. [cited December 29, 2015]. ezralevant.com/pumping _up_the_volume.

18. Ezra Levant. *Ethical Oil: The Case for Canada's Oil Sands*. McClelland and Stewart, 2010, pp. 233–234.

19. CBC's *Power & Politics with Evan Solomon*, January 11, 2012.

20. See a website by the same name. [online]. [cited October 21, 2015]. exxonhatesyourchildren.com/learnmore.html.

21. Ezralevant.com. "Ethical Oil in the Globe and Mail Again." January 15, 2011. [online]. [cited December 29, 2015]. ezralevant.com/ethical _oil_in_the_globe_and_m/.

22. Conference Board of Canada. *Environment*. [online]. [cited October 21, 2015]. conferenceboard.ca/hcp/details/environment.aspx.

23. World Wildlife Fund. "Canada Ranked Last in G8 on Climate Action." July, 2009. [online.] [cited December 29, 2015.] wwf.ca /newsroom/?4000.

24. Ramez Naam. "Arctic Sea Ice: What, Why and What Next?" *Scientific American Blog*, September 21, 2012. [online]. [cited December 29, 2015]. blogs.scientificamerican.com/guest-blog/arctic-sea-ice-what -why-and-what-next/.

25. Bill C-38, Jobs, Growth and Long-term Prosperity Act, 1st Sess., 41st Parl, 2012 (as amended 24 September 2014). [online]. [cited October 27, 2015]. canlii.ca/t/8qvz.

26. Jodi Stark. "Forty Per Cent of Australian Oceans Protected: What About Canada?" *David Suzuki Foundation Blog*, June 14, 2012. [online]. [cited December 29, 2015]. davidsuzuki.org/blogs/healthy-oceans -blog/2012/06/australia-protects-40-per-cent/.

27. Jesse Coleman. "LEAKED: What You Should Know About Edelman and TransCanada's Attack Plan." *Greenpeace Blog*, November 14, 2014. [online]. [cited December 29, 2015]. greenpeace.org/usa/leaked -edelman-transcanadas-pr-attack-plan/.

28. Shawn McCarthy. "Greenpeace Sees Dirty Tricks in PR Firms TransCanada Plan." *Globe and Mail*, November 17, 2014. [online]. [cited December 29, 2015]. theglobeandmail.com/report-on-business /industry-news/energy-and-resources/greenpeace-sees-dirty-tricks -in-pr-firms-transcanada-plan/article21630761/.

29. Edelman. "TC Energy East: Grassroots Advocacy Vision Document." May 15, 2014. [online]. [cited December 29, 2015]. assets.document cloud.org/documents/1362369/tc-energy-east-grassroots-advocacy -vision-document.pdf.

30. Richard Edelman. "A Commitment." *Edelman 6 A.M. Blog*, October 16, 2006. edelman.com/p/6-a-m/a-commitment/; Pallavi Gogoi. "Wal-Mart's Jim and Laura: The Real Story." *Bloomberg Business*, October 9, 2006. bloomberg.com/bw/stories/2006-10-09/wal-marts -jim-and-laura-the-real-storybusinessweek-business-news-stock -market-and-financial-advice: Both [online]. [cited December 29, 2015].

31. Brendan DeMelle. "Lobbyists for Big Oil Organizing Most 'Grassroots' 'Energy Citizens' Rallies." *DeSmogBlog*, August 24, 2009. [online]. [cited October 21, 2015]. desmogblog.com/directory/vocabulary/4451.

32. Kate Sheppard. "Here's What Big Oil Has in the Pipes If Keystone Fails." *HuffingtonPost*, November 17, 2014. [online]. [cited December 29, 2015]. huffingtonpost.com/2014/11/17/transcanada-pipeline-oil_n _6174570.html.

33. Edward Walker. *Grassroots for Hire: Public Affairs Consultants in American Democracy*. Cambridge University Press, 2014.

34. Eric Lipton. "Hard-Nosed Advice from Veteran Lobbyist: 'Win Ugly or Lose Pretty': Richard Berman Energy Industry Talk Secretly Taped." *New York Times*, October 30, 2014. [online]. [cited October 21, 2015]. nytimes.com/2014/10/31/us/politics/pr-executives-western -energy-alliance-speech-taped.html?_r=0.

35. James Hoggan and Richard Littlemore. *Climate Cover-Up: The Crusade to Deny Global Warming*. Greystone, 2009.

36. Christopher Stevens. "The Pea-Souper That Killed 12,000: How the Great Smog Choked London 60 Years Ago This Week." *The Daily Mail*, December 6, 2012. [online]. [cited December 29, 2015]. dailymail.co.uk/news/article-2243732/Pea-souper-killed-12-000-So -black-screen-cinemas-So-suffocatingly-lethal-ran-coffins-How-Great -Smog-choked-London-60-years-ago-week.html#ixzz3vlK4wtBV.

37. This is down from 24,000 deaths in 2004 due to stricter regulations and enforcement: Clean Air Task Force. "Death and Disease from

Power Plants." 2010. [online]. [cited December 29, 2015]. catf.us/fossil /problems/power_plants/.

38. Union of Concerned Scientists. "Environmental Impacts of Coal Power: Air Pollution." [online]. [cited December 29, 2015]. ucsusa.org /clean_energy/coalvswind/c02c.html#.VoMxtVL9BUE.

39. Richard Conniff. "The Myth of Clean Coal." *Yale Environment 360*, June 3, 2008. [online]. [cited December 29, 2015]. e360.yale.edu /feature/the_myth_of_clean_coal/2014/.

40. Brendan DeMelle. "ACCCE Coal Lobby Drops Bonner & Associates Over Forged Letters." *DeSmogBlog*, August 21, 2009. [online]. [cited October 22, 2015]. desmogblog.com/accce-coal-lobby-drops-bonner -associates-over-forged-letters.

Chapter 11: Assault on Democracy

1. Source for quotations from Alex Himelfarb, personal communication.

2. Since 2005, Hoggan & Associates has participated in a series of ongoing surveys and dialogue-based research studies on the Canadian public's understanding, values and attitudes toward sustainability. Findings suggest that a strong majority say climate change is very serious, is happening now and receives inadequate action from Canada's leaders and that government and business should address both economic and environmental challenges as a top priority, and support addressing the growing gap between rich and poor as a social injustice. Participants identified three key barriers to acting more sustainably: mistrust of government and business, belief that individual actions have no meaningful impact on the big picture, and lack of reliable, relevant information. More about the studies and their findings are available here: Hoggan website. "Sustainability Research."

3. "Margaret Thatcher in Quotes." *The Spectator*, April 8, 2013. [online]. [cited October 26, 2015]. blogs.new.spectator.co.uk/2013/04/margaret -thatcher-in-quotes/.

4. Debra Marshall. "C. Wright Mills: The Sociological Imagination." YouTube, December 24, 2012. [onoline]. [cited October 26, 2015]. youtube.com/watch?v=dMR74ytkXKI.

5. Meagan Fitzpatrick. "Harper on Terror Arrests: Not a Time for 'Sociology.'" *CBC News*, April 25, 2013. [online]. [cited October 26, 2015]. cbc.ca/news/politics/harper-on-terror-arrests-not-a-time-for -sociology-1.1413502.

Chapter 12: Silencing the Voices of Others

1. Jason Stanley, "Democracy and the Demagogue." *New York Times,* October 12, 2015. [online]. [cited October 26, 2015]. opinionator.blogs .nytimes.com/author/jason-stanley/?_r=o.
2. Newshounds. "Fox News Regular Suggests Obama Is a Muslim." YouTube, August 19, 2010. [online]. [cited October 26, 2015]. youtube .com/watch?v=qCog5l9kq94.
3. Source for all quotations from Jason Stanley, personal communication.
4. George Orwell. *Nineteen Eighty-Four.* Penguin Books, 1949.
5. Victor Klemperer, trans. Martin Chalmers. *I Shall Bear Witness: The Diaries of Victor Klemperer, 1933–41.* Weidenfeld & Nicolson, 1998; Victor Klemperer, trans. Martin Chalmers. *To the Bitter End: The Diaries of Victor Klemperer, 1942–1945.* Weidenfeld & Nicolson, 1999.
6. Ben Zimmer. "Truthiness." *New York Times Magazine,* October 13, 2010. [online]. [cited December 28, 2015]. nytimes.com/2010/10/17 /magazine/17FOB-onlanguage-t.html?_r=o.

Chapter 13: Gaslighting Blurs Our Reality

1. Bryant Welch. *State of Confusion: Political Manipulation and the Assault on the American Mind.* Thomas Dunne, 2008.
2. *Gaslight,* directed by George Cukor. MGM, 1944.
3. Source for quotations from Bryant Welch, personal communication.
4. Stephen Colbert, 2006 White House Correspondents' Association Dinner. [online.] [cited: December 8, 2015.] c-span.org/video/?192243 -1/2006-white-house-correspondents-dinner.
5. Welch counts Karl Rove, Republican political consultant and former Senior Advisor and Deputy Chief of Staff to George W. Bush, among America's most effective "gaslighters," influential people who actively create and exploit confusion in the minds of Americans. In *State of Confusion,* Welch casts Rove as the "creative genius" behind Bush's political success and discusses the many "tricks" he uses to manipulate the public; see pp. 122–128 and 133–134.
6. Franklin D. Roosevelt. "The Only Thing We Have to Fear Is Fear Itself." Great Speeches of the 20th Century, *The Guardian,* April 25, 2007. [online]. [cited October 28, 2015]. theguardian.com/theguardian /2007/apr/25/greatspeeches.

Chapter 14: Summary: The Polluted Public Square

1. Mark Stoll. "Personal Attacks on Rachel Carson." *Rachel Carson's Silent Spring: A Book That Changed the World*. Environment and Society Portal, Virtual Exhibitions 2012 no. 1. [online]. [cited October 30, 2015]. environmentandsociety.org/exhibitions/silent-spring/personal-attacks-rachel-carson.

2. Deborah Tannen. "We Need Higher Quality Outrage." *Christian Science Monitor*. October 20, 2004. [online.] [cited: December 29, 2015.] faculty.georgetown.edu/tannend/csm102204.html.

3. Source for quotes from Bryant Welch, personal communication.

4. "Marshall Ganz on Making Social Movements Matter." *BillMoyers.com*, May 10, 2013. [online]. [cited November 2, 2015]. billmoyers.com/segment/marshall-ganz-on-making-social-movements-matter/.

5. Source for quotes from Marshall Ganz, personal communication.

6. On1Foot: Jewish Texts for Social Justice. "Arguing for the Sake of Heaven." Mishnah, *Pirkei Avot* 5:17. [online]. [cited November 2, 2015]. on1foot.org/sourcesheet/arguing-sake-heaven.

Chapter 15: Power and Love

1. Books by Adam Kahane: *Solving Tough Problems: An Open Way of Talking, Listening, and Creating New Realities*. Berrett-Koehler, 2007; *Power and Love: A Theory and Practice of Social Change*. Berrett-Koehler, 2010; *Transformative Scenario Planning: Working Together to Change the Future*. Berrett-Koehler, 2012.

2. Blurbs quoted from Kahane. *Transformative Scenario Planning*.

3. Source for quotations from Adam Kahane, personal communication.

4. Paul Tillich. *Love, Power, and Justice: Ontological Analyses and Ethical Applications*. Oxford, 1954.

5. Martin Luther King, Jr., ed. James Washington. *A Testament of Hope: The Essential Writings and Speeches of Martin Luther King, Jr*. Harper-SanFrancisco, 1990, p. 247.

Chapter 16: No Fish? No Fish Sticks

1. American systems scientist Peter Senge is a major figure in the organizational development field. He was named Strategist of the Century by the *Journal of Business Strategy*, and *Harvard Business Review* has referred to his vision of a learning organization from his 1990 book, *The Fifth Discipline*, as one of the seminal management ideas of the previous 75 years. *The Fifth Discipline: The Art and Practice of a Learning Organization*. Deckle Edge, 2006.

2. Source for quotations from Peter Senge, personal communication.

3. For example: Mike Gaworecki. "China to Create National Cap-and-Trade Program As Obama Admin Must Bypass U.S. Senate on Climate." *DeSmogBlog*, September 25, 2014. [online]. [cited November 4, 2015]. desmogblog.com/2014/09/23/china-create-national-cap-and-trade-program-obama-admin-must-bypass-u-s-senate-climate.

4. "Video Message from Xie Zhenhua, Vice Chairman of the National Development and Reform Commission (NDRC), China." Globe International Second Climate Legislation Summit, February 27–28, 2014. [online]. [cited November 4, 2015]. globelegislators.org/2gcls-proceedings/videomessage-from-xie-zhenhua-china.

5. Jack Clark. "IT Now 10 Percent of World's Electricity Consumption, Report Finds." *The Register*, August 16, 2013. [online]. [cited November 4, 2015]. theregister.co.uk/2013/08/16/it_electricity_use_worse_than_you_thought/.

6. Paul Gilding. *The Great Disruption: Why the Climate Crisis Will Bring on the End of Shopping and the Birth of a New World.* Bloomsbury, 2012; "The Earth Is Full." TED talk, February 2012. [online]. [cited November 4, 2012]. ted.com/talks/paul_gilding_the_earth_is_full.

Chapter 17: Listen Deeply

1. Willian J. O'Brien. *Character at Work: Building Prosperity Through the Practice of Virtue.* Paulist Press, 2008.

2. Source for quotations from Otto Scharmer, personal communication.

3. Otto Sharmer website. [online]. [cited November 6, 2015]. ottoscharmer.com; C. Otto Scharmer. *Theory U: Leading from the Future As It Emerges.* Berrett-Koehler, 2009; Otto Scharmer and Katrin Kaufer. *Leading from the Emerging Future: From Ego-System to Eco-System Economies.* Berrett-Koehler, 2013.

4. Otto Scharmer. "Shaping the Future." World Economic Forum, Tianjin, September 13–15, 2010. [online]. [cited November 6, 2015]. ottoscharmer.com/publications/videos.

Chapter 18: What Are They Thinking?

1. Anthony Leiserowitz et al. *Climate Change in the American Mind: March 2018*, Yale Program on Climate Change Communication, April 17, 2018.

2. Source for Leiserowitz and Maibach quotations, personal communication.

Chapter 19: The Myth of Apathy

1. "Archive." Renee Lertzman website. [online]. [cited November 6, 2015]. reneelertzman.com/archive/.
2. Source for quotations from Renee Lertzman, personal communication.
3. Harold F. Searles. "Unconscious Processes in Relation to the Environmental Crisis." Psychoanalytic Review, 59 (1972).
4. Hanna Segal. (1987, 1997) "Silence Is the Real Crime." In Hanna Segal, Psychoanalysis, Literature and War: Papers 1942–1995. Routledge, 2005.
5. Kari Norgaard. *Living in Denial: Climate Change, Emotions, and Everyday Life*. MIT Press, 2011.
6. Renée Lertzman. "The Myth of Apathy." *The Ecologist*, June 19, 2008. [online.] [cited: December 25, 2015.] theecologist.org/blogs_and_comments/commentators/other_comments/269433/the_myth_of_apathy.html.

Chapter 20: Psychic Numbing

1. Paul Slovic biography. Decision Research website. [online]. [cited November 9, 2015]. decisionresearch.org/researcher/paul-slovic-ph-d/.
2. Source for quotations from Paul Slovic, personal communication.
3. United Human Rights Council. "Genocide in Darfur." [online]. [cited November 9, 2015]. unitedhumanrights.org/genocide/genocide-in-sudan.htm.
4. Paul Slovic and Elke U. Weber. "Perception of Risk Posed by Extreme Events." Paper prepared for discussion at the conference Risk Management Strategies in an Uncertain World, Palisades, New York, April 12–13, 2002. [online]. [cited November 9, 2015]. ldeo.columbia.edu/chrr/documents/meetings/roundtable/white_papers/slovic_wp.pdf.
5. Paul Slovic. *The Feeling of Risk: New Perspectives on Risk Perception*. Routledge, 2010.
6. Daniel Kahneman. *Thinking, Fast and Slow*. Farrar, Straus and Giroux, 2013.
7. Daniel Kahneman, Paul Slovic and Amos Tversky, eds. *Judgment Under Uncertainty: Heuristics and Biases*. Cambridge, 1982.

Chapter 21: Sometimes David Wins

1. Source for quotations from Marshall Ganz, personal communication.

Chapter 22: The Golden Rule

1. "Karen Armstrong Religious Scholar." Speakers, TED.com. [online]. [cited November 11, 2015]. ted.com/speakers/karen_armstrong.

2. Source for quotations from Karen Armstrong, personal communication.

3. 1 Corinthians 13:4 and 6.

Chapter 23: Tending Our Inner Ecology

1. Source for quotations from Joan Halifax, personal communication.

Chapter 24: Speak the Truth, But Not to Punish

1. Source for quotations from Thich Nhat Hanh, retreat and interview, Awakening the Heart Retreat, UBC, August 8–13, 2011.

2. Peter Solomon in "Happiness Machines," Episode One, *The Century of Self*, BBC Two England, 2002.

3. A koan is a Zen parable, statement or paradox that is given to a student to meditate and reflect upon. The practice of focusing upon the koan is hoped to bring enlightenment.

Chapter 25: We Need Warmheartedness

1. Barry Saxifrage. "Wikileak: Dalai Lama Says Climate Change in Tibet More Urgent Than Political Solution. Why?" *Vancouver Observer*, January 25, 2011. [online]. [cited December 26, 2015]. vancouverobserver. com/blogs/climatesnapshot/2011/01/25/wikileak-dalai-lama-says -climate-change-tibet-more-urgent-political; World Wildlife Fund. "Glaciers in China and Tibet Fading Fast." *ScienceDaily*, February 22, 2009. [online]. [cited December 26, 2015]. sciencedaily.com/releases /2009/02/090220185537.htm.

2. Baiqing Xu et al. "Black Soot and the Survival of Tibetan Glaciers." *Proceedings of the National Academies of Sciences*, 106 (52) (2009). [online]. [cited December 25, 2015]. pnas.org/content/106/52/22114 .full.pdf; James Hansen. "Science Briefs: Survival of Tibetan Glaciers." NASA GISS Website, December 2009. [online]. [cited December 25, 2015]. giss.nasa.gov/research/briefs/hansen_14.

3. Future Generations China. "Four Great Rivers Project." [online]. [cited November 17, 2015]. china.future.org/conservation-tibet/four -great-rivers.

4. Claudio O. Delang and Zhen Yuan. *China's Grain for Green Program: A Review of the Largest Ecological Restoration and Rural Development Program in the World*. Springer, 2014.

5. Mind and Life Conference XXIII. [online]. [cited November 18, 2015]. mindandlife.org/dalai-lama-dialogues/.

6. T. S. Eliot, "Little Gidding," Part V.

7. Source for quotations from the 14th Dalai Lama, retreat and interview, Mind and Life Conference XXIII: Ecology, Ethics, and Interdependence. Office of His Holiness the Dalai Lama, October 17–21, 2011.

8. Source for quotations from Sallie McFague, personal communication.

9. Source for quotations from Peter Senge, personal communication.

Epilogue: Hope, Compassion, and Courage

1. Source for quotations from Alex Himelfarb and Miles Richardson, personal communication.

2. Rosalie Abella, "Rosalie Abella: An Attack on the Independence of a Court Anywhere Is an Attack on All Courts." *Globe and Mail*, October 26, 2018.

3. Source for quotations from Adam Kahane, personal communication.

4. Adam Kahane, *Collaborating with the Enemy: How to Work with People You Don't Agree With or Like or Trust*. Berrett-Koehler, June 2017.

5. Source for all quotations: Paul Slovic, personal communication.

Index

About the Author

JAMES HOGGAN is a best-selling author and president of an award-winning public relations firm in Vancouver, British Columbia. Jim writes and speaks widely on public relations, communication and incivility in the public sphere, especially focusing on lessons from his most recent book *I'm Right and You're an Idiot: The Toxic State of Public Discourse and How to Clean It Up.*

Hoggan has spent more than a decade studying today's warlike approach to public discourse, looking at how unyielding one-sidedness defeats our efforts to resolve global problems, and how self-awareness, empathy and pluralistic advocacy can help us cut through this toxic barrier to change.

He is seen as one of the gurus in his field, whether defending the reputations of civil society organizations, public institutions, prominent corporations or the leaders who run them. A tireless advocate for improved ethics in public discourse, he founded the influential online news site DeSmogBlog, which reports on public relations trickery. It was named one of the internet's best blogs in 2011 by *Time Magazine*.

Hoggan is former chair of the David Suzuki Foundation and Al Gore's Climate Project Canada. He has served on numerous national and international boards and advisory committees including Shell Global's External Review Committee in The Hague, the Dalai Lama Centre for Peace and Education and the Four Great Rivers Society.

He is the author of two other books, *Do the Right Thing: PR Tips for a Skeptical Public* and *Climate Cover-Up: The Crusade to Deny Global Warming.*

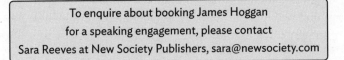

To enquire about booking James Hoggan
for a speaking engagement, please contact
Sara Reeves at New Society Publishers, sara@newsociety.com

ABOUT NEW SOCIETY PUBLISHERS

New Society Publishers is an activist, solutions-oriented publisher focused on publishing books for a world of change. Our books offer tips, tools, and insights from leading experts in sustainable building, homesteading, climate change, environment, conscientious commerce, renewable energy, and more—positive solutions for troubled times.

We're proud to hold to the highest environmental and social standards of any publisher in North America. This is why some of our books might cost a little more. We think it's worth it!

- We print all our books in North America, never overseas

- All our books are printed on **100% post-consumer recycled paper**, processed chlorine-free, with low-VOC vegetable-based inks (since 2002)

- Our corporate structure is an innovative employee shareholder agreement, so we're one-third employee-owned (since 2015)

- We're carbon-neutral (since 2006)

- We're certified as a B Corporation (since 2016)

At New Society Publishers, we care deeply about *what* we publish—but also about *how* we do business.

Download our catalog at https://newsociety.com/Our-Catalog or for a printed copy please email info@newsocietypub.com or call 1-800-567-6772 ext 111.

New Society Publishers
ENVIRONMENTAL BENEFITS STATEMENT

For every 5,000 books printed, New Society saves the following resources:[1]

30	Trees
2,743	Pounds of Solid Waste
3,018	Gallons of Water
3,936	Kilowatt Hours of Electricity
4,985	Pounds of Greenhouse Gases
21	Pounds of HAPs, VOCs, and AOX Combined
8	Cubic Yards of Landfill Space

[1] Environmental benefits are calculated based on research done by the Environmental Defense Fund and other members of the Paper Task Force who study the environmental impacts of the paper industry.

Certified **B** Corporation

FSC MIX Paper from responsible sources FSC® C016245 www.fsc.org

new society PUBLISHERS www.newsociety.com